SAN FRANCISCO

AND

NEARBY

ATTRACTIONS

HOW TO USE THIS GUIDE

The first section consists of useful general information—Facts at Your Fingertips—designed to help you plan your trip, as well as local facts, business hours, local holidays, time zones, and customs that will be of use while you are traveling.

Following this section comes the detailed breakdown of the area, geographically. Each chapter begins with a description of the place or region, broadly describing its attraction for the visitor; this is followed by Practical Information to help you explore the area—detailed descriptions, addresses, directions, phone numbers, and so forth for hotels, restaurants, tours, museums, historical sites, and more.

Two vital ways into this book are the Table of Contents at the beginning and the Index at the end.

FODOR'S TRAVEL GUIDES

are compiled, researched, and edited by an international team of travel writers, field correspondents, and editors. The series, which now almost covers the globe, was founded by Eugene Fodor in 1936.

OFFICES
New York & London

Fodor's San Francisco:

Area Editor: TONI CHAPMAN
Editorial Contributors: PHIL ELWOOD, TROY GARRISON, VERN
   HAWKINS, JACQUELINE KILLEEN, ROBERT TAYLOR, CASEY
   TEFERTILLER, BARRY WOOD, LARRY WOOD
Editor: DEBRA BERNARDI
Editorial Associate: STEVE BREWER
Illustrations: TED BURWELL
Maps and Plans: JON BAUCH, MARK STEIN, DYNO LOWENSTEIN

SAN FRANCISCO

and

Nearby Attractions

1985

FODOR'S TRAVEL GUIDES
New York

All the following Guides are current (most of them also in
the Hodder and Stoughton British edition).

**FODOR'S COUNTRY
AND AREA TITLES:**

AUSTRALIA, NEW
ZEALAND AND
SOUTH PACIFIC
AUSTRIA
BELGIUM AND
LUXEMBOURG
BERMUDA
BRAZIL
CANADA
CANADA'S MARITIME
PROVINCES
CARIBBEAN AND
BAHAMAS
CENTRAL AMERICA
EASTERN EUROPE
EGYPT
EUROPE
FRANCE
GERMANY
GREAT BRITAIN
GREECE
HOLLAND
INDIA, NEPAL, AND
SRI LANKA
IRELAND
ISRAEL
ITALY
JAPAN
JORDAN AND HOLY
LAND
KOREA
MEXICO
NORTH AFRICA
PEOPLE'S REPUBLIC
OF CHINA
PORTUGAL
SCANDINAVIA
SCOTLAND

SOUTH AMERICA
SOUTHEAST ASIA
SOVIET UNION
SPAIN
SWITZERLAND
TURKEY
YUGOSLAVIA

CITY GUIDES:

AMSTERDAM
BEIJING,
GUANGZHOU,
SHANGHAI
BOSTON
CHICAGO
DALLAS AND FORT
WORTH
GREATER MIAMI
HONG KONG
HOUSTON
LISBON
LONDON
LOS ANGELES
MADRID
MEXICO CITY AND
ACAPULCO
MUNICH
NEW ORLEANS
NEW YORK CITY
PARIS
ROME
SAN DIEGO
SAN FRANCISCO
STOCKHOLM,
COPENHAGEN,
OSLO, HELSINKI,
AND REYKJAVIK
TOKYO
TORONTO
VIENNA
WASHINGTON, D.C.

FODOR'S BUDGET SERIES:

BUDGET BRITAIN
BUDGET CANADA
BUDGET CARIBBEAN
BUDGET EUROPE
BUDGET FRANCE
BUDGET GERMANY
BUDGET HAWAII
BUDGET ITALY
BUDGET JAPAN
BUDGET LONDON
BUDGET MEXICO
BUDGET
SCANDINAVIA
BUDGET SPAIN
BUDGET TRAVEL IN
AMERICA

USA GUIDES:

ALASKA
CALIFORNIA
CAPE COD
COLORADO
FAR WEST
FLORIDA
HAWAII
NEW ENGLAND
PACIFIC NORTH COAST
PENNSYLVANIA
SOUTH
TEXAS
USA (in one volume)

GOOD TIME TRAVEL GUIDES:

ACAPULCO
MONTREAL
OAHU
SAN FRANCISCO

CONTENTS

The Bay Area Outside San Francisco

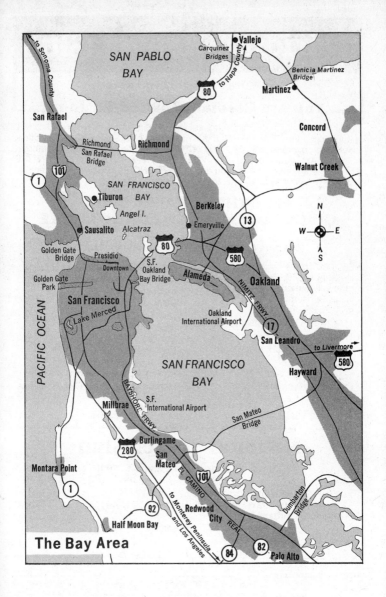

The Bay Area

SAN PABLO BAY

to Sonoma County

Vallejo

Carquinez Bridges

to Napa County

Benicia Martinez Bridge

80

Martinez

Concord

San Rafael

Richmond San Rafael Bridge

Richmond

Walnut Creek

101

1

SAN FRANCISCO BAY

Tiburon

Angel I.

BerKeley

13

Sausalito

Alcatraz

Emeryville

80

580

Golden Gate Bridge

Presidio

Downtown

S.F. Oakland Bay Bridge

Alameda

Oakland

NIMITZ FRWY

Golden Gate Park

San Francisco

Lake Merced

Oakland International Airport

17

San Leandro

to Livermore

580

PACIFIC OCEAN

SAN FRANCISCO BAY

Hayward

Millbrae

BAYSHORE FRWY

S.F. International Airport

San Mateo Bridge

Montara Point

1

280

Burlingame

San Mateo

EL CAMINO REAL

101

Dunbarton Bridge

92

to Monterey Peninsula and Los Angeles

Redwood City

Half Moon Bay

84

82

Palo Alto

N
W E
S

FOREWORD

San Francisco has been labeled "Everybody's Favorite City." Our purpose in this Guide is to show you, point by point, why—so that you will be able to choose the things to do and see that will please *you* the most.

This book is designed to be your tool for creating the best vacation in the Bay Area to fit your time, your budget, and your interests. We have therefore concentrated on giving you the widest **range** of choices the city and surrounding areas offer, and within that range to present you with **selections** that will be safe, solid, and of value. The descriptions we provide are just enough for you to make your own intelligent choices from among our selections.

All selections and comments in *Fodor's San Francisco* are based on the editors' and contributors' personal experiences. We feel that our first responsibility is to inform and protect you, the reader. Errors are bound to creep into any travel guide, however. We go to press in the middle of the year, and much change can and will occur in the Bay Area even while we are on press, and certainly also during the succeeding twelve months or so when this edition is on sale. We cannot, therefore, be responsible for the sudden closing of a restaurant, a change in a museum's days or hours, a shift of hotel ownership (for the worse), and so forth. We sincerely welcome letters from our readers on these changes, or from those whose opinions differ from ours, and we are ready to revise our entries for next year's edition when the facts warrant it.

Send your letters to the editors at **Fodor's Travel Guides, 2 Park Avenue, New York, NY 10016.** Continental or British Commonwealth readers may prefer to write to Fodor's Travel Guides, 9-10 Market Place, London W1N 7AG, England.

FACTS AT YOUR FINGERTIPS

 FACTS AND FIGURES. The third-largest state in size, California's population topped 25 million in 1984. It hosts millions of visitors yearly, and in 1984 earned about $30 billion from them; the Summer Olympic fans spent about $1 billion.

It stretches almost 1,000 miles from the Oregon border in the north to the Mexican border in the south. It is an exciting blend of Spanish/Mexican, European, Asian, and Yankee spirits.

It is the Golden State, showering a wealth of natural scenic splendors, superb climates, sophisticated cities and citizens, and fresh, often zany lifestyles.

It is two Californias. The northern part covers almost two-thirds of the length of the state. It is the home of the world's oldest trees, the mighty coast redwoods; legendary Mount Shasta and spectacular, granite-walled 1,200-square-mile Yosemite National Park—and its center is the world-popular San Francisco.

The San Francisco Bay Area (comprising San Francisco proper, the peninsula communities south of San Francisco—such as Palo Alto, Santa Cruz, and San Jose—and East Bay cities such as Berkeley and Oakland) has a combined population of about 5 million. San Francisco itself has a population of approximately 700,000.

 PLANNING YOUR TRIP. If you don't want to bother with reservations on your own, a travel agent won't cost you a cent, except for specific charges like telegrams. He gets his fee from the hotel or carrier he books for you. A travel agent can also be of help for those who prefer to take their vacations on a "package tour"—thus keeping your own planning to a minimum. If you prefer the convenience of standardized accommodations, remember that the various hotel and motel chains publish free directories of their members that enable you to plan and reserve everything ahead of time.

If you don't belong to an auto club, now is the time to join one. They can be very helpful about routings and providing emergency service on the road. If you plan to route yourself, make certain the map you get is dated for the current year (highways and thruways are appearing and being extended at an astonishingly rapid rate). Some of the major oil companies will send maps and mark preferred routes on them if you tell them what you have in mind. Try: *Exxon Touring Service,* Exxon Corporation, 1251 Avenue of the Americas, New York, NY 10020; *Texaco Travel Service,* P.O. Box 1459, Houston, TX 77001; or *Mobil Oil Corp Touring Service,* P.O. Box 25, Versailles, KY 40383. In addition, most areas have their own maps, which pinpoint attractions, list historical sites, parks, etc. City chambers of commerce are also good sources of information. Specific addresses are given under *Tourist Information.*

Plan to board the pets, discontinue paper and milk deliveries, and tell your local police and fire departments when you'll be leaving and when you expect to return. Ask a kindly neighbor to keep an eye on your house; fully protect your swimming pool against intruders. Have a friend keep your mail, or have it held at the post office. Look into the purchase of trip insurance (including baggage), and make certain your auto, fire, and other insurance policies are up-to-date. Today, most people who travel use credit cards for important expenses such as gas, repairs, lodgings and some meals. Consider converting the greater portion of your trip money into traveler's checks. Arrange to have your lawn mowed at the usual times, and leave that kindly neighbor your itinerary (insofar as is possible), car license number, and a key to your home (and tell police and firemen he has it). Since some hotel and motel chains give discounts (10–25 percent) to senior citizens, be sure to have some sort of identification along if you qualify. Usually AARP or NRTA membership is best. (See below at the end of the *Hotels and Motels* section.)

 VISITOR INFORMATION. Contact the *California Office of Tourism,* 1030 13th Street, Suite 200, Sacramento, CA 95814, for list of their publications. Visitor information is available through this office, and at the many convention and visitors bureaus or chambers of commerce throughout the state. See individual sections for listings.

 TIPS FOR BRITISH VISITORS. Passports. You will need a valid passport and a U.S. Visa (which can only be put in a passport of the 10-year kind). You can obtain the visa either through your travel agent, or directly from the *United States Embassy,* Visa and Immigration Department, 24 Grosvenor Sq., London W1 (tel. 01-499 3443).

No vaccinations are required for entry into the U.S.

Customs. If you are 21 or over, you can take into the U.S.—200 cigarettes, 50 cigars or 3 lbs. of tobacco; 1 U.S. liter of alcohol; duty-free gifts to a value of $100. Be careful not to try to take in meat or meat products, seeds, plants, fruits, etc. And avoid narcotics like the plague.

Insurance. We heartily recommend that you insure yourself to cover health and motoring mishaps, with *Europ Assistance,* 252 High St., Croydon CRO 1NF (tel. 01-680 1234). Their excellent service is all the more valuable when you consider the possible costs of health care in the U.S.

Tour Operators. The price battle that has raged over transatlantic fares has meant that most tour operators now offer excellent budget packages to the U.S. Among those you might consider as you plan your trip are—

American Express, 6 Haymarket, London SW1.
Thomas Cook Ltd., Thorpe Wood, Peterborough, PE 3 6SB.
Cosmos, Cosmos House, 1 Bromley Common, Bromley, Kent BR2 9LX.
Cunard, 8 Berkeley St., London W1.
Jetsave, Sussex House, London Rd., East Grinstead RH19 1LD.
Page and Moy, 136–138 London Rd., Leicester LE2 1EN.
Speedbird, 200 Buckingham Palace Rd., London SW1.

Air Fares. We suggest that you explore the current scene for budget flight possibilities. All the main transatlantic carriers have stand-by tickets, available a short time before the flight only, as well as APEX and other fares at a considerable saving over the full price. Quite frankly, only business travelers who don't have to watch the price of their tickets fly full-price these days—and find themselves sitting right beside an APEX passenger!

Hotels. You may have need of a fast booking service to find a hotel room. One of the very best ways to do this is to contact *HBI-HOTAC,* Globegate House, Pound Lane, London NW10 (tel. 01–451 2311). They book rooms for most of the large chains (Holiday Inns, Hilton, Ramada etc.), so you can have a multiple choice with only one contact. HBI-HOTAC specialize in booking for business firms, but they also deal with the general public.

 WHEN TO GO. With the Humboldt Current (cold) swirling toward the south of this region, and the Japanese current (warm) nudging northern coastal strips, with America's highest, coolest mountains and its deepest, sun-sizzled valleys, the humidity and temperature readings in this region are as varied as the patterns on your grandmother's favorite patchwork quilt. Here and there sea breezes cause a temperature variance of as much as 5 to 15 degrees within the limits of a single city.

San Francisco nonetheless has a delightfully mild year-round climate. In summer, the usual morning and evening fog will cause extremes. In June, for example, the highs will range from the 60s to 90s, with the lows in the 50s. September through October is usually warm, with a normal rainy season—about twenty-five inches a year—between December and March, when it is often overcast for days at a time. Across the Bay, in either Marin or Oakland, the temperatures can be significantly higher. High winds and well-below normal overnight temperatures often occur in April. Winds along the coast often reach more than 50 miles an hour. Those traveling in campers should be especially wary and should check with the California Highway Patrol.

 PACKING. *What to take, what to wear.* Make a packing list for each member of the family. Then check off items as you pack them. It will save time, reduce confusion. Time-savers to carry along include extra photo film (plenty), suntan lotion, insect repellent, sufficient toothpaste, soap, etc. Always carry an extra pair of glasses, including sunglasses, particularly if they're prescription ones. A travel iron is always a good tote-along, as are some plastic bags (small and large) for wet suits, socks, etc. They are also excellent for packing shoes, cosmetics, and other easily damaged items. If you fly, remember that despite signs to the contrary airport security X-ray machines do in fact damage film rolls in about 17 percent of the cases. Have them inspected separately or pack them in special protective bags. Fun extras to carry include binoculars, a compass, and a magnifying glass—to read fine-print maps.

All members of the family should have sturdy shoes with nonslip soles. Keep them handy in the back of the car. You never know when you may want to stop and clamber along a rocky trail. Carry the family raingear in a separate bag, in the back of the car (so no one will have to get out and hunt for it in a downpour en route).

Women will probably want to stick to one or two basic colors for their holiday wardrobes, so that they can manage with one set of accessories. If possible, include one knit or jersey dress or a pants suit, and for the winter months take a *light-weight* coat. For dress-up evenings, take along a few "basic" dresses you can vary with a simple change of accessories. That way you can dress up or down to suit the occasion.

Be sure to check what temperatures will be like along the route. Traveling in mountains can mean cool evenings, even in summer—and so can traveling through the desert. An extra sweater is always a safe thing to pack, even if just to protect you from the air conditioning.

Men will probably want a jacket along for dining out, especially for San Francisco. T-shirts are now accepted almost everywhere during the daytime; in some resort areas they're worn evenings, as well. Don't forget extra slacks.

Pack lightly, but keep weather extremes in mind. The morning and evening fogs and frequent windy gusts suggest having a sweater or jacket always available; plus a scarf, for special hairstyles.

Planning a lot of sun time? Don't forget something to wear en route to the pool, beach, or lakefront, and for those few days when you're getting reacquainted with the sun on tender skin.

 CLIMATE. Seasons in the Bay Area are not as defined as in most other temperate areas of the world. December through February brings heavy rains, so count on needing an umbrella during your trip in the winter. But in June, July, August, and September there is almost no rain at all. Fogs, especially in the morning but sometimes in the evening, are common during the summer but may occur throughout the year. The fog usually clears during the day. Summer does not usually bring high temperatures; very rarely does the temperature even hit 80 degrees F. The Bay Area has varying micro-climates: the Napa Valley, a half-hour's drive to the north, may have temperatures as much as 20 degrees higher than downtown San Francisco in the summer, and when it is overcast and nippy in town Carmel to the south may be basking in sunshine and

65-degree temperatures. The coastal mountains often hold the fogs away from inland areas just a couple of miles away.

	Average Daily Temp.	Rainfall in Inches
January	50.1 F.	4.03
February	53.0	3.91
March	54.9	2.78
April	55.7	1.49
May	57.1	0.59
June	59.1	0.15
July	58.9	0.01
August	59.3	0.01
September	61.6	0.13
October	61.0	1.07
November	57.2	2.27
December	51.9	4.07

WHAT WILL IT COST? This is obviously a crucial question and one of the most difficult. The American Automobile Association estimates that in 1984 expenses for a couple driving across the country would average out around $50.00 per day for meals, $51.00 for lodging, and about $7.00 for each 100 miles for gasoline (at 22 miles to the gallon). We hope you can do it for less, and we have included a number of concrete and practical suggestions for cutting costs wherever you can. A couple can travel comfortably in California for about $140 a day (not counting gasoline or other transportation costs), as you can see in the table below.

In some areas, you can cut expenses by traveling off-season, when hotel rates are usually lower. The budget-minded traveler can also find bargain accommodations at tourist homes or family-style YMCA's and YWCA's. Both California state and national parks offer limited lodgings; book early. Colleges offer dormitory accommodations to tourists during the summer vacations at single-room rates of $2.00–$10.00 per night, with meals from $0.60–$3.50. A directory of some 200 such opportunities all over the U.S. is *Mort's Guide to Low-Cost Vacations and Lodgings on College Campuses, USA-Canada,* from CMG Publishing Co., P.O. Box 630, Princeton, NJ 08540, $5.00 postpaid.

Another way to cut down on the cost of your trip is to look for out-of-the-way resorts. Travelers are frequently rewarded by discovering very attractive areas which haven't as yet begun to draw quantities of people.

If you are budgeting your trip (who isn't?), don't forget to set aside a realistic amount for the possible rental of sports equipment (perhaps including a boat or canoe), entrance fees to amusement and historical sites, etc. There are no tolls on the highways, but allow for modest bridge tolls, extra film for cameras, and souvenirs.

Typical Expenses for Two People

Room at moderate hotel or motel	$60.00
Breakfast at hotel or motel, including tip	12.00
Lunch at inexpensive restaurant, including tip	12.00
Dinner at moderate restaurant, including tip	30.00
Sightseeing bus tour	17.00
Evening drink	5.00
Admission to museum or historic site	5.00
	$141.00

After lodging, your next biggest expense will be food, and here you can make very substantial economies if you are willing to get along with only one meal a day (or less) in a restaurant. Plan to eat simply, and to picnic. It will save you time and money, and it will help you enjoy your trip more. That beautiful scenery does not have to whiz by at 55 miles per hour. There are picnic and rest areas, often well-equipped and in scenic spots, even on highways and thruways, so finding a pleasant place to stop is usually not difficult. Before you leave home put together a picnic kit.

If you like a drink before dinner or bed, bring your own bottle. Most hotels and motels supply ice free or for very little, but the markup on alcoholic beverages in restaurants, bars, lounges and dining rooms is enormous, and in some states peculiar laws apply regarding alcohol consumption. And in any case, a good California dry white wine makes a fine apéritif and can be far cheaper than a cocktail.

HINTS TO THE MOTORIST. Probably the first precaution you will take is to have your car thoroughly checked by your regular dealer or service station to make sure that everything is in good shape. Secondly, you may find it wise to join an auto club that can provide you with trip planning information, insurance coverage, and emergency and repair service along the way. Thirdly, if you must have your car serviced look for a repair shop displaying the *National Institute for Automotive Service Excellence* seal. *NIASE* tests and certifies the competence of auto mechanics in about 10,000 repair shops nationwide.

Driving in California is probably more unpredictable and challenging than in any other part of the nation. With an auto registration of some 9 million, the Golden State easily outranks its two closest contenders, New York and Texas, each issuing about 5.5 million license plates. If you enter a California freeway, be sure you have a full gas tank. When you park in San Francisco, turn your wheels to the curb. If you park downhill, turn your steering wheel to put your tires into the curb. If you park uphill, do the opposite. Turning your wheels to the curb in hilly San Francisco is the law, even on level stretches, because runaway automobiles have been a problem, and it's hard to tell where the hills end and the level stretches begin.

California speed limits comply with federal law—55 mph. Tops for cars hauling trailers is 50, but lower limits sometimes are posted. General speed limit for school zones and residential and business districts is 25—again, except when posted. And there are special speed zones ranging from 25 to 55, depending on what the sign says at the entrance to such zones. Watch the signs: there is no state requirement for posting warning signs on radar, mechanical, or electrical speed-checking devices.

DESERT DRIVING

If you are driving westward into Northern California, you will encounter some stretches of desert driving. Service industries across the desert have grown in number during the past decade to the point that the hazards of desert driving have been minimized. A principal point to check before crossing the hot desert should be your tires. Put them at normal driving pressure or slightly below. Heat builds pressure. If your car seems to be bouncing too readily, stop to let your tires cool. If you have a good radiator, don't bother about extra water—except for Death Valley—but keep an eye on the water gauge. Be alert for sudden sandstorms and rainstorms. If you have a car radio, keep it tuned to local stations for information about unusual weather conditions.

MOUNTAIN DRIVING

Unless you venture onto exotic mountain roads, you should have little trouble with mountain driving. Today's mountain roads are engineered for the ordinary driver. They are normally wide, well graded, and safe. Be especially wary of exceeding the speed limit posted for curves. Keep to the right. If your normal driving is at low altitudes, have a garage mechanic check your carburetor. It may need adjusting for mountain driving. If your car stalls, and your temperature gauge is high, it could mean a vapor lock. Bathe the fuel pump with a damp cloth for a few minutes.

If you get stuck on any kind of road, pull off the highway onto the shoulder, raise the hood, attach something white (a handkerchief, scarf, or a piece of tissue) to the door handle on the driver's side, and sit inside and wait. This is especially effective on limited-access highways, usually patroled vigilantly by state highway patrol officers. A special warning to women stalled at night: Remain inside the car with doors locked, and make sure the Good Samaritan is indeed a Good Samaritan. It's easier to find telephones along the major highways these days since their locations are more frequently marked than they used to be.

PULLING A TRAILER

Most states have special safety regulations for trailers, and these change frequently. If you plan to operate your trailer in several states, check with your motor club, the police, or the state motor vehicle department about the rules. Also talk it over with the dealer from whom you buy or lease your trailer.

Generally, speed limits for cars hauling trailers are lower, parking of trailers (and automobiles) is prohibited on expressways and freeways, and tunnels often bar trailers equipped with cooking units which use propane gas.

 WHAT TO DO WITH THE PETS. Traveling by car with your pet dog or cat? More and more motels and hotels accept them. Some turn them down, some want to look first, some offer special facilities. Check first before you register. If it's a first trip with your pet, accustom it to car travel by short trips in your neighborhood. And when you're packing, include its favorite food, bowls, and toys. Discourage your dog from riding with its head out the window. Wind and dust particles can permanently damage its eyes. Dogs are especially susceptible to heat stroke. Don't leave your dog in a parked car on a hot day while you dawdle over lunch. Keep your dog's bowl handy for water during stops for gas; gasoline attendants are usually very cooperative about this. Make sure your pet exercises periodically; this is a good way for you and the kids to unwind from unbroken traveling, too.

 HOTELS AND MOTELS. *General Hints.* Don't take potluck for lodgings. You'll waste a lot of time hunting and often won't be happy with the accommodations you finally find. If you are without reservations, by all means begin looking early in the afternoon. If you have reservations, but expect to arrive later than 5 or 6 P.M., advise the hotel or motel in advance. Some places will not, unless advised, hold reservations after 6 P.M. And if you hope to get a room at the hotel's minimum rate, be sure to reserve ahead or arrive very early.

In San Francisco, or any resort area in Northern California, try to reserve *well* in advance. Include a deposit for all places except motels (and for motels if they request one). Many chain or associated motels and hotels will make advance reservations for you at affiliated hostelries of your choosing along your route.

A number of hotels and motels have one-day laundry and dry-cleaning services, and many motels have coin laundries. Most motels, but not all, have telephones in the rooms. If you want to be sure of room service, however, better stay at a hotel. Many motels have swimming pools, and even beachfront hotels frequently have a pool. Even some motels in the heart of large cities have pools. An advantage at motels is the free parking. There's seldom a charge for parking at country and resort hotels.

Hotel and motel chains. In addition to the hundreds of excellent independent motels and hotels throughout the state, there are also many that belong to national or regional chains. A major advantage of the chains, to many travelers, is the ease of making reservations en route, or at one fell swoop in advance. If you are a guest at a member hotel or motel one night, the management will be delighted to secure a sure booking at one of its affiliated hotels at no cost to you. Chains also usually have toll-free WATS (800) lines to assist you in making reservations on your own. This, of course, saves you time, money, and worry.

For directory information on (800) lines, dial (800) 555–1212 to see if there is an (800) number for the hotel you want to reach.

Since the single biggest expense of your whole trip is lodging, you may well be discouraged and angry at the prices of some hotel and motel rooms, particularly when you know you are paying for things you neither need nor want, such as a heated swimming pool, wall-to-wall carpeting, a huge color TV set, two huge double beds for only two people, meeting rooms, a cocktail lounge, maybe even a putting green. Nationwide, motel prices for two people now average $40.00 a night; hotel prices start at $45.00, with the average around $65.00. This explains the recent rapid spread of a number of budget motel chains whose rates average $20.00 for a single and $25.00 for a double, an obvious advantage.

The main national motel chains are Holiday Inn, Howard Johnson's, Quality Inns, Ramada Inns, Sheraton Motor Inns, and TraveLodge. Other popular family-type motel chains include: Best Western, Friendship Inn Hotels, Rodeway Inns, Vagabond Motor Hotels, and Motel 6.

HOTEL AND MOTEL CATEGORIES

Hotels and motels in all the Fodor's guidebooks to the U.S.A. are divided into five categories, arranged primarily by price but also taking into some consideration the degree of comfort, the amount of service, and the atmosphere which will surround you in the establishment of your choice. Our ratings are flexible and subject to change. In every case, however, the dollar ranges for each category are clearly stated before each listing of establishments. We should also point out that many fine hotels and motels had to be omitted for lack of space.

Super Deluxe: This category is reserved for only a few hotels. In addition to giving the visitor all the amenities discussed under the deluxe category (below), the super deluxe hotel has a special atmosphere of glamour, good taste, and dignity. Its history will inevitably be full of many anecdotes, and it will probably be a favored meeting spot of local society. In short, super deluxe means the tops.

Deluxe: The minimum facilities must include bath and shower in all rooms, valet and laundry service, suites available, a well-appointed restaurant and a bar (where local law permits), room service, TV and telephone in room, air conditioning and heat (unless locale makes one or the other unnecessary), pleasing décor, and an atmosphere of luxury, calm, and elegance. There should be ample and personalized service. In a deluxe *motel,* there may be less service rendered by employees and more by automatic machines (such as refrigerators and ice-making machines in your room), but there should be a minimum of do-it-yourself in a truly deluxe establishment.

Expensive: All rooms must have bath or shower, valet and laundry service, restaurant and bar (local law permitting), at least some room service, TV and telephone in room, attractive furnishings, heat and air conditioning (locale not precluding). Although décor may be as good as that in deluxe establishments, hotels and motels in this category are frequently designed for commercial travelers or for families in a hurry and are somewhat impersonal in terms of service. As for *motels* in this category, valet and laundry service will probably be lacking; the units will be outstanding primarily for their convenient location and functional character, not for their attractive or comfortable qualities.

(**Note:** We often list top-notch ultra-modern hotels in this category, in spite of the fact that they have rates as high as deluxe hotels and motels. We do this because certain elements are missing in these hotels—usually, the missing element is service. In spite of automated devices such as ice-cube-making machines and message-signaling buzzers, service in these hotels is not up to the standard by which we judge deluxe establishments. Room service is incredibly slow in some of these places, and the entire atmosphere is often one of expediency over comfort, economy of manpower and overhead taking precedence over attention to the desires of guests.)

Moderate: Each room should have an attached bath or shower, there should be a restaurant *or* coffee shop, TV available, telephone in room, heat and air conditioning (locale not precluding), relatively convenient location, clean and comfortable rooms, and public rooms. *Motels* in this category may not have attached bath or shower, may not have a restaurant or coffee shop (though one is usually nearby), and, of course, may have no public rooms to speak of.

Inexpensive: Nearby bath or shower, telephone available, clean rooms are the minimum.

Free parking is assumed at all motels and motor hotels; you must pay for parking at most city hotels, though certain establishments have free parking, frequently for occupants of higher-than-minimum-rate rooms. *Babysitter* lists are always available in good hotels and motels, and *cribs* for the children are always on hand—sometimes at no cost, but more frequently at a cost of $1.00 or $2.00 per night. The cost of a *cot* in your room, supplementing the beds, will also be around $3.00 per night, but moving an *extra single bed* into a room will cost from $7.00 in better hotels and motels.

Senior Citizens may in some cases receive special discounts on lodgings. The Days Inn chain offers various discounts to anyone 55 or older. Holiday Inns give a 10 percent discount year-round to members of the NRTA (write to National Retired Teachers Association, Membership Division, 701 North Montgomery St., Ojai, CA 93023) and the AARP (write to American Association of Retired Persons, Membership Division, 215 Long Beach Blvd., Long Beach, CA 90802). Howard Johnson's Motor Lodges give 10 percent off to NRTA and AARP members (call 800–654–2000); and the ITT Sheraton chain gives 25 percent off (call 800–325–3535) to members of the AARP, the NRTA, the National Association of Retired Persons, The Catholic Golden Age of United Societies of U.S.A., and the Old Age Security Pensioners of Canada.

San Francisco's Bed-and-Breakfast inns are a rather new approach to visitor accommodations. Presently, unlike their European counterparts, most Bay Area inns are in the expensive to deluxe category. However, each offers its very special, highly personalized service and charm to the guest. All are smallish, reservations a must. Décors run to handsome brass beds; mellow Victorian chests; pewter and brass lamps, and nostalgic accessories highlighted with daily fresh flowers and fluffy towels. Often, a decanter of sherry and a good-night sweet tempt at the bedside. Breakfast is usually special, with tasty croissants or San Francisco sourdough-toast, fresh fruits and juices, wonderful coffee, teas.

In the Bay Area, *Bed & Breakfast International,* 151 Ardmore Rd., Kensington, CA 94707, will arrange lodging in private homes ($25–$75.00), with a three-night minimum, and breakfast or contact *Bed & Breakfast Innkeepers of San Francisco,* 710 Fourteenth St., San Francisco, CA 84114 (415) 626–8777. Styles and standards vary widely, of course; generally private baths are less common and rates often are moderate. In many small towns such guest houses are excellent examples of the best a region has to offer of its own special atmosphere. Each one will be different, so that their advantage is precisely the opposite of that "no surprise" uniformity which motel chains pride themselves on. In popular tourist areas, state or local tourist information offices or chambers of commerce usually have lists of homes that let out spare rooms to paying guests, and such a listing usually means that the places on it have been inspected and meet some reliable standard of cleanliness, comfort, and reasonable pricing. A nationwide *Guide to Guest Houses and Tourist Homes USA* is available from Tourist House Associates of America, Inc., P.O. Box 355-A, Greentown, PA 18426. A list of nearly 200 California bed-a̤ ̣ıd-breakfasts can be obtained by sending a self-addressed, stamped (37¢), number 10 envelope to the California Office of Tourism, Dept. BB, 1030 13th St., Suite 200, Sacramento, CA 95814.

Youth Hostels. The San Francisco Bay Area section of the California Coast Hostel Chain consists of six hostels spaced 20 to 30 miles apart. When completed the chain will space 38 hostels along the coastline from Mexico to Oregon. Advance reservations are suggested for San Francisco International Hostel, in historic Fort Mason. It serves 130 guests nightly, and turns away over 50 daily. Hostel customs include: 3-day limit of stay; no illegal drugs or alcohol; smoking prohibited indoors; hostel closed during day. Accommodations are simple, dormitories are segregated by sex, common rooms and kitchens are shared, and everyone helps with the clean-up. Lights out at 11:00 P.M. (or a midnight curfew) until 7:00 A.M. In season it is wise to reserve ahead; write or phone directly to the particular hostel you plan to stay in. Fees range from $3.50 to $8.00 per person per day. Other Bay Area locations include: Point Reyes National Seashore; Golden Gate Hostel, in the Marin headlands; Montara Lighthouse, on the San Mateo coast; and Pigeon Point Lighthouse in Pescadero. Fifty miles south of San Francisco is the Saratoga Hostel, a 1908 log house, set in the redwoods. The oldest hostel in the West is Hidden Villa, in the Los Altos Hills, about forty miles south of the city. Though almost 80 percent of the visitors to the San Francisco Hostel are from other countries, anyone is welcome, and a hostel pass is unnecessary, though the lodging may be a few dollars more. No age limit. For more information, write to AYH Golden Gate Council, Building 240, Fort Mason, San Francisco, CA 94123. Or check your library for *The Official American Youth Hostels Handbook Hosteling–USA,* which lists 270 or more U.S. hostels with maps; published in 1983, cost $7.95. Alternatively—and you need not be a member—write to American Youth Hostel Association, Inc., 1332 Eye St., N.W., 8th Fl., Washington, DC 20005. If you do join the Association, a copy of the *Hostel Guide and Handbook* will be included in materials sent you.

San Francisco's YMCA Embarcadero Center is an ideal budget accommodation for students, men, women, and married couples from all over the world. They offer full athletic facilities (pool, sauna, gym); restaurant, TV lounge, and self-service laundries. Located in the Financial District, at 166 The Embarcadero (94111), it is four blocks east of the Trans-Bay Bus Terminal (Amtrak, Continental, Bay Area buses); two blocks from the cable cars, and an easy stroll to Fisherman's Wharf and Chinatown. Nearby are the Sausalito/Larkspur ferry landings. BART (Bay Area Rapid Transit) Embarcadero station is about two blocks away. Write for their free brochure, *Discover San Francisco—The Y's Way,* offering 3- to 6-day packages including lodging, some meals, city sightseeing, and on the 5- to 6-day packages, trips to Muir Woods, Sausalito, and even the Napa Valley Wine Country.

 DINING OUT. For evening meals, the best advice is to make reservations in advance whenever possible anywhere in the Bay Area, but certainly in San Francisco and the Wine Country.

Some restaurants are fussy about customers' dress, particularly in the evening. For women, pants and pants suits are now almost universally acceptable. For men, tie and jacket remains the standard. Shorts are almost always frowned on for both men and women. Standards of dress are becoming more relaxed, so a neatly dressed customer will usually experience no problem. If in doubt about accepted dress at a particular establishment, call ahead.

If you're traveling with children, you may want to find out if a restaurant has a children's menu and commensurate prices (many do).

When figuring the tip on your check, base it on the total charges for the meal, not on the grand total, if that total includes a state sales tax. Don't tip on tax.

RESTAURANT CATEGORIES

Restaurants located in San Francisco proper are categorized in this volume by type of cuisine: French, Chinese, etc., with restaurants of a general nature listed as Continental-International. Restaurants in less populous areas are divided into price categories as follows: *deluxe, expensive, moderate,* and *inexpensive.* As a general rule, expect restaurants in metropolitan areas to be higher in price, although many restaurants that feature foreign cuisine are often surprisingly inexpensive. We should also point out that limitations of space make it impossible to include every establishment. We have, therefore, included those which we consider the best within each type of cuisine and price range.

Although the names of the various restaurant categories are standard throughout this series, the prices listed under each category may vary from area to area. In every case, however, the dollar ranges for each category are clearly stated before each listing of establishments.

Deluxe: This category will be pertinent to San Francisco and a few select resort areas. This indicates an outstanding restaurant which is lavishly decorated, which may delight in the fear it inspires among the humble. Sometimes overpriced and overrated, it will charge the customer at least $15.00 for soup, entrée, and dessert. The average price for the same is apt to be closer to $20.00, although some will run much higher than this. As in all our other categories, this price range *does not include* cocktails, wines, cover or table charges, tip, or extravagant house specialties. The price range here indicates a typical roast beef (prime ribs) dinner. The restaurant in this category must have a superb wine list, excellent service, immaculate kitchens, and a large, well-trained staff. Many a fine restaurant around the Bay Area falls into this category. It will have its own well-deserved reputation for excellence, perhaps a house specialty or two for which it is famous, and an atmosphere of elegance or unique décor.

Expensive: In addition to the expected dishes, it will offer one or two house specialties, wine list, and cocktails, air conditioning (unless locale makes it unnecessary), a general reputation for very good food and an adequate staff, an elegant décor, and appropriately dressed clientele.

Moderate: Cocktails and/or beer, air conditioning (when needed), clean kitchen, adequate staff, better-than-average service. General reputation for good, wholesome food.

Inexpensive: The bargain place in town, it is clean, even if plain. It will have when necessary air conditioning, tables (not a counter), and clean kitchen, and will attempt to provide adequate service.

Chains: There are now several chains of restaurants, some of them nationwide, that offer reliable eating at excellent budget prices. Some of the ones that operate in California are: *Denny's; Shakey's Pizza Parlors,* 21 kinds of pizza; and *Sambo's,* simple food, surprisingly inexpensive. *Sheraton* and *Holiday Inn* motels and hotels have all-you-can-eat, fixed-price buffets on certain days.

TIPPING. Tipping is a personal expression of your appreciation of someone who has taken pleasure and pride in giving you attentive, efficient, and personal service. Because standards of personal service are highly uneven, you should, when you get genuinely good service, feel secure in rewarding it, and when you feel that the service you got was slovenly, indifferent, or surly, don't hesitate to show this by the size, or withholding, of your tip. Remember that in many places the help are paid very little and depend on tips for the better part of their income. This is supposed to give them incentive to serve you well. These days, the going rate on *restaurant* service is 15% on the amount *before* taxes. Tipping at counters is not universal, but many people leave 25¢ on anything up to $1.00, and 10% on anything over that. For *bellboys,* 25¢ per bag is usual. However, if you load him down with all manner of bag, hatboxes, cameras, coats, etc., you might consider giving an extra quarter or two. In many places the help rely on tips for a goodly portion of their income. For one-night stays in most *hotels* and *motels* you leave nothing. If you stay longer, at the end of your stay leave the maid $1.00–$1.25 per day, or $5.00 per person per week for multiple occupancy. If you are staying at an *American Plan* hostelry (meals included), $1.50 per day per person for the waiter or waitress is considered sufficient, and is left at the end of your stay. However, if you have been surrounded by an army of servants (one bringing relishes, another rolls, etc.), add a few extra dollars and give the lump sum to the captain or maître d'hotel when you leave, asking him to allocate it.

For the many other services you may encounter in a big hotel or resort, figure roughly as follows: doorman, 25¢ for taxi handling. 50¢ for help with baggage; bellhop, 25¢ per bag, more if you load him down with extras; parking attendant, 50¢; bartender, 15%; room service, 10–15% of that bill; laundry or valet service, 15%; pool attendant, 50¢ per day; snackbar waiter at pool, beach, or golf club, 50¢ per person for food and 15% of the beverage check; locker attendant, 50¢ per person per day, or $2.50 per week; golf caddies, $1.00–$2.00 per bag, or 15% of the greens fee for an 18-hole course, or $3.00 on a free course; barbers, 50¢; shoeshine attendants, 25¢; hairdressers, $1.00; manicurists, 50¢.

Transportation: Give 25¢ for any taxi fare under $1.00 and 15% for any above; however, drivers in San Francisco *expect* 20%. Limousine service, 20%. Car rental agencies, nothing. Bus porters are tipped 25¢ per bag, drivers nothing. On charters and package tours, conductors and drivers usually get $5.00–$10.00 per day from the group as a whole, but be sure to ask whether this has already been figured into the package cost. On short local sightseeing runs, the driver-guide may get 25¢ per person, more if you think he has been especially helpful or personable. Airport bus drivers, nothing. Redcaps, in resort areas, 35¢ per suitcase, elsewhere, 25¢. Tipping at curbside check-in is unofficial, but same as above. On the plane, no tipping.

Railroads suggest you leave 10–15% per meal for dining-car waiters, but the steward who seats you is not tipped. Sleeping-car porters get about $1.00 per person per night. The 25¢ or 35¢ you pay a railway station baggage porter is not a tip but the set fee that he must hand in at the end of the day along with the ticket stubs he has used. Therefore his tip is anything you give him above that, 25–50¢ per bag, depending on how heavy your luggage is.

SENIOR CITIZEN AND STUDENT DISCOUNTS. Some attractions throughout the Bay Area offer considerable discounts to Senior Citizens and students. Some may require special city-issued Senior Citizen identification, but in most cases showing a driver's license, passport, or some other proof of age will suffice—"senior" generally being defined as 65 or over for men and 62 or over for women. Museums, first-run and neighborhood movie theaters and even some stores will often post special Senior Citizen rates. Those places offering student discounts are generally somewhat more stringent in their proof requirements—a high school or college ID, international student traveler card, or evidence of age may be requested. Unfortunately, there is no uniformity on these matters.

DRINKING LAWS. In California, the minimum age for the consumption of alcohol is 21. In San Francisco, alcoholic beverages—by the bottle or by the drink—may be purchased from 6:00 A.M. to 2:00 A.M. daily. Package sales are made in liquor stores, some groceries and drugstores. Most restaurants, bars, nightclubs and pubs are licensed to serve a full line of beverages, while some have permits to serve beer and wine only. The legal age for the purchase of alcoholic beverages is also 21; proof of age is required. One quart of alcohol may be imported or transported from another state or country.

 BUSINESS HOURS, HOLIDAYS, AND LOCAL TIME. San Francisco and the areas up and down the coast, like the rest of the United States, are on Standard Time from the last Sunday in October until the last Sunday in April. In April the clock is advanced one hour for Daylight Savings Time, and in October is turned back an hour. The entire state lies within the Pacific Time Zone, which is 3 hours earlier in the day than the Eastern Time Zone, 8 hours earlier than Greenwich Mean Time, and more or less 18 hours earlier on the clock and calendar than Sydney, depending on whether Sydney is on Daylight Savings Time.

Business hours for banks are pretty much like the rest of the country, by and large 9:00 to 3:00, with some opening earlier or staying open later. Shops open at 9:00 A.M. and department stores at 10:00 or 10:30 A.M. Offices operate from 8:30 to 4:30 or 9:00 to 5:00.

Most businesses, banks, and many restaurants will be closed the following holidays (the dates are for 1982): New Year's Day, January 1; Washington's Birthday (observance), February 15; Easter Sunday, April 11; Memorial Day (observance), May 31; Independence Day, July 4; Labor Day, September 6; Thanksgiving Day, November 25; and Christmas Day, December 25.

In addition, banks and some businesses may be closed on Lincoln's Birthday, February 12; Good Friday (from noon), April 8; Columbus Day (observance), October 11; Election Day (partially), November 2; and Veterans Day, November 11.

 SUMMER SPORTS. Northern California spectator sports include the well-publicized Pebble Beach Concours' d'Elegance, starring vintage Bentleys, Rolls Royces, and Bugattis with their celebrity owners, and the annual state fair in Sacramento, "Cal Expo," featuring an aquatic park with the world's largest waterslide, rodeo, and California wine-tasting as well as traditional attractions found at county fairs. Both events are in late August.

Golf enthusiasts crowd the Monterey Peninsula each January for the prestigious Crosby Pro-Am and play at the outstanding public, private and military courses in the area. Enjoy a round or two of golf at Napa's Silverado, with its two Robert Trent Jones courses and twenty **tennis** courts, eight **swimming** pools, plus **bike** and **horseback riding**, and **wine tours**.

In Sonoma, record crowds attest to the popularity of world-class **sports car racing** at Sears Point. And for over one hundred years, the 450 square miles of water in San Francisco Bay have lured weekend sailors in a variety of crafts.

Stream fishing experts suggest the Sacramento River above Lake Shasta. Try Sims Camp, Conant Road, Soda Creek, and Cantara Loop. Each area features different kinds of water. All have riffle water, and Conant and Cantara also have very deep pools. All are well fished. The trout range from 9 to 13½ inches in the riffle water. Additional information is available from: Dept. of Fish and Game, 1416 9th St., 12th Fl., Sacramento, CA 95814, (916) 445–3531, and the Dept. of Forestry, 1416 9th St., 15th Fl., Sacramento, CA 95814, (916) 445–9920.

All along the coast there are **sportfishing** landings and public fishing piers.

Point Reyes National Seashore's 68,000 acres offers miles of beaches, spectacular cliffs, and rugged terrain for **hikes** or short walks. No swimming; very rough surf. However, swimming is permitted at Marin's Stinson Beach from mid-May to mid-September. This area, of the new Golden Gate National Recreation Area, hosts over a million guests annually. Avoid crowded weekends.

Lake Tahoe is a mecca for **water-skiers, boaters, fishermen,** and followers of Lady Luck who flock to the many **gambling** casinos around the lake. Rental houseboats are popular on the Delta and Lake Shasta. **Ballooning** is lush Napa Valley's latest craze, offered at Yountville's Napa Valley Balloons and Adventures Aloft; cost averages $100 an hour, per person. It's fun to float or photograph. The return to terra firma is celebrated with champagne.

Sample **white-water rafting** along the Klamath, Stanislaus, Kern, and Tuolumne rivers. For information, contact: ARTA River Trips, 445 High St., Oakland, CA 94601; OARS, Highway 49, Angels Camp, CA 95222; Outdoor Adventures, 3109 Fillmore, San Francisco, CA 94123; and Wilderness Adventures, P.O. Box 938, Redding, CA 96099.

There is summer **thoroughbred racing** at Albany's Golden Gate Fields, and thoroughbred and **quarter-horse** races at San Mateo's Bay Meadows.

Vacationers will find **yachting** and **speedboating races** and **regattas** (San Francisco Bay), a number of exciting **rodeos,** here and there **polo** matches, **wild burro races,** and **horse shows. Horseback riding** is particularly popular in the San Francisco and Santa Barbara areas.

All up and down the coast, participant sports include **golf, swimming, surfing** (at many places you can rent boards, get instruction), **sailing, saltwater fishing, skindiving, fishing tournaments, water skiing,** and, in the north, **clam digging.** Unfortunately, bad storms in 1983 have eroded stretches of beach, but by 1985 the sand should certainly be replenished through natural processes. In any event, there are still plenty of beaches left to visit.

Bicycling. For free maps or information regarding bike routes in the state, write to: Bicycle Facility Unit, Division of Highways, P.O. Box 1499, Sacramento, CA 95807, (916) 322–4314. For a copy of the 100-page guide of the Pacific Coast Bicentennial Bike Route, send $2.00, plus 12¢ tax (total $2.12) to: Caltrans, 6002 Folsom Blvd., Sacramento, CA 95819.

WINTER SPORTS. Northern California is a **skier's** paradise. The Lake Tahoe area, about 4 hours from San Francisco by car, is the most highly developed ski area here, with numerous resorts; see the Reno-Lake Tahoe section for details. The Sierra's 300-plus inches of average annual snowfall make powder-skiing assured in season, which is roughly from mid-November to mid-April.

Cross-country skiing and **snowshoeing** are growing in popularity in Yosemite's backcountry. However, the harsh Sierra winter environment demands proper planning, special precautions, and appropriate equipment and food. Two- and 3-day cross-country ski trips are offered to Glacier Point and snow camps teach the basics of winter camping and survival. A free snow skiing publication is available from the California Office of Tourism, 1030 13th St., Suite 200, Sacramento, CA 95814.

 ROUGHING IT. More, and improved, camping facilities are springing up each year in California—in national parks, national forests, state parks, private camping areas, and trailer parks, which by now have become a national institution.

A current *California State Park Camping Guide* is available for $1.00 at most state parks or $2.00 by mail from the Department of Parks and Recreation, P.O. Box 2390, Sacramento, CA 95811, (916) 445-6477. This very comprehensive brochure pinpoints all sites throughout the state, but includes specific details as to whether the campsites are developed, primitive, or trailer hookups. Sites especially set aside for hikers and bicyclists are noted. Parks able to accommodate group camping and those which have boat landings are designated.

For information on camping in the National Park System in California, the Department of Interior offers a free booklet, available from the Western Regional Office, National Park Service, Ft. Mason, Bldg. 201, San Francisco, CA 94123, or phone (415) 556-4122.

Throughout this guide, in the various sections on the Redwood Empire, the Monterey–Carmel–Big Sur area and listings for the national and state parks, there is specific information on some of the popular campsites.

The *Redwood Empire Visitors' Guide* lists a number of public campgrounds in their country and advises that there are over 3,000 public campgrounds plus private campgrounds scattered along the Redwood Route. (Send $1.00 to: Redwood Empire Association, One Market Plaza, Suite 1001, San Francisco, CA 94105, for this invaluable guide.)

Reservations are recommended for the state parks, especially in summer. There is a reservation charge plus the campsite fees; write: Ticketron, P.O. Box 26430, San Francisco, CA 94126, or phone (415) 393-6914, elsewhere (800) 952-5580.

To camp in a national park or forest, there is a small fee; people are usually taken on a first-come, first-served basis. Yosemite is an exception, and in summer the valley campgrounds are on a reservation basis. Reservations are taken at the Western Regional Office, National Park Service, Ft. Mason, Bldg. 201, San Francisco, CA 94123, (415) 556–4122, or through Ticketron, P.O. Box 26430, San Francisco, CA 94126.

For information on national forest camping write: U.S. Forest Service, 630 Sansome St., San Francisco, CA 94111, (415) 556–0122. PG&E offers picnic and camping facilities from the Mokelumne River northeast of Stockton to Iron Canyon Reservoir above Shasta Lake, with fishing, boating and biking. All areas are available on a first-come basis. Contact: PG&E-Land Dept., 77 Beale St., Room 2C10, San Francisco, CA 94106. To obtain a free *Plan-Ahead Guide*, listing over 100 private parks and campgrounds in California, write: Leisuretime Reservation Systems, Inc., P.O. Box 532, Citrus Heights, CA 95610. The AAA publishes a *California-Nevada Camping Guide*, available to all members; it is revised annually.

RECREATIONAL VEHICLE PARKS. *San Francisco R.V. Park* (downtown); 250 King St. Almost 200 sites; pets allowed on leash.

Marin Mobile Home Park; 2130 Redwood Hwy., San Rafael. 170 spaces; pets, pool.

Send $2.00 to: California Travel Parks Association, P.O. Box 348, Auburn, CA 95603, for its guide listing almost 200 privately owned RV parks and campgrounds in California.

 FARM VACATIONS, GUEST RANCHES, HEALTH SPAS, AND RESORTS. Farm vacations continue to gain adherents, especially among families with children. Some accommodations are quite deluxe, some extremely simple. Here and there a farm has a swimming pool, while others have facilities for trailers and camping. For a directory of farms that take vacationers (including dates, accommodations, rates, etc.) write to Adventure Guides, Inc., 36 East 57th St., New York, NY 10022, for their 240-page book *Farm, Ranch, and Country Vacations.*

Bodega Bay, just 65 miles north of San Francisco, has a 700-acre working cattle ranch, the *Chanslor Ranch,* that accommodates twenty-four guests for bed-and-breakfast. Furnishings are homey, the lounge is well stocked with books, games, and an autographed picture of Liberace, the most celebrated of the guests. Bunkhouse accommodations for ten over a weekend range from $150.00 and include a fully equipped kitchen and a backyard barbecue. The ranch also rents horses for trail rides. For information write: P.O. Box 327, Bodega Bay, CA 94923, or phone (707) 875–3386.

Quite another type of vacation is offered at the historic *Highlands Inn,* five miles south of Carmel. For the past thirty years, the landmark has attracted honeymooners. Today, after a $30 million transformation, it offers elegant two-story townhouses equipped with private spas with hydromassage tubs, to discriminating guests. A two-level, glass-walled dining room, the Pacific's Edge, will feature California cuisine. Situated on a Monterey pine hillside, the resort's views of the Big Sur coast and the rugged Monterey coastline are awesome. For information write: Box 1700, Carmel, CA 93921, or phone (408) 624–3801.

The Bay Area's only resort is the handsome *Claremont Hotel,* twenty minutes from downtown San Francisco, in Oakland. Recently refurbished, this grande dame hostelry offers 10 day/night tennis courts, an Olympic-sized pool, saunas, a whirlpool, over 20 acres of attractive gardens, and fabulous views of San Francisco Bay. For information write to: The Claremont Resort, Ashby and Domingo Ave., Oakland, CA 94623, or phone (415) 843–3000.

Travelers en route to the Gold Country may select to escape to the deluxe *Rancho Murieta Country Club.* About ½-hour drive from downtown Sacramento, Murieta's recreational amenities include two 18-hole championship golf courses, six lighted tennis courts, a sauna and two spas, jogging track, boating and fishing, an equestrian center and private airport, plus gourmet dining. Although used often for smallish executive-type conferences, all the club's facilities are open to the public. Write to: Country Club, 14813 Jackson Rd., Rancho Murieta, CA 95683, or phone (916) 985–7200.

Another great escape is an hour away from San Francisco in the Napa Valley wine country. The elegant *Silverado Country Club* and Resort offers attractive condominium-type accommodations and everything needed for a relaxing sojourn. The club is situated on 1,200 acres and is dotted with 22 tennis courts, eight swimming pools, two Robert Trent Jones golf courses, a sauna, and a Jacuzzi. Nighttime festivities center in the luxurious Royal Oak Room with its gourmet menu and large selection of local Napa Valley wines. Write to: Silverado Country Club and Resort, 1600 Atlas Peak Rd., Napa, CA 94558, or phone (707) 255–2970.

If traveling up through the Redwood Country, consider pausing at the *Benbow Inn* in Garberville, about 225 miles north of the Bay Area. The Tudor-style building was built in the 1920s by a well-known San Francisco architect, Albert Farr. Antiques are scattered throughout the low-key comfortable inn. Tennis courts, golf, swimming, fishing, hunting and hiking are handy. After-dinner action is the taproom or lounge with its blazing fire. Write to: Benbow Inn, 2675 Benbow Dr., Garberville, CA 95440, or phone (707) 923–2124.

Carmel is one of the most beautiful and busy towns in the state. For a away-from-town resort, *Quail Lodge,* with tennis courts, swimming pools, hot tubs, and an exceptional Continental restaurant, is the answer. Write to: Quail Lodge, 8205 Valley Greens Dr., Carmel, CA 93923, or phone (408) 624–1581.

Situated at the foot of an extinct volcano, Calistoga has been a popular spa since 1859 when Samuel Brannan (leader of the Mormon Battalion that arrived in San Francisco in 1846) opened the first mineral bathhouse. The town is popular year-round, and reservations are necessary on weekends. There are a number of establishments offering mud baths, steamrooms, mineral baths, and massages. *Dr. Wilkinson's,* 1507 Lincoln, is popular with families; phone (707) 942–4102. The *Roman Spa Health Resort* is also family-oriented, and offers hot mineral baths, massage, and whirlpool. It is located at 1300 Washington St.; phone (707) 942–4441.

Sonoma County's newest and most opulent resort/spa is the *Sonoma Mission Inn*. The grand style of the 1930s has been expensively restored to this pink hideaway just 40 miles north of San Francisco. The seven-acre resort is a bit difficult to find without precise directions. We suggest crossing the Golden Gate Bridge, continuing north on 101. Turn right on Hwy. 37, then a left to Hwy. 121 until you reach the historic town of Sonoma. At the plaza, turn left and continue for about 2.5 miles, until the main gates appear. This is really not for a family, but is great for couples—and the spa is growing very popular with San Franciscans anxious to shed a few pounds fast. The exercise is the latest and the best. Exercise and gym area, steamroom, hydrotherapy tubs, massage areas, and beauty salon are all handsomely decorated. This is super deluxe all the way.

 HUNTING. For current information on fees, which animals you may hunt, and seasons, write to: Department of Fish and Game, 1416 9th St., Sacramento, CA 95814, or phone (916) 445-3531. Some of the state's wildlife is protected. Deer and black bear hunting licenses are required. Pheasant, dove, grouse shoots are often in private shooting reserves. No firearms are allowed in either the national or state parks, so big-game hunting is usually in national forests or public lands.

 FISHING. Fishing is an all-season sport and business in the Golden State. Commercial fishermen netted over $230 million in 1980. For the sportsfisherfolk, the state's lakes and rivers abound with a great variety of freshwater fish. Several varieties of trout, salmon, bass, and catfish are especially plentiful. Saltwater catches include salmon, yellowtail, rockfish, and bass. For information, write to the Department of Fish and Game in Sacramento, as above under *Hunting*.

 STATE PARKS. Reservations for state parks may be made through the central reservation system. For forms write: Department of Parks and Recreation, P.O. Box 2390, Sacramento, CA 95811. Reservations must be made two weeks in advance of the dates requested.

Reservations may also be made by applying in person to a local Ticketron outlet. In San Francisco the phone is (415) 393-6914.

In the northern coast and Redwood Empire, the *Del Norte Coast Redwood State Park* is a 6,000-plus-acre redwood, rain forest, and seacoast retreat. Springtime is a splendor of azalea and rhododendron displays. The campground is closed November through March. Very popular in summer is the *Jedediah Smith Redwoods State Park*, about ten miles east of Crescent City. Like Del Norte it is closed during the winter because of heavy rainfall. Fishing, camping, hiking, swimming plus 18 memorial redwood groves are the top attractions. Other state parks in the Del Norte/Humboldt counties are: *Prairie Creek Redwoods; Dry Lagoon; Patrick's Point; Grizzly Creek; Humboldt Redwoods,* and

Richardson Grove. For details on these facilities see the *Redwood Empire* section. Or write the Redwood Empire Association, One Market Plaza, San Francisco, CA 94105, and enclose $1.00 for their comprehensive *Visitor's Guide.*

In the Mendocino area, *Russian Gulch* and *Van Damme State Parks* offer camping, fishing, and hiking. Summer fogs are usual; in winter, expect heavy rainfall. It is noted for dramatic scenery, including pygmy forests. *Hendy Woods'* 700 acres is great for day-use as well as overnight. Write: Mendocino Area State Parks, P.O. Box 127, Mendocino, CA 95460, phone (707) 937–5804, for further information.

The Central Valley's Lake County is just two hours from San Francisco and is the center of water-oriented vacations with year-round fishing, water-skiing, boating, and deer hunting. *Clear Lake State Park,* four miles from Kelseyville, is located along the largest natural body of water entirely within California. At the south end of Clear Lake is the new 900-acre Anderson Marsh. A birdwatchers' paradise, it is rich in archeological sites dating back 10,000 years.

Napa Valley means Wine Country USA to some; others seek out its hot springs at Calistoga and often the all-year camping, recreational facility at *Bothe–Napa Valley State Park,* four miles north of St. Helena.

One of the most unusual and underdeveloped state parks is *Salt Point,* seven miles from historic Fort Ross. Tide pools, caves, and an "ecologically-rich" shoreline attract naturalists. Rock-fishing is good, and skindivers seek the prized abalone. For information on this area, write: Russian River State Parks, P.O. Box 385, Guerneville, CA 95446.

San Francisco and Marin counties are studded with state parks and beaches as well as national seashore and recreational areas. *Tomales Bay State Park,* four miles northwest of Inverness, is a reserve for the photogenic Bishop pine and its trails overlook Tomales Bay. Often windy and cold, the park has its best weather during spring and fall. Just south is out-of-this-world *Point Reyes National Seashore;* see the *Marin County* section.

Mount Tamalpais State Park is almost the city's backyard. The park surrounds Muir Woods with its famous coast redwood groves. Great for hiking; be prepared for winds and often chill, even in summer. A black sand beach at *Fort Cronkhite's Rodeo Cove* is open to the public and is fine for sunbathing and beach strolls (no swimming allowed); the *Marin Headlands State Park,* just west of the Golden Gate Bridge, is adjacent to the Fort Cronkhite beach.

Notable Bay area state parks include *Angel Island, Knowland State Arboretum and Park* (operated by the city of Oakland), and San Francisco's *Maritime Park* at the foot of Hyde St. There are two state beach parks within the city—*Baker* and *Phelan,* though swimming is permitted at Phelan, it is usually the hardy souls who take to the surf.

Those driving south to the Monterey/Big Sur wonderworld often pause at either *Big Basin Redwoods* or *Henry Cowell Redwoods State Parks.* Big Basin attracts hundreds of thousands of campers annually; weekends and summer are very crowded. Cowell is mostly used daytimes as it offers an excellent self-guided walk through impressive groves of pines and redwoods; located near Felton off Hwy. 9. Boulder Creek is the entry for Big Basin. The Santa Cruz area hosts two beach parks—*New Brighton,* open all year with campsites, surf fishing, swimming, and clamming, just four miles below Santa Cruz off Hwy. 1, and *Seacliff,* five miles farther along on Hwy. 1. Seacliff is a day-use area, and is Northern California's most popular beach park, with over a million visitors annually. For information on Monterey Area State Parks, write to: 210 Olivier St., Monterey, CA 93940.

Information on all state parks is available from the Department of Parks and Recreation, P.O. Box 2390, Sacramento, CA 95811, or phone (916) 445–6477.

 NATIONAL PARKS. Each year more and more visitors and residents are taking time out to escape to one of a number of national parks, monuments, seashore, and wilderness areas scattered throughout Northern California. For most, it is their closest encounter with the wild sea, majestic peaks, lush meadowlands, and emerald woods of this fortunate state.

Visiting any of these natural treasures is possible year-round, preferably off-season. The summer season (July 4–early September) is usually a nightmare of too many people, vehicles, and noise in the more popular and easily accessible areas. Spring and fall offer fine weather as well as nature's seasonal color changes. Winter in Yosemite is spectacular, with an awesome quiet hanging over the snow-covered peaks, only occasionally marred by the intrusion of snowcats and snow-bunnies.

There are one-day bus tours from San Francisco to *Yosemite* (Express Tours Unlimited, P.O. Box 77267, San Francisco, CA 94107; phone 415–621–7738); as well as overnight trips. The park hosted over 2.5 million guests in 1980, and is an easy three- to four-hour drive from San Francisco. Thousands of campsites and trailer sites are available and may be reserved through Ticketron (415–393–6914; there is a small service charge). The historic Ahwahnee Hotel offers fine dining and charming accommodations (see the *Yosemite* section for more detailed information).

A 200-mile drive north from the Bay Area through the Redwood Empire brings one to the 166-square-mile *Redwood National Park,* established in 1968. Coast redwoods grow in dense groves and many of the towering giants are a thousand years old. Three state parks within the national park provide campgrounds for some of the half-million yearly visitors. (See the *Redwood Empire* section for more detailed information.)

Lassen Volcanic National Park in north central California is a fascinating moonscape of hot springs and pools, mud pots and cinder cones, twisted remains of trees—all the aftermath of a devastating eruption in 1915. Accommodations are open only spring till October (one guest ranch; campgrounds). Only a part of Lassen is open in winter, for cross-country skiing and winter sports.

Lava Beds National Monument is about a two-hour drive northeast from San Francisco. The mini-park (72 square miles) is honeycombed by lava-tube caves in the southern part. Most of the 19 caves are open to visitors and accessible by automobile. Rangers suggest sturdy shoes, protective headgear, and several lights. If you come unprepared, they will lend you two large flashlights free. The rugged terrain was used as a natural fortress by the Indians during the Modoc War (1872–73). General E. R. S. Canby, the only American general killed in post-Civil War action against the Indians, was assassinated near Tule Lake. A cross marks the site. (For information write to the monument at Tulelake, CA 96134.)

The *Golden Gate National Recreational Area* (GGNRA) is a large urban park that encompasses the western shores of San Francisco and extends north into Marin County. It includes historic sites, 100 miles of trails, picnic spots, beach and yacht facilities, plus rural rolling hills and redwoods almost within sight of the city.

One of the most historic spots in the city is the brick *Fort Point National Historic Site,* at the base of the Golden Gate Bridge. Built at the time of the Civil War, it houses a small museum, open daily. Rangers describe life as a soldier in that long-ago conflict.

Just a half-hour drive north from San Francisco takes one to the closest stand of coastal redwoods at *Muir Woods,* in Mill Valley in Marin County. This 500-acre monument was dedicated in 1908 as a tribute to the naturalist John Muir. In 1898, Muir wrote: "Thousands of tired, nerve-shaken, over-civilized people are beginning to find out that going to the mountains is going home; that wilderness is a necessity." Several tour operators have daily trips to Muir Woods, Sausalito, and Mount Tamalpais.

The *Point Reyes National Seashore* is one of the most rewarding all-day trips out of San Francisco. About 35 miles northwest, this 71,074-acre retreat is a magical world of rolling grasslands with black-and-white Holsteins, a Great Beach, 11 miles of pristine white sand (no swimming, very powerful undertows), sea and shore birds as well as seals, and, during their migrations north and south, the great California gray whales. Usually only the hardy manage the 100-plus steps to the old lighthouse perched over swirling surf.

For information on any of the above national parks, write directly to the park or: National Park Service, Ft. Mason, Bldg. 201, San Francisco, CA 94102, or phone (415) 556–4122. Information on the Golden Gate National Recreation Area: Fort Mason, San Francisco, CA 94123, or phone (415) 556–0560.

 THEME PARKS. *Marriott's Great America,* about 45 miles south of the city, is a total family entertainment complex. *Winchester Mystery House, Gardens and Historical Museum,* 525 South Winchester Boulevard, between Stevens Creek Blvd. and I-280, near State Highway 17 intersection, San Jose, CA 95128; (408) 247–2000. Guided tours daily from 9 A.M. (except Christmas). Last tour departs: Summer, 6 P.M.; Winter, 4 P.M. weekdays and 4:30 P.M. weekends; and Spring and Fall, 5 P.M. For more information, see the *Children's Activities* section in San Francisco Practical Information.

HINTS TO HANDICAPPED TRAVELERS. California has been the bellwether for much of the social reform in the past twenty-five years. In July 1978, the state's new laws concerning special privileges for handicapped people became effective. Presently, handicapped people are issued license plates allowing special parking privileges. The law also applies to vehicles carrying blind passengers and to people with serious heart problems. Handicapped people are now permitted to park in special blue-marked parking spaces, to park for unlimited periods in limited-time spaces, and to park free in metered spaces.

For travel tips for the handicapped, write: Consumer Information Center, Pueblo, CO 81109. Hints include always requesting specially equipped hotel and motel accommodations and making reservations. Allow plenty of time if meeting bus, train, or plane schedules. Be sure your wheelchair is clearly identified if it is carried with other luggage. Check out restroom facilities and, if driving, allow frequent, refreshing breaks. Travel lightly and informally.

Additional information can be obtained by writing to the Society for the Advancement of Travel for the Handicapped, 26 Court St., Brooklyn, NY 11242. This organization has presented awards to both Ramada and Holiday Inns for their programs to provide wheelchair ramps and room modifications for handicapped guests.

Access to the National Parks, a handbook for the physically disabled, describes facilities and services at all U.S. National Parks and costs $3.50. *Access Travel,* a brochure, provides information on 220 worldwide airport facilities. These publications are available from U.S. Government Printing Office, Washington DC 20402. A booklet especially for people with lung problems is available for $1.25 from George Washington University, Rehabilitation Research and Training Center, Ross Hall, Suite 714, 2300 Eye St., N.W., Washington DC 20037.

For a free copy of Amtrak's *Access Amtrak,* a guide to their services for elderly and handicapped travelers, write: Amtrak, National Railroad Passenger Corporation, 400 North Capitol St., N.W., Washington, DC 20001. Handicapped travelers and Senior Citizens are entitled to 25% off regular coach fare, when the one-way coach fare is at least $40.00. A special children's handicapped fare is also available, offering qualifying children aged 2 to under 12 years a special savings—37.5% of the applicable one-way regular adult coach fare.

In San Francisco, BART (Bay Area Rapid Transit System), has all stations equipped with elevators. Contact the station agent via the white courtesy telephone for this service. Also, any required assistance for processing your ticket will be provided by the station agent. Stations are equipped with accessible restrooms, telephones, and drinking fountains. Parking lots provide reserved spaces for the handicapped persons. However, automobiles using these places must display special-issue plates for disabled persons or a handicap placard available from any local Department of Motor Vehicles. For information on a Bay Region Transit Discount Card, phone BART's Office of Passenger Service, (415) 465–4100, ext. 569.

The following hotels and motels will make special efforts to comply with needs of handicapped guests. Phone or write in advance for reservations and mention any special needs or requests. *The Bedford,* 761 Post St. Best Western Airport Inn, 380 South Airport Blvd., South San Francisco; wheelchair units, steam baths. *Cable Motel,* 1450 Lombard St.; one ground room especially designed for paraplegics. *Clift Hotel,* Geary and Taylor Sts.; several rooms have wider entrances to bathroom. *De Ville Motel,* 2599 Lombard St. *Fairmont Hotel,* California and Mason Sts. *Holiday Inn–Civic Center,* 50 8th St., has several rooms designed for paraplegic guests. Also the *Holiday Inns* at *Fisherman's Wharf, Golden Gateway,* and *San Francisco Airport. Hyatt on Union Square. Hyatt Regency,* 5 Embarcadero, has specially designed accommodations for paraplegics. *Cathedral Hill,* Van Ness and Geary Blvd. *Laurel Motor Inn,* California and Presidio Aves.; shuttle bus service to local hospitals for visitors. *Mark Hopkins Hotel,* California and Mason Sts. *Miyako Hotel,* 1625 Post St. *Ramada Inn at Fisherman's Wharf* and *San Francisco Airport* have rooms especially designed for paraplegics. *Rancho Lombard,* 1501 Lombard; wheelchair units. *San Francisco Hilton,* Mason and Farrell Sts. *Seal Rock Inn,* 545 Point Lobos. *Sheraton at Fisherman's Wharf;* several rooms designed for paraplegics. *Sheraton Palace,* 639 Market; 4 wheelchair units. *Sheraton–San Francisco Airport;* 10 rooms especially designed for paraplegics. *Sir Francis Drake,* 450 Powell. *Stanford Court,* 905 California St. *St. Francis,* Powell and Geary Sts. *Grosvenor Inn,* 1050 Van Ness. *Chelsea Motor Inn,* 2095 Lombard; all rooms have wide doors, bars in bath. *Quality Inn–San Francisco,* 2775 Van Ness Ave. *Vagabond Airport,* 1640 Bayshore Hwy.

 POSTAGE. At press time, rates for international mail from the United States are as follows: *Surface* letters to Canada and Mexico are at the U.S. domestic rate: 20¢ for 1 ounce or under, 37¢ for 2 ounces or under, but these rates actually get airmail carriage to those countries. Surface letters to other foreign destinations are 30¢ for the first ounce and 47¢ for up to 2 ounces. Airmail letters to foreign destinations other than to Canada, Mexico, and some Caribbean and South American countries are 40¢ ½ ounce, 80¢ 1 ounce, $1.20 1½ ounces, $1.60 2 ounces. Postcards (except for Canada and Mexico, which go airmail for 13¢) are 19¢ for surface mail and 28¢ for airmail to any foreign destination. Standard international aerogram letters, good for any foreign destination, are 30¢, but of course nothing may be enclosed in them. Postal rates are no exception in this period of inflation, so check before you mail, in case they have gone up since press time.

SECURITY. The San Francisco Convention and Visitors Bureau recently stopped distributing a free guide to Victorian houses in the city, and other maps and materials that either directed tourists through a high-crime area, the *Western Addition,* or made it appear that Golden Gate Park is within walking distance of the Civic Center, thus taking tourists into the Western Addition. The Western Addition, an area roughly bounded by Geary Blvd. on the north, Hayes

St. on the south, Gough St. on the east, and Steiner St. on the west, is a low-income area within minutes of popular Japantown and St. Mary's Roman Catholic Cathedral, as well as near many expensive high-rise apartments and attractive old Victorians. *Avoid the Western Addition,* which is unsafe for outsiders.

San Francisco is a disarming place, and looks safer than it really is. The Union Square area, with its world-famous hotels, is bounded on the west and south by some seamy areas—and the hotels themselves are a magnet for professional thieves. As in most other places in the world these days, don't leave money or valuables in your hotel room. Be sure always to lock your door—even when you are inside. For valuables, use the safe-deposit boxes offered by hotels; they are usually free.

Carry most of your funds in traveler's checks, and be sure to record the numbers in a separate, secure place. Watch your purse or wallet, *especially* on buses or trolleys—a popular scene for pickpockets, who are highly skilled and usually don't look at all like sinister criminals. Enjoy casual acquaintances—but at a distance. Never leave your car unlocked, or valuable articles in plain sight in the car even if it is locked. It's wise to keep your car locked even when you're inside it; motorists have been known to be robbed while stopped at red lights. Again, avoid the Western Addition, where many such robberies have occurred. The Hunters Point area, too, has been a popular spot for "red-light robbers." Terminal counters and hotel check-in desks are also favored spots for lurking opportunists.

Avoid walking along Market St. outside the downtown area, or in the nearby Tenderloin District south of Market. Broadway at night, east of Columbus, is also to be avoided, if only because of the sleazy porno shops centered there. Also avoid Polk and Larkin Sts. in the evening or at night; those areas, along with the heavily Latino Mission District, attract street criminals who prey on the homosexuals who patronize the area, and on any tourists unwise enough to wander along.

It isn't hard to have a safe vacation in San Francisco—but it is too bad to let a little carelessness spoil it.

 EMERGENCY TELEPHONE NUMBERS. In San Francisco proper, the emergency number for *fire, police, ambulance,* and *paramedics* is 911. Or, dial "0" for Operator, and ask the person's help in connecting you immediately with the appropriate agency.

EXPLORING SAN FRANCISCO

by
TONI CHAPMAN

*Toni Chapman is a San Francisco travel and feature writer whose
articles have appeared in major national and international publications.
A member of the Society of American Travel Writers, she also co-
produces and hosts a cable television travel program in the Bay Area. A
specialist in writing on art, architecture, fashions and shopping. Ms.
Chapman is also a certified appraiser.*

A very special and exciting way to arrive in San Francisco is by sea.
Unfortunately, few visitors, except seasonal cruise-ship passengers and
yachting parties, experience the thrill of sailing through the Golden
Gate—with the hills of the city on the south and the steep Marin
Headlands on the north. Though the strait is a mile wide and three

miles long, it is often shrouded in the "stynkinge fogges" mentioned by
Sir Francis Drake's chronicler in 1579. It wasn't until almost two
hundred years had passed that a wandering party of Spaniards in 1769
discovered the Bay. They were searching for Monterey but quickly
recognized the importance of their accidental find.

Today's tourists have daily the opportunity of enjoying exhilarating
cruising on the Bay. Two local tour companies offer an array of excursions, ranging from hour runs to special Sunday Brunch and Thursday-
evening barbecue parties featuring Country-and-Western music. The
Blue and Gold Fleet, berthed at Pier 39, provides its passengers with
validated parking across the street. Among the cruises of the Red and
White Fleet, based at Fisherman's Wharf, is the highly popular Alcatraz trip—a two-hour guided tour of the former federal prison, and
round-trip transportation to the island in the Bay. The cruises follow
similar courses, using taped narrations as one sails westward toward
the Gate and the stunning single span suspension bridge, completed in
1937. The much-painted and photographed bridge connects the city
with Marin County and the Redwood Empire country farther north.

Snacks are available aboard and we suggest this as a first-thing-in-
the-morning outing (departures are from 10:00 A.M.). On a clear day
(which is often) the morning light casts a warm glow on the different-
hued homes climbing Russian Hill, the weather-aged fishing boats
cluttered at Fisherman's Wharf, rosy Ghirardelli Square and its fairytale clock tower, and on the swelling seas beyond the entrance. Return
vistas include Alcatraz, from afar; Treasure Island (a U.S. Navy base
which took over the site of the 1939 World's Fair), the landmark Ferry
Building with another prominent clock tower, and the burgeoning
Embarcadero.

The Northern Waterfront

Following the cruise, start strolling. Those passengers using the Blue
and Gold Fleet, from Pier 39, will find much to attract and entertain
them at this newest of San Francisco's waterfront diversions. Dozens
of shops with almost irresistible, though often useless, merchandise will
tempt. A myriad of eateries confuse some parents seeking only a traditional Coke and burger stop. On-going free entertainment, accessible
validated parking, as well as nearby public transportation, assure
crowds most days.

Meanwhile, a bit farther down to mainstream Fisherman's Wharf
(the eastern end is Pier 43, where the Cape Horn square-rigged *Balclutha,* a floating maritime museum, beckons with early photographs and
marine memorabilia), where the Red and White Fleet passengers
alight, a bounty of amusements for all ages awaits. Dining choices run

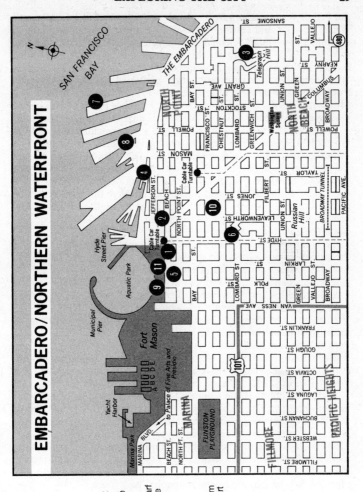

EMBARCADERO/NORTHERN WATERFRONT

Points of Interest

1) Buena Vista Café
2) The Cannery
3) Coit Tower
4) Fisherman's Wharf
5) Ghiradelli Square
6) Lombard Street
   ("Crookedest
   Street")
7) Pier 39
8) Balclutha
9) Maritime Museum
10) San Francisco Art
    Institute
11) Victorian Park

the gamut from memorable fresh fish at Alioto's at #8 Fisherman's Wharf to tasty and thrifty "walk-away" shrimp or crab cocktails at bustling street stalls. Selective shopping is offered at three dramatic complexes. The first, Ghirardelli Square, is a charming series of brick former factory buildings. Until the early 1960s, the Ghirardelli Chocolate Company's aromatic production perfumed the northern waterfront. The outstanding ethnic restaurants there now include The Mandarin, in a stunning Chinese setting; Paprikás Fono, an Hungarian food and folk art festival, and Modesto Lanzone's Italian pastadom.

The town's newest novelty—Maxwell's Plum—shines down from Ghirardelli Square with acres of twinkling lights, brilliant Tiffany glass, wondrous animals, and forgettable objets d'art. Restaurateur Warner LeRoy (son of movie mogul Mervyn LeRoy) created New York's Tavern on the Green, reputed to be the nation's second-highest-grossing restaurant. The dynamic showman dazzled the San Francisco media and many local folk with the biggest, brightest, circus-cum-restaurant the Barbary Coast has ever seen. You can skip the food, but catch the action for sure.

An older but equally "famous for everything but the food" haunt is the mellow Buena Vista Café, at 2765 Hyde. Birthplace of Irish Coffee stateside; local columnist Stan Delaplane is credited with importing the Gaelic concoction. The BV opens at 9:00 A.M., serves a delicious full breakfast, and is always crowded. Try to get a view table overlooking nostalgic Victorian Park with its cable-car turntable.

Historic sights close to Ghirardelli Square worth investigating include the marine memorabilia at the Maritime Museum in Aquatic Park and the restored vessels usually docked at the Hyde Street Pier. Ripley's Believe It Or Not Museum, 175 Jefferson, displays over 500 curiosities. The wharf's newest museum, the Guiness Museum of World Records, 235 Jefferson, abounds in educational exhibits.

A near neighbor is the Cannery, the second complex of red-brick former factories. The three-story structure was built in 1894 to house the Del Monte Fruit and Vegetable Cannery. Shops, art galleries, bookstores, and unusual restaurants now ring the olive-tree courtyard. The Hungry Tiger on the top floor combines sweeping views and a moderate family-favorites menu. Slip into Spanish mood and food at the striking El Greco, with nightly flamenco music. Spicy Szechuan favorites can be enjoyed at the roof-top Shang Yuen.

The City of the Hills

San Francisco is a city born of the sea and sand. Geologists explain that two main fault zones divide the city into three blocks, each composed of different kinds of rocks. When the blocks move suddenly along the larger faults, the result is an earthquake. The San Andreas Fault, responsible for the 1906 quake, does not appear within San Francisco proper, but rather it crosses the ocean floor just off the Golden Gate. The San Andreas Fault extends 600 miles from Cape Mendocino (north of the city) to the Gulf of California.

The sandstone bedrock that underlies much of San Francisco is visible at Telegraph Hill. Geologists call it "graywacke"—originally gray, but time and weather turn it light brown and finally a soft orange. The three most famous hills in town, Russian, Telegraph, and Nob, have a foundation of "graywacke" or sandstone, shale, and volcanic rock. Called by geologists the Franciscan Formation, the rock is first seen on entering the Bay from the Pacific Ocean at Point Lobos.

Telegraph Hill rises from the east end of Lombard St. to about 300 feet, and is capped with the landmark Coit Tower, built in 1933 as a monument to the city's volunteer firemen. Early in the Gold Rush, one of the city's most memorable eccentrics arrived: Lillie Hitchcock Coit. Legend relates that at age seventeen Lillie deserted a wedding party and chased down the street after her favorite engine, Knickerbocker No. 5, clad in her bridesmaid finery. Soon after, she was made an honorary member of the Knickerbocker Company. Ever after she signed herself Lillie Hitchcock Coit 5—in honor of her favorite fire engine.

Lillie died in 1929 at the age of eighty-six, leaving the city $125,000 to erect the 210-foot tower. Many of the city's foremost artists worked on the fifteen frescoes decorating the rotunda.

Over the years Telegraph Hill has been home for a colorful collection of people. During the Gold Rush, fishermen and would-be Comstock tycoons huddled there in makeshift shacks and tattered tents. Later, the first of the artistic colonies took root, attracted by sublime Bay and Golden Gate views, cheap rents, and the central location. Later still, more substantial houses were built on the tops of the cliffs.

For a period of six years extensive quarrying was carried on to provide fill for the Embarcadero. It exposed the face of Telegraph, and the dynamiting caused several houses to topple. Homeowners were understandably incensed, and two people were shot to death during the violent protests. The dynamiting of the thick Franciscan formation was quickly stopped.

New life and vitality is coming to the hill. Expensive pier-front condominiums, handsome commercial structures, including the impressive new Levi Strauss headquarters, attractive restaurants, and young affluent residents are making Telegraph a very desirable habitat.

Just west is *Russian Hill.* In the early days the summit was a cemetery for Russian sailors. Now the hills are covered with an astounding array of housing: simple studios, sumptuous pied-à-terres, Victorian flats, and costly boxlike condos. Don't miss the spectacular artist Dong

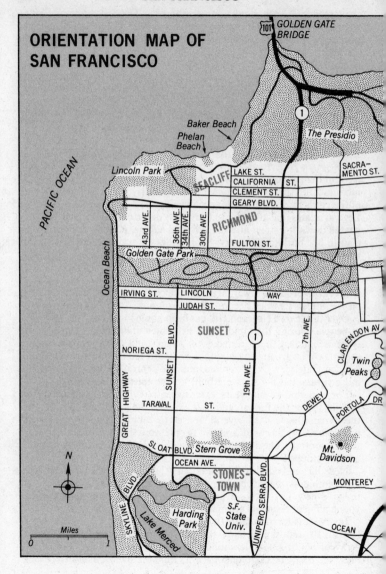

ORIENTATION MAP OF SAN FRANCISCO

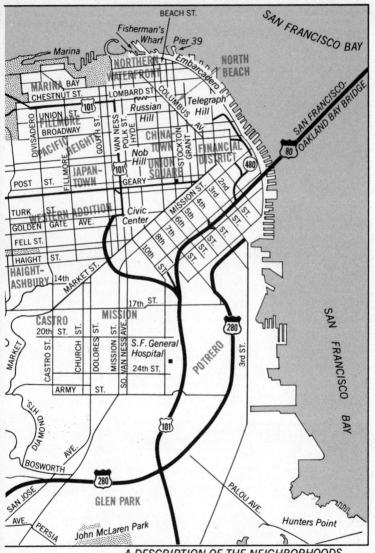

*A DESCRIPTION OF THE NEIGHBORHOODS
FOLLOWS ON THE NEXT PAGE.*

Northern Waterfront. The No. 1 area for visitors, with Fisherman's Wharf, Pier 39, Ghirardelli Square, and the Cannery, all with boutiques and view dining; plus the Maritime Museum and square-rigger *Balclutha*. Fun to stroll anytime from Jefferson to Beach Sts.

North Beach. The City's most European-flavored neighborhood, with growing Asian influence. Fine and reasonable dining; cafés and coffee houses; Italian food shops; jazz clubs. Busy daytimes; some nighttime strolling along Columbus Ave. and parts of Broadway. Eastern Broadway has strip and sex clubs. Grant Ave. in North Beach is now shabby.

Chinatown. Good restaurants; very crowded most of the time. Shopping and strolling on Grant Ave. High-density but run-down neighborhood; sweatshop factories.

Union Square/Downtown. From Sutter on north to Market on south; from Mason on west to Financial District on east. The center of the City's fashionable shopping. Deluxe hotels. Adjacent theater district along Geary St. Boutiques, bars, and restaurants.

Financial District. The Pacific Coast Stock Exchange; major banking, insurance firms in skyscrapers. Excellent restaurants. Rather deserted late evenings and weekends.

Japantown. Good restaurants; 2 major hotels; interesting shopping and strolling at 5-acre Japan Center. Adjacent area **(Western Addition)** not safe.

Pacific Heights. Many of the City's loveliest and most expensive Victorians and mansions. Most diplomatic missions quartered here. Superb views, restaurants, shopping throughout.

Fillmore. Many of the Victorian gingerbreads and Queen Anne gothics here are being restored, and there is a growing number of small shops and restaurants. Avoid south of Sutter St.

Marina. One of the City's loveliest upper-middle-class neighborhoods; Mediterranean-style homes built in the 1920s on landfill for the 1915 Panama-Pacific Exhibition (the Palace of Fine Arts is its only survivor). Chestnut St. has interesting shops and restaurants.

Civic Center. City, state, and federal buildings, plus the Opera House, S.F. Museum of Modern Art, and the new Davies Symphony Hall. Nearby Tenderloin, notorious for dangerous street people, is being upgraded. Mason and Turk Sts. dubbed "Transvestite Center."

Castro. The heart of the City's gay community, with trendy shops, restaurants, bars. Weekend crowds include straight visitors. The side streets are lined with two- and three-story Victorians originally tenanted by Irish, German, and Scandinavian (as in "I Remember Mama") working-class families. Strolling is safe any time. Nearby Noe Valley's 24th St. has inexpensive restaurants and unusual small businesses.

Richmond. The City's "new" Chinatown is in a middle-class area of row houses and small apartments. Russians, Irish, Filipinos, Koreans, and Japanese coexist. Clement St. has an international array of restaurants and shops, some late-night action at clubs. **Sea Cliff** is a gorgeous and exclusive area of large homes.

Sunset. Mostly middle-class; many senior citizens. Irving St. has an international bazaar air. Little to offer most visitors.

Lake Merced/Stonestown. Stonestown, completed in 1952, was the City's first shopping mall. Low- and high-rise apartments ring the lake, a popular jogging scene. S.F. State University, the Zoo, golf courses, and beaches are nearby.

Mission. A heavily populated Latino area. 24th St. offers Spanish/Mexican/Central American food, and one of the City's liveliest nightclubs, Cesar's, is nearby. There has been friction between gays (moving into the area's Victorians) and Latin men. At night Mission St. becomes a parade of Latin "low riders"—cruising custom cars.

Potrero is mostly a working-class neighborhood. Some affluent professionals are moving into the area for its good views of the City. Light industry is scattered throughout; not much for visitors.

South of Market. The George Moscone Convention Center, opened in December 1981, is expected to change this rundown district ringed by freeways and piers, with its unsavory S&M bars and punk-rock hangouts. Except for the Convention Center and the adjacent Yerba Buena Center, an as-yet-unrealized cluster of shops and restaurants, there is presently little for visitors here.

Kingman-type views of the bay from Lombard ("the world's crooked-est") St. There are eight twisting turns in the one-block run from Hyde to Leavenworth. Hardy souls often tackle the nearby two hundred steps down the flower-decorated maze.

Dropping off to the south of Russian Hill is *Nob Hill*. Some of San Francisco's top hotels (Fairmont, Mark Hopkins, Stanford Court, and the Huntington) crown this mount. Expensive restaurants and apartments complement the exclusive Pacific Union Club, once the home of bonanza king James C. Flood.

Many visitors opt for a skyroom-restaurant night view of San Francisco from Nob Hill's Fairmont or Mark Hopkins Hotels or the nearby Carnelian Room topping the Bank of America's world headquarters.

A new spot to explore is *Levi's Plaza*, below Telegraph Hill. Cargo West, a brick landmark from which unwary sailors were shanghaied during the heydays of the infamous Barbary Coast, and the former Italian Swiss Colony wine depot were remodeled and are part of the three-building waterfront complex. Landscape architect Lawrence Halprin's dramatic fountain and treescapes make this a delightful dell in which to "brown bag" lunch or enjoy Garo's, the fine seafood restaurant.

The Flavor of North Beach

Like neighboring Chinatown, North Beach, centered around Columbus Avenue north of Broadway, is best explored on foot. Much of the old-world ambience still lingers in this easy-going and polyglot Bohemia. In the early days there truly was a beach. At the time of the Gold Rush the Bay extended into the hollow between Telegraph and Russian Hills, forming a beach. A semaphore crowned Telegraph Hill, signaling the arrival of ships off the Golden Gate. Since the 1930s, Coit Tower has dominated this view site. The tower was built as a monument to the city's brave firefighters and is named after the first female volunteer fireperson, colorful Lillie Hitchcock Coit. Murals executed by WPA artists depict the local artistic scene circa 1934.

Among the first immigrants to Yerba Buena in the early 1840s were young men from the northern provinces of Italy. By 1848, the village, now renamed San Francisco, became an overnight boom town with the discovery of gold. Thousands more poured into the burgeoning area seeking the golden dream.

For many, the trail ended in San Francisco. The Genoese started the still-active fishing industry, as well as much-needed produce businesses. Later, the Sicilians emerged as leaders of the fishing fleets, and eventually as proprietors of the seafood restaurants lining Fisherman's Wharf.

Meanwhile, their Genoese cousins established banking and manufacturing empires.

Washington Square may well be the daytime social heart of what was once considered "Little Italy." By mid-morning, groups of conservatively dressed elderly Italian men are sunning and sighing on the state of their immediate world—North Beach. Nearby, laughing Chinese and Caucasian playmates race through the grass with Frisbees or colorful kites. Multi-national jeans-clad mothers exchange shopping tips and ethnic recipes. Tourists tend to focus their lens on the imposing Romanesque splendor of Saints Peter and Paul, often called "the Italian Cathedral." The twin-turreted terra cotta towers are local landmarks. The church has a busy calendar of traditional weddings, funerals, and festivals. On the first Sunday in October, the annual Blessing of the Fishing Fleet is celebrated with Mass, followed by a parade to Fisherman's Wharf. Another very popular event is the annual Columbus Day pageant.

North Beach is a picturesque blend of savory Italian delicatessens and recently arrived Chinese markets. A rich variety of good eating is displayed. Wonderful aromas waft the air. Coffee beans roasting at Graffeo at 733 Columbus are shipped to customers all over the U.S. Stop in the Panelli Brothers deli at 1419 Stockton, between Columbus and Vallejo, for a memorable meat and cheese sandwich to go, at a reasonable price. Nearby, Gloria's at 635 Vallejo, between Stockton and Columbus, features garlic sausage, prosciutto, and mortadella as well as over seventy-five tasty cheeses. And sandwiches to go.

The finest produce reigns at Rossi's, just next to Gloria's. Stop by and pick up the best of the season. Especially notable are their fancy grape and Bing cherry offerings. Right around the corner is Molinari's, established in 1896, and perhaps the Beach's most widely known deli. There is usually a wait for service, but it is well worth the time. Molinari's is rated as having the best salami in town, and it is shipped all over the country.

Sprinkled throughout the area are Chinese merchants specializing in exotic teas and spices, hard-to-find Oriental favored vegetables, and daily displays of freshly caught fish.

Over the years, North Beach has attracted creative individualists. The combination of low rents, tolerant attitudes, and the camaraderie of kindred souls attracted early Bohemians. Just after World War II, international attention focused on the North Beach area: The Beat Renaissance of the 1950s was born, grew up, flourished, then faltered in this then predominately Italian neighborhood. The Beat gathering places are gone. Only a few of the original leaders remain, notably poet Lawrence Ferlinghetti. His City Lights Books, at 261 Columbus, near Broadway, is the remaining rendezvous. Eastern visitors like Allen

Ginsberg, Gregory Corso, and Jack Kerouac, and local habitues Kenneth Rexroth and Brother Antoninus (William Everson) gathered at the bookstore to exchange thoughts.

Times have changed, and much of the counterculture shocks of the 1950s and 1960s are part of today's mainstream society. The face of the Beach is changing: rents are soaring, and some of the city's top restaurants draw more affluent outsiders to this urbane habitat.

The goodness of the North Beach lifestyle is reflected by the ever-increasing number of cafés. In true European manner, they offer informal, relaxing atmospheres to enjoy an espresso or glass of wine while chatting with friends or perusing the daily papers. All serve light foods, and many serve wine and beer in addition to a wide range of coffees, teas, and chocolates. There are more than a dozen in North Beach. Extremely popular are Café Roma, 414 Columbus, and across the street at 411, Café Puccini. The granddaddy of them all, and the "21" of such cafés, is Enrico's at 504 Broadway. Their sidewalk tables are great for people watching from noon to 3:00 A.M. Even the honky-tonk air of Broadway's brash barkers, shoddy and expensive sex-show clubs and their clientele hasn't tarnished the lure of Enrico's. Nightly, neighbor Finocchio's draws bus loads of curious tourists to its lavish production featuring female impersonators. This after-dark neon-dazzle is best viewed from the security of a car, or a nightcap at Enrico's, preferably before midnight.

Chinatown

This city-within-a-city is the largest Chinese community outside Asia. Approximately 75,000 Chinese live in the sixteen-block downtown area just south of North Beach (and in Richmond's "New" Chinatown). Some unofficial sources estimate the number at over 100,000 in the city, with thousands more living in the Bay Area.

Downtown Chinatown is officially defined as "Bay Street south, to California and from Sansome at the edge of downtown west to Van Ness"—which includes much of Russian and Nob Hills.

But most visitors see only the tip of pagodaland. The bustling, noisy, and colorful stretches of Grant and Stockton Sts. north of Bush are sometimes difficult to navigate. As in Hong Kong, most families shop *daily* for fresh meats and vegetables, bakery products, and often the traditional herbal medicines and ointments displayed on dusty shelves.

Visitors usually enter this land of magic through the ornate dragon-crowned gate at Bush and Grant Ave., and, to savor Chinatown best, explore it on foot. This street world shines with much good-luck crimson and gold; giant beribboned floral wreaths mark openings of new bakeries, bazaars, and banks. Nighttime is as busy here as the daytime.

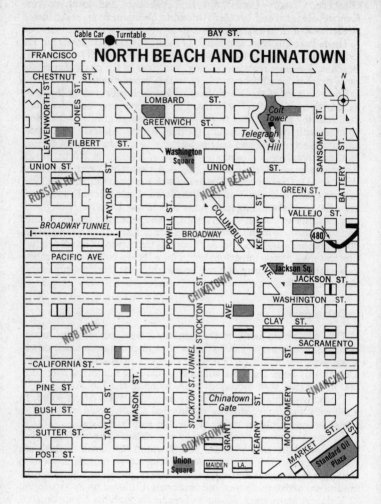

NORTH BEACH AND CHINATOWN

All day, a variety of cafes and restaurants satisfy any culinary craving. Most are tiny and crowded, their food tasty and cheap. A few are elegant, rather self-consciously Chinoiserie in design and décor, but commanding in serving memorable Mandarin, Cantonese, and Szechuan specialities.

Skip a Big Mac; opt instead for *dim sum,* the Chinese version of smorgasbord, a variety of pastries filled with meat, fish, and vegetables. Over a dozen Chinatown restaurants feature this unusual lunch/brunch adventure from about 11:00 A.M. to 3:00 P.M. Usually, stacked food-service carts patrol the premises. Customers select from the varied offerings, and the final bill is tabulated by the number of different plates on the table. *Dim sum* restaurants tend to be big, crowded, cheap, and noisy. The crowd is friendly, and suggestions are often offered by nearby strangers as to what is inside the tempting morsels. Two favorites on Pacific Ave. are Asia Garden at 772 and Tung Fong, at 808. Noodle fans frequent Tong Kee at 854 Washington and also at 710 Kearny; those specialize in tantalizing wonton noodles. Many of the smaller, inexpensive Chinese restaurants and cafés do not accept credit cards; some serve wine and beer. Usually a full bar is found in the more expensive establishments, who also accept most major credit cards.

Chinese immigration was first spurred by the Gold Rush of 1849. Many of the illiterate "Celestials" made their way to Sacramento and eventually to the foothills of the Mother Lode to work the mines. Hundreds remained in dusty San Francisco, which they called in Chinese "Great City of the Golden Hill." Life was hard in the teeming, crime-ridden pre-earthquake ghetto inhabited by a wholly male society. Hostility and violence has marked much of the Chinese 125-year history in California.

In the 1880s, historian Hubert Howe Bancroft commented, "Sacramento Street was already becoming known as Little China, from the establishment of some Mongol merchants upon its north side, on either side of Dupont Street. . . . " Dupont St. is now Grant Ave., renamed in 1906 for the eighteenth President of the United States, Ulysses Simpson Grant.

Today, shopping surrounds the stroller along Grant Ave. Much of what is offered in the countless curio shops is worthless, and discerning visitors may be dismayed by the wealth of gaudy and glittery gimcrackery. In recent years, however, a growing number of large department-store-type operations have opened. Most feature an ever-growing array of products from Mainland China. Many attractively priced souvenirs or gifts are appearing: hand-painted porcelain prizes from teacups to complete dinner services; exquisite hand-embroidered table and bed linens; whimsical straw animals from Shanghai; and precious goose-down comforters from Peking.

At the northeast corner of Grant and California St., Old St. Mary's Church served as the city's Catholic cathedral until 1891. Granite quarried in China was used in the structure, dedicated in 1854. Diagonally across is St. Mary's Park, a tranquil setting for the late local sculptor Beniamino (Benny) Bufano's stainless-steel and rose-colored granite heroic Sun Yat Sen. The 12-foot statue of the founder of the Republic of China was dedicated in 1937.

The original Chinatown burned down after the 1906 earthquake, and the first building to set the style for the "new" Chinatown is the three-tiered pagoda called the Old Chinese Telephone Exchange, 743 Washington Street, built in 1909. Also worth a visit, is Buddha's Universal Church, 720 Washington Street. It is a five-story hand-built temple decorated with murals and tile mosaics.

Turn down the corner at Grant Ave. and Clay St. At this corner, the city's first house was built in 1836. A short walk brings one to Portsmouth Square, the potato patch that became the plaza for Yerba Buena and where Montgomery raised the American flag in 1846. Note the bronze galleon in memory of Robert Louis Stevenson, who often visited the site during his 1879–80 residence on the Square. Walk over to the Holiday Inn, 750 Kearny St., to the Chinese Culture Center, open Tuesdays through Saturdays from 10 to 5. Frequent exhibitions of Chinese-American artists are displayed as well as traveling exhibitions of Chinese culture. Saturday-afternoon walking tours of historic points in Chinatown are offered by the Center.

The other main Chinatown shopping street for everyday needs is Stockton, an easy half-hour walk from downtown Union Square via the tunnel at Sutter and Stockton Sts. One emerges into a typical Hong Kong thoroughfare. Usually the street is difficult to navigate due to the throngs of locals laden with bulging shopping bags crammed with fresh meats and vegetables, bakery products and, at holidays, flowering branches. On Sunday mornings one often sees a live duck or goose being tucked in a corner of a carryall, after being purchased from the battered pick-up of a nearby farmer.

Here, too, one rubs elbows with emigrant grandmothers, traditional in somber padded jackets, tiny Mary-Jane-slippered feet, and ivory-hued enigmatic expressions. Exuberant youngsters sporting Superman T-shirts, jeans, and cowboy boots indifferently jostle their elders. Trendy teenagers crowd Walgreen's magazine racks, culling the latest fashion, sporting, and entertainment news from popular periodicals.

Inspect the colorful rows of oranges, tangerines, snow peas, winter melons, and ginger roots piled in windows and countertops. Examine the tanks full of fish and the many butcher shops decorated with strings of glazed Peking ducks. Slip into one of the tiny herb shops with dusty, crowded shelves harboring strange-looking roots and creatures in glass containers, large and small.

Recently, Superior Court Judge Harry Low of San Francisco remarked, " . . . it has only been in recent years that Chinese-Americans have fully participated in community life. Our participation and influence is yet developing and has yet to reach full maturity."

Visitors to the Napa Valley wine country tour the limestone wine-aging tunnels and admire the handsome stone and rock walls, constructed without cement or mortar, and built by anonymous Chinese artisans. Also widely recorded is the labor of the 12,000 Chinese workers who helped complete the transcontinental railroad between 1865 and 1869. The first of California's Asian immigrants contributed greatly to the state's economic growth.

San Francisco's Chinese-American community continues to add a rich cultural and commercial asset to the city.

Union Square

Much of the glamour and gloss of the city is centered in this one-block spree of high-fashion stores, international hotels, and some drifters sunning, preaching, and panhandling in the carefully cared-for park three or four blocks south of Chinatown. Ringing the greenery is the elegant St. Francis Hotel. Its recently opened Art Deco Compass Rose is a charming retreat for tea or a light repast. In addition to fine dining, there are some outstanding shops in the hotel, including Maison Mendessolle, for fine ladies' apparel, Fox's for gems big and small, and the City Gallery for oils, graphics and sculpture. Saks Fifth Avenue opened its modern, rather stark new store in late 1981, and it was an immediate smashing success. A few doors down, Bullock and Jones has a well-established reputation for fine British apparel, including Burberry's for both sexes. At Post and Stockton, the Hyatt On Union Square Hotel sports a distinctive fountain by artist Ruth Asawa. Notice the detailed scenes on her work. Hyatt's Napper Tandy or the new Napper Too are good choices for lunch. Opposite the hotel is I. Magnin, noted for fine fashions for women, an excellent gift department, and—just new—a lower level with a gourmet food department and tiny café operated by famous Narsai David, local restaurateur and TV celebrity chef. When you exit Magnin on Geary, turn left to enter Macy's. This full department store has imported furniture, Oriental rugs, and bed and linen departments. It also promotes high fashion and trendy men's and women's togs. The Cellar features gourmet cookware, a bakery, post office, and one of the city's most popular eateries, Mama's.

Shopping really reigns in this part of downtown. The controversial checkerboard facade and dazzling, restored glass rotunda made the

Neiman-Marcus store an immediate tourist attraction when it opened in 1983. On the corner of Post and Stockton is a branch of Alfred Dunhill and a charming Wedgwood china boutique. Just down the block Gumps, Elizabeth Arden, Eddie Bauer, and Celine await your presence. Maiden Lane is a two-block shopping distraction. Orvis stocks the finest sports equipment for outdoorsy types; Britex displays a world of luxe fabrics for the home dressmaker. Also here are Courrèges featuring French exclusives, and San Francisco's leading pet shop, Robinson's.

There are a number of alleys or small lanes in the downtown area, often charming and good for window shopping: Maiden Lane, off Union Square, the best known; Belden Lane; and Tillman Place, with a fine bookstore featuring children's literature.

Civic Center

San Francisco's Civic Center stands today as one of the county's great city, state, and federal building complexes with handsome adjoining cultural institutions. The concept is really the fulfillment of the plans envisioned by Chicago architect Daniel H. Burnham and other turn-of-the-century advocates of the "City Beautiful." The City Hall, facing Polk St., between Grove and McAllister Sts., modeled after the Capitol in Washington, D.C., is a Baroque masterpiece of granite and marble. Its dome is higher than the Washington version, and dominates the area. Facing the building are formal gardens with seasonal flowerbeds, fountains, and pleasant walkways. Opposite it on Van Ness Ave. are the Opera House, which opened in 1932, and the Veteran's Building, whose upper floors house the San Francisco Museum of Modern Art with its impressive permanent collection of Henri Matisse, Jackson Pollock, Alexander Calder, Robert Motherwell, and Clyfford Still. The new home of the San Francisco Symphony is the 3,000-plus-seat Louise M. Davies Symphony Hall (it looks like a giant beartrap). Tours of the Performing Arts Center (Davies Hall, the Opera House, and the Herbst Theater) are offered on Mondays, from 10:00 A.M. to 2:00 P.M.; every half hour. In addition, San Francisco Symphony volunteers offer tours of Davies Hall on Wednesday and Saturday at 1:00 and 2:00 P.M.; phone 552–8338. Tour fees: Adults, $3.00; seniors/students, $2.00.

Other public buildings in this area include the Civic Auditorium, and the main branch of the Public Library with an outstanding San Francisco and California research department.

Opera Plaza, featuring $200,000 condos and the Modesto Lanzone restaurant with its million dollars worth of very modern art, debuted in 1982. Three residential towers of 463 condominium units will be surrounded by restaurants and cafés, shops and offices, landscaped grounds—and 24-hour security.

The prime location unfortunately has some disadvantages. It is adjacent to the low-cost housing of the crime-plagued Western Addition, an area visitors should avoid at all times. Increased police patrol has been promised for this district, especially at evening performances at both Davies Hall and the Opera House. Visitors should be alert and if possible travel with others, when visiting the Civic Center or Japantown districts, as both are on the periphery of the Western Addition. Bands of young toughs have attacked tourists waiting at bus stops along Fillmore, Webster Sts., and even on Geary Blvd. in this vicinity.

Japantown

Japanese-Americans began gravitating to the neighborhood known as the Western Addition prior to the 1906 quake. Many more followed after fire destroyed their wooden homes in other parts of the stricken city. The pioneers opened shops, restaurants and markets and established Shinto and Buddhist temples.

Japantown, or "Nihonmachi," is centered on the slopes of Pacific Heights, north of Geary Blvd. between Fillmore and Laguna. In 1968, the multimillion-dollar Japan Center opened. This five-acre site became the ethnic center for the more than 60,000 Issei and Nisei (first- and second-generation) to the highly Americanized Sansei (third) and Yonsei (fourth) who live in the Bay Area.

Westin's Miyako Hotel and the Kyoto Inn both offer Japanese and Western accommodations. The three-block cluster includes an 800-car public garage, shops, and showrooms selling electronic products, cameras, records, porcelains, pearls, and paintings.

A five-tiered Peace Pagoda overlooks the plaza where seasonal festivals are staged. Art and cultural exhibits are scattered throughout the Center. On the Webster Street Bridge, a window displays rotating exhibits of Japanese treasures from the Avery Brundage Collection of the Asian Art Museum.

Kinokuniya, the giant bookstore, may have the finest selection of English-language books on Japanese subjects in the U.S. There are books on food and *ikebana,* the art of flower arranging, and handsomely bound editions of Japanese philosophy, religion, literature, and art.

Also on the second floor, next to the bookstore, is Shige Kimonos. Art-to-wear collectors search here for antique hand-painted silk-embroidered kimonos and the all-important waist sash—the *obi.* The methods of tying the obi indicate the wearer's age, marital status, and even the special events to be attended, such as weddings and funerals. The Arita porcelains, silk calligraphy scrolls, tea-ceremony utensils,

Points of Interest

1) Alcoa Building
2) Bank of America Building
3) City Hall
4) Civic Center
5) Coit Tower
6) Curran Theater
7) Davies Symphony Hall
8) Embarcadero Center
9) Ferry Building
10) Flood Building
11) Geary Theater
12) Moscone Convention Center
    *(Yerba Buena Center under
    construction)*
13) Golden Gate Center
14) Grace Cathedral
15) Museum of Modern Art
16) Old U.S. Mint
17) Opera House
18) St. Mary's Cathedral
19) St. Patrick's Church
20) San Francisco Art Institute
21) Stock Exchange
22) Transamerica Pyramid
23) Visitor Information Center

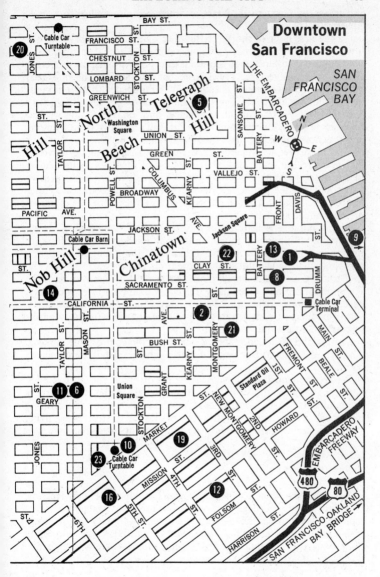

and treasured lacquerware boxes at Shige will also appeal to knowledgeable collectors.

On the first floor of the West Building, Asakichi specializes in antique blue-and-white Imari porcelains and handsome Tansu (chests).

Within a seven-block area are about thirty restaurants, most offering
simple, inexpensive fare. Try a sushi bar and sample the bite-sized
portions of lightly seasoned rice and seaweed topped with various kinds
of seafood, usually raw. Try to manage the chopsticks, dip (*don't*
drench) your portion in the soy sauce, and experience this typical
Japanese favorite. One warning—the final bill is counted piece by piece,
and it is not unusual to run up a $20.00 tab, per person. Tea, sake, or
fine Japanese beer accompanies these morsels. Sashimi, made with tuna
and octopus, are often also offered. Many of the restaurants display
plastic reproductions of various dishes for the guest. An inexpensive
and popular snack are noodle dishes (*ramen*). The noodles are either
boiled and served in a broth or prepared toss-fried with bits of greens
or meat added for flavor.

Serene Nippon is featured in the free travel-oriented films shown
Wednesday afternoons at the Japan Information Service office. If future
real or imagined travels include the Land of the Rising Sun, select a
sampling of their well-illustrated brochures and maps.

If touring has about done you in, we suggest a brief respite at the
Kabuki Hot Springs. Open daily, the communal bath is for men only,
except on Sunday, when it is Ladies' Day. Sign up for a *shiatsu* massage; this method concentrates on pressure points in the body and is
guaranteed to get one back in the race.

Samuri-film aficionados should check out the comfortable Kokosai
Theater, at Post and Buchanan. English subtitles detail the on-screen
carnage.

We recommend Japantown as a daytime diversion for most visitors.
Though the hotel and restaurant areas are safe in the evenings, it is
often difficult to avoid long waits at isolated bus stops or find a cruising
empty cab. The proximity of the often-hostile ghetto street gangs living
in the Western Addition could cause unpleasant incidents.

Pacific Heights

Though Japantown may be centered on the slopes of Pacific Heights,
it is light years and mega-yen away from the many splendored mansions and townhouses that still dominate some of the city's most expensive and viewable real estate. Here, west of Van Ness Ave., grand old
Victorians, expensively face-lifted, grace tree-lined streets, though here
and there glossy glass-walled condo high-rises cut out the view.

Old money and some new; trade and diplomatic personnel; personalities in the limelight and those who prefer absolute media anonymity occupy the city's most prestigious residential enclave. Rolls-Royces, Mercedes, and security systems are commonplace. Few visitors see anything other than the pleasing façades of Queen Anne charmers, English Tudor imports, and Baroque bastions.

But strolling can still be a jackpot. The area encompasses a variety of great and small private homes, and some of the city's smartest shopping and dining along the Cow Hollow's Union St. At the time of the Gold Rush, the open country from Van Ness to the Presidio between Pacific Ave. and the Bay was known as Golden Gate Valley. Within its northwestern confines was the city's dairy farms—Cow Hollow. As newcomers needed more appealing housing, many moved west and began building spacious houses with splendid views. Many of the most elaborate Victorians still grace this neighborhood.

You might like to begin a stroll at Webster and Pacific, deep in the heart of the heights, and easily accessible by public transportation.

Start walking north on Webster to 2550, a huge Georgian brick mansion designed by local architect Willis Polk, responsible for many of the most traditional and impressive commercial buildings and private homes from the pre-earthquake days until the early 1920s. (His most outstanding construction is the famous all-glass façade of the 1917 Hallidie Building, downtown at 130 Sutter St.) Polk's Pacific Heights gem was built in 1896 for William B. Bourn, the president of the Spring Valley Water Company, who had inherited a Mother Lode gold mine. Frequently, charity benefits provide San Franciscans an opportunity to savor the treasures inside this grand house. Polk also designed the palatial Peninsula estate, Filoli, for Mr. Bourn just before the United States entered World War I. (Recently, this elegant country home and its superb gardens were given to the National Trust for Historic Preservation; reserved tours are offered from mid-February to mid-November; phone (415–364–2880.)

Neighbors include a consulate, and across on the northwest corner stand two classic showplaces. 2222 Broadway is the three-story Italian Renaissance palace built by Comstock mine heir James Flood. Uptown Broadway, unlike its North Beach stretch, is big league socially. The former Flood residence was given to a religious order. Ten years later, the Convent of the Sacred Heart purchased the Baroque brick Grant home at 2220, and both serve as school quarters today. A second top-drawer school, the Hamlin, occupies 2120 Broadway, yet another Flood property.

At the next corner, go right on Buchanan, and on up to 2090 Jackson St. One of the most elegant nineteenth-century houses in the state, the former Whittier Mansion is headquarters for the California Historical

Society. Period furnishings enhance this fine 1894 beauty, which is viewable Wednesday, Saturday and Sunday from 1:00 to 5:00 P.M. There is an admission fee. The adjoining library, Schubert Hall, occupies a 1905 Baroque wood and stucco pearl, at 2099 Pacific.

Proceed to Laguna and turn right onto Washington St. and survey Lafayette Square, a green park-land once part of an early estate. The most imposing residence is the formal French Spreckels palace at 2080 Washington. Sugar heir Adolph Spreckels was so pleased he commissioned architect George Applegarth to design the city's all-French museum, the California Palace of the Legion of Honor in Lincoln Park.

Continue south to Gough St. (pronounced "Goff"), where a number of Queen Anne Victorians have been lovingly restored. Continue to California St. and go east on Franklin to 2007, the Haas-Lilienthal Victorian. Built in 1886, this grand Queen Anne survived the 1906 fire and earthquake. Operated by the Foundation for San Francisco's Architectural Heritage, tours are given by docent volunteers Wednesday from noon to 4:00 P.M., Sunday, 11:00 A.M. to 4:30 P.M. There is an entrance fee.

Union Street

By now it is time to relax over lunch or coffee, and the ideal area to head for is near Cow Hollow: Union St., its ten blocks from Van Ness to Fillmore. It is a great escape to patio dining, to gingerbread Victorians turned into trendy boutiques and galleries, all for great shopping, seeing, dining, and drinking—and lots of the beautiful people and so-so types found worldwide in similar settings.

The *Shopping* and *Dining Out* sections will clue you into much necessary information. We suggest this be a day and evening experience.

Down-east preppie types, Brioni-suited young achievers, and chamois-shirted urban boys frequent Perry's, at 1944 Union. Competition is keen at this heterosexual singles' scene, a respected dispenser of Anchor Steam Beer. Breakfast is a good introduction to the setting. Another breakfast or brunch stop is Doidge's, at 2217. It is best to reserve at this crowded Fillmore favorite. Visit Crane & Kelley at 2111 and sample their wine of the day with a bit of fine pâté or unusual cheese, or carry some of both back to your lodgings.

Take a short walk down Fillmore to Greenwich, where a number of small fascinating shops are moving in. Two of the city's top Oriental dealers have settled here, and two of the town's currently "in" moderate restaurants face each other: the casual and always crowded Balboa Café, at 3199, and the earthy Osteria Romana, at 2183 Greenwich.

Pacific Heights' affluent gays pack the Pacific Exchange, 2225, and the Alta Plaza at 2301 Fillmore. Handsome décor matches the tastes of their clientele.

The Marina and the Presidio

San Francisco's rosy rococo Palace of Fine Arts at Baker and Beach Sts. is at the very end of the picture-pretty residential district fronting the Bay. The only building remaining from the 1915 Panama-Pacific Exposition, the Roman Classic beauty was designed by Bernard Maybeck. A local philanthropist later contributed over two million dollars to preserve the striking monument. The massive columns, great rotunda, swan-filled lagoon are familiar in fashion layouts as well as many recent films. The interior houses *not* a fine arts museum, but a fascinating hands-on museum, the Exploratorium. The curious of all ages flock to this barnlike setting, open Wednesday–Friday from 1:00 to 5:00 P.M.; Wednesday evenings from 7:00 to 9:30 P.M.; Saturday and Sunday from noon to 5:00 P.M. Admission is $2.50 (under 18 free), except on Wednesday, when it is free.

If you have a car, now is the time to drive through the Presidio, since 1776 a military garrison. Headquarters of the United States Sixth Army, its over 1,500 acres of rolling hills and majestic woods and attractive red-brick barracks and stables present an air of serenity in the middle of the city. A small museum displays historical memorabilia of the early Spanish and U.S. occupants. Dramatic slices of the Bay and the Golden Gate frequently come in view on the winding drive.

Watch for the sign indicating Fort Point, the impressive masonry fortification built at the entrance to the Bay in the 1850s. Part of the vast (39,000-acre) Golden Gate National Recreation Area, the fort is located directly below the Golden Gate Bridge. Half-hour guided tours are offered on weekends, as are self-guided ecowalks. Sturdy shoes and warm outerwear are essential for those planning a walk along the dramatic seawall.

The GGNRA is designed to appeal to urban dwellers as well as backpackers looking for a semiwilderness experience. It is designed to appeal to all ages and varied educational and financial backgrounds. It offers a wide variety of free recreational activities easily reached by public transport. Many well-known locales—Ocean Beach, Cliff House, Aquatic Park, and Angel Island—are included, as well as Baker and Phelan Beaches in the city, and Marin County's Muir and Stinson Beaches. GGNRA headquarters are at Fort Mason, where a number of booklets, maps and information on special programs for children, the elderly, and the disabled visitors are available. Phone (415) 556–

0560 for information on weekdays from 9:00 A.M. to 4:30 P.M. Closed weekends and holidays.

Cliff House and Ocean Beach

San Francisco still has wilderness and shoreline to walk and explore. Land's End, with two main trails, follows the coastline. However, this is not for the faint-hearted or unsteady; danger lurks in the steep cliff edges and the frequent landslides.

No other American city provides such close-up viewing of the power and fury of the surf attacking the shore. Waves on the Pacific coast are far more powerful than those on the eastern seaboard because of the prevailing westerlies—the band of winds blowing from the west around the globe.

Several miles of Ocean Beach stretch south from the Cliff House look-outs. Extreme caution is advised if strolling or climbing the ruins of nearby Sutro Baths. The Victorian recreational palace was dedicated in 1896. In its heyday, six indoor saltwater pools, seats for 7,000 spectators, and lounging areas decorated with palms and Egyptian art attracted throngs. Closed in 1952, the neglected ruins were destroyed by fire in 1966. Plans to erect public housing on this prime real estate at the end of Geary St. on the ocean front have never materialized.

The original Cliff House built in 1858 was a restaurant. Fire destroyed it as well as several other, later structures in 1894. On a clear day one is able to see the Farallon Islands. Most days hundreds of California sea lions are sunning or sleeping on the sharply pointed Seal Rocks. Cliff House now has a gift shop, a bar, and a restaurant.

Richmond District and Clement Street: The "New" Chinatown

The area between the Presidio and Golden Gate Park, known as the Richmond, was a flat area of wind- and fog-swept dunes, relatively undeveloped until World War I. It is now composed mostly of modest single-family row houses and low-rise apartment houses.

Clement (pronounced Cle-MENT) St. is a major shopping artery for the area, and its character has been shaped by the variety and vitality of its residents. Until the mid-1970s, the mores and manners of Eastern Europe dominated. Neighborhood stores, modest restaurants, and annual celebrations reflected the tastes and needs of immigrants from Armenia, Czechoslovakia, the Ukraine, Russia, and especially the thousands who had fled Hitler's slaughter.

A wave of new people began moving in about five years ago; of Asian backgrounds, some were second- and even third-generation Chinese-

Americans seeking more spacious and affordable housing. Later came Thai and Indochinese refugees as well as industrious Korean and Japanese small businessmen.

All contribute to the solid but culturally rich district called Richmond (*Rich mun kuy* by the Chinese), or Park Presidio. A mile-and-a-half walk along Clement St. reveals a stretch of unpretentious commercial storefronts, many with bilingual signs: interesting ethnic clothing emporiums; the Miniature Bakery offering Russian delights; Label's Deli crammed with Kosher products; and the Sixth Avenue Cheese Shop serve a varied and discriminating clientele.

At least fifty other inexpensive ethnic restaurants dot the neighborhood, mostly in the 20s blocks. Most are operated by expatriate families, and most of the weekday patrons live nearby. Weekends are very busy, with knowledgeable Bay Area people sampling the exotic fare and strolling the wide Sunday-quiet street.

One respected local restaurant critic included three Richmond restaurants in his top 15 Bay Area eateries: for Thai dining, Khan Toke, 5937 Geary Blvd. at 24th; Spanish and Mexican classics at Alejandro's, 1840 Clement St. between 19th and 20th Aves.; and Vietnamese specialities at Mai's at 316 Clement St. near 4th Ave.

Nightlife blooms at the Holy Cow Zoo, a showcase for aspiring comics, and its neighbor, the Last Chance Saloon, a bastion of country and rock fans.

Parking is always difficult, so we suggest using public transportation or a taxi. And try not to miss a short stroll through this lively international settlement.

A bit north of Clement St. in the 30th St area is an extremely posh area of villas and mansions—the Sea Cliff section—overlooking the Presidio and the Bay.

Golden Gate Park

In 1868 the city acquired title to about 1000 acres of "outside lands," mostly bare sand dunes, at a cost of $800,000. Three years later an engineer, William Hammond Hall, was appointed superintendent. He laid out the basic road system, and for five years he worked to eradicate the sand dunes, first by planting barley and beach grass and later Monterey pine and cypress and eucalyptus. When political opponents slashed his budget in 1876 he resigned.

Hall was instrumental in selecting John McLaren, a Scottish gardener employed on a San Mateo estate, to become park superintendent in 1890. "Uncle" John lived in the rustic McLaren Lodge at the Fell and Stanyan Sts. entrance to the Park from 1896 until his death in 1943 at age ninety-six. The lodge is now headquarters for the Park Commission, and the huge cypress on the lawn, Uncle John's Christmas tree, is decorated annually.

McLaren followed Hall's concept of a natural, rustic retreat for city-dwellers. He had wells dug and found fresh water, which for many years was pumped by the windmills at the west end. The old Dutch Windmill at the northeast corner of the park was installed in 1902 and provided power to pump 20,000 gallons of water each hour from wells beneath the rocky shores of the Richmond district.

In November 1981, the completely restored Dutch Windmill was reopened. For twenty years Eleanor Rossi Crabtree had labored to collect funds from private sources to repair the historic mill. In 1976, additional federal and local appropriations added to her private funds, plus free skilled labor offered by the Seabees, launched the project. Crews of skilled Seabees have worked free of charge two days a month since 1976.

At the commemorative ceremonies, a bronze plaque to Robert W. Carroll, a Marin electrical contractor and a Naval Reserve petty officer who contributed skills and leadership to the work crews, was unveiled. In 1980, when the Seabees had been removing scaffolding, Carroll was supervising from a temporary footing near the top of the 85-foot mill-house when he fell and was killed.

Because San Francisco's budget can't afford a millkeeper to raise and lower the traditional canvas sails, the mill is expected to operate with bare spars. Although Mrs. Crabtree's original plan was to restore both windmills, presently she feels there are still too many problems with the Dutch Mill, so work on the Murphy Windmill, installed in 1907 at the southwest corner of the park, must be shelved for the time.

McLaren imported seeds, plants, and cuttings from around the world, and planted more than a hundred species of conifers. He also realized that he had to allow buildings, playgrounds, and statues, which he called "stookies," in his domain.

A Midwinter Fair in 1894 was centered in the eastern part of the park around the Music Concourse, and the chief remnant of the fair is the still-popular Japanese Tea Garden. Today, the de Young and Asian Museums of Art face the California Academy of Science across the concourse. Frequent concerts are held in the nearby open-air shell bandstand. A charmer in this part of the park is the Victorian Conservatory, a copy of London's famous Kew Gardens. The ornate greenhouse was originally brought around the Horn for the estate of James Lick in San Jose.

The story of the life of the city's greatest miser, and before his death the city's greatest benefactor, is one of San Francisco's legends. Lick arrived two years before the discovery of gold, sailing in from South America with a fortune of forty thousand dollars made in hides and imported pianos in Argentine. The gaunt loner was considered mad as he invested in a cowpath (later Montgomery St.). He sold his holdings during the boom of 1848–49, rebuying more lots and a huge tract of arid land near Mission San Jose. The miser millionaire nightly gathered bones and scraps from restaurants, later using them as fertilizer for his fruit-tree orchard in San Jose. This was the beginning of the Santa Clara Valley fruit industry in what has now become the richest fruit orchard region in the world.

At seventy-seven Lick decided to distribute his huge fortune. San Jose's Lick Observatory, a division of the University of California, Santa Cruz, is one of his memorials. The Park's Conservatory, bought with popular subscription funds, also recalls this friendless eccentric.

The western half of Golden Gate Park offers miles of wooded greenery and open spaces for all types of spectator or participant sports. Don't miss the buffalo paddock, the Polo Field, and the Equestrian Center, where rental horses are available.

The eastern section of the park, with its museum complex, is closed to vehicles on Sunday, making it a pleasant place for joggers, walkers, bicyclists, or roller skaters.

Almost any day is great for a picnic in the world's largest man-made park.

The Sunset District and Stern Grove

The attractive Sunset residential area borders Golden Gate Park on the Park's south and the Pacific Ocean on the area's west. During the 1930s, hundreds of stucco row houses were built, and today they are well-cared for with extensive landscaping.

On a sunny summer Sunday, thousands flock to the free concerts held at the Sigmund Stern Grove at Sloat Blvd. and 19th Ave. Many music lovers tote a picnic basket to the natural amphitheater, sheltered by stately eucalyptus and redwoods.

Lake Merced and San Francisco State University

South of the Sunset is the San Francisco Zoo at Sloat Blvd. at the Ocean. More than a thousand exotic animals and birds are housed in realistically landscaped enclosures. The newest attraction is Gorilla World, a two-million-dollar African-styled habitat. For more complete information see the Zoos entry later in the book.

Lake Merced (the Lake of Our Lady of Mercy) is located in the southwest corner of the city and county of San Francisco. The three-mile-long lake is a popular jogging area for residents of the nearby Park

Merced, an enormous housing development built by the Metropolitan Life Insurance Company in 1951.

Nearby is the architecturally undistinguished campus of San Francisco State University. The coeducational state liberal-arts college was originally the State Teachers College until 1935, when it became San Francisco State College.

Moved to its present location after World War II, it enjoyed a Golden Age through the early 1960s. The San Francisco "Beatnik" literary renaissance was centered on the polarities of State College and North Beach. This was a period of impressive creativity, especially in the fields of poetry and the humanities. The English Department, staffed by S. I. Hayakawa, Leonard Wolff, and Walter Von Tillburg Clark, enjoyed a national reputation.

In 1969, there was a violent strike which split the school's student body into ideological factionalism. The bitter days were fortunately short-lived, but the earlier glory of the institution were never regained. In 1972 it became San Francisco State University. As it enters the 1980s, especially with the establishment of the Urban Mission, directed by Professor Arthur Chandler, the Lake Merced-area campus hopes to become a more vital part of the city.

Twin Peaks

Twin Peaks Blvd. offers a 360° panorama of the city that should be viewed both by day and at night, although heavy fogs often cloud this residential area. These hills, once known as *Los Pechos de la Chola* ("The Breasts of the Indian Girl"), are crowded with all manner of urban housing, their greatest charm being the spectacular overview of the city, especially the nightly carpet of twinkling lights.

The University of California Medical Center is located in this district. Its two hospitals and several research institutes are world-acclaimed. The huge campus is at Third and Parnassus Aves.

San Francisco's Gay Community: Castro and Elsewhere

Many visitors do not appreciate the very open, permissive attitude toward the gay men and lesbians for which San Francisco is famous. Yet increasing numbers of straight people are venturing into the packed and emotionally charged Castro district.

The gay center consists primarily of two blocks of Castro St. south of Market, two blocks of 18th St. adjacent to Castro, and the immediate residential side streets. Perhaps the most well known of the clothing stores is the All-American Boy, 463 Castro. It established the "Castro" look: Levi jeans, plaid shirts, and bright T-shirts. American- and European-designed sportswear is widely available, and there are several stores stocking the fads and fashions of the forties and fifties.

Leatherworld, 4084 18th St., is a one-stop shopping bonanza of all things leather. Headlines at 549 Castro (and 1217 Polk) sells funky clothes, fun accessories, and carnival-colored gym bags to the beat of the latest hit records.

Pop into Does Your Mother Know, 4079 18th St., a very different card store from the usual Hallmark variety. Certainly the most beautiful shop is the mirrored-walled Obelisk, 489 Castro, with fine crystal and glass objects.

There are florists, cheese and wine specialists, bookstores, and interesting small restaurants, some of which are located in beautifully restored and cared-for Victorians.

Snow Peas, 4072 18th St., serves Continental food in an attractive upstairs dining room. Perhaps the most popular restaurant, and with attractive prices, is Burton's at 2223 Market, very close to Castro.

Any visitor who wishes to walk along Castro is quite safe, especially in daytime. Discretion is suggested in the use of a camera and in conversations in public places.

While San Francisco is touted as "everyone's favorite city," it most definitely has a special appeal to gays from all over this country as well as abroad. Gays are visible in every profession and occupation in the Bay Area: doctors and dockworkers, police officers and preachers, teachers and truckers. Reliable estimates suggest that up to a half-million homosexuals or lesbians were among the city's 3,300,000 visitors in 1980.

Last year, a Bay-area-based newspaper published the *Gay Visitor's Guide to San Francisco*. Sales nationwide are brisk, and the *Advocate*'s marketing director attributes its appeal to the fact that "gay people think of San Francisco as a comfortable place."

Presently, 19 gay-oriented hotels and bed-and-breakfast inns, plus a staggering 200 reported gay bars and perhaps 40 homosexual restaurants, welcome this free-spending audience.

Polk St. from about Geary Blvd. to Washington is also a popular, though less crowded, gay shopping street, with a number of clothing stores catering to this trade. The street has many straight neighborhood businesses and restaurants as well. Many of the more affluent gay residents of Nob or Russian Hills or posh Pacific Heights patronize the area. Recently, a number of young male hustlers are being seen on the street daytimes as well as late evenings. We do not suggest strolling Polk St. any evening. Certainly avoid the South-of-Market-St. district anytime. Also avoid Folsom St., which is the site of most of the city's highly dangerous leather-and-chain (S&M) haunts.

The Guerneville (pronounced GURN-vill) area, seventy miles north of San Francisco, has changed dramatically the last several years. The former summer resort for families had deteriorated in recent years. Recently it has become a year-round vacationland for gays, not only from the city's burgeoning gay community, but for gay customers from Australia, England, Germany, and Scandinavia.

Like Provincetown or the Hamptons on Long Island, the Russian River—with its pastoral views, towering redwoods and laid-back ambience—is enjoying an economic explosion. Down-at-the-heels 1920s family resorts are being refurbished for the new clientele. A seven-acre gay resort, The Woods, sports a $300,000 sound-and-light system. The local real-estate boom is bringing offers of over $100,000 for modest 1940s $6,500 cottages. Many long-time residents as well as straight and gay merchants agree: "We're here to stay, the river's big enough for all of us."

"What we're looking at is another Sausalito or Monterey—a vacation spot that is also something of a bedroom community," says Leonard Matlovich, the former Air Force sergeant who made the cover of *Time* magazine six years ago for his court battle against the military's ban on homosexuals. Now the owner of Stumptown Annie's pizza parlor on Guerneville's Main St., he feels "Guerneville could be an experiment for the future, showing you can grow and still keep your natural beauty."

During the 1970s the local gay community made enormous changes in San Francisco's social, political, and economic attitudes. The important role gays have played in the refurbishing of decaying parts of the city (gentrification), with subsequent increases in real-estate values and rentals, has, however, caused on-going tension with many of the low-income minorities. The 1978 assassination of Mayor George Moscone and gay supervisor Harvey Milk focused worldwide attention on the important role gays play in the life of San Francisco. Since then, the gay community seems more organized, especially politically.

South of Market: The Moscone Center

South of Market is the Mission District, one of the oldest and most polyglot areas of San Francisco. Between the Mission and the Bay is the Potrero District, mostly industrial but with a growing residential area of refurbished Victorians and low-rise apartments. Both Mission and Potrero are on the whole still rather seedy. The neighborhood of Mission Dolores (16th & Dolores Sts.; see *Historical Sites* in Practical Information) attracted many gay and Latino arrivals in the '70s. Today, Valencia St. is Mecca for the city's lesbians and feminists. The neighborhood also hosts Filipinos, Southeast Asians, American Indians, Samoans, and senior citizens. Around 16th and Mission are new-wave shops and Mexican, Cuban, Chinese, and Salvadoran restaurants, many with colorful wall murals decorating their façades.

San Francisco's dramatic new Moscone Center south of Market opened December 2, 1981. The convention center features a 270,000-square-foot exhibit floor that is 37 feet below street level and 11 feet below the water table. The exterior of the building is distinguished by a contemporary glass-and-girder lobby at street level and a landscaped mound over the roof. The superblock at Third and Howard covers 11 acres, while the exhibit floor alone accounts for 6 acres.

Two blocks between the Center and Market St. were leveled years ago, but it took twenty years of politics before the project was realized. This district was once filled with sleazy residential hotels, a variety of small businesses, and light industry.

A long-range redevelopment plan calls for a 24-acre Yerba Buena Gardens. The $750-million complex includes a 1,500-room Marriott Hotel near Fourth and Market Sts., due for completion in 1986. Air France's luxury hotel, the 35-story Meridien opened last year at 50 Third Street.

Nearby is a new nine-story apartment complex for low-income elderly and handicapped residents. Additional residential, shopping, and entertainment areas are planned to attract people day and night. Because of the assured convention space now available, more than 5,000 additional hotel rooms in the city are planned for the next five years.

PRACTICAL INFORMATION FOR

SAN FRANCISCO

HOW TO GET THERE. There are, of course, four ways to get about in the United States: plane, train, bus, and car. Usually, if you plan to travel long distances, it is cheaper to go by plane than by rail. But for distances under 300 miles, the train is cheaper and may be faster too because the station often is in the middle of town and you don't have that long ride to the airport. Also, if you are traveling to enjoy the scenery, you will see almost nothing of it from a plane, and quite a lot of it from the train.

For short trips between cities, buses have the same advantages as going by train, are usually cheaper than the train, and may have more frequent services.

By bus. *Continental Trailways* and *Greyhound* bus routes form the warp and woof of a vast pattern of scheduled trips, allowing travelers from all U.S. areas to come close to their vacation destinations and often reach them directly.

Greyhound's Ameripass offers travel passes at $189.00 for 7 days; $249.00 for 15 days; $349.00 for 30 days. Each pass can be extended, at $10 each additional day, up to a total of 60 days. Children under 12 pay half-price, and under 5 travel free. The great distances involved in travel in this region could make these passes very advantageous.

Check your travel agent or nearby Greyhound or Trailways office for information on special tours to and in the area you wish to visit. Also ask your travel agent about special tours to the area you plan to see. But keep in mind you can only spend as much time in any one place as is allotted by the tour itinerary.

By air. The major cities in this area with the most frequent, most direct air service are San Francisco and Oakland. Among major airlines serving either or both of these cities are *American, Alaska Air, Continental, Delta, Eastern, Republic, Frontier, TWA, United,* and *Western.* Among international carriers serving San Francisco are *Air Canada, Canadian Pacific, Japan Air Lines, British Airways, China Airlines, Qantas, Air New Zealand, Mexicana,* and *Pan American.*

Regional airlines serving this area offer many scheduled flights from the above-mentioned cities, as well as from other metropolitan areas, to additional cities and to vacation areas. Regional airlines include *WestAir, PSA, Air Cal,* and *Southwest.*

Discounts are offered by many airlines to members of families traveling together. Thirty-day excursion fares, youth fares for college students, and special low fares for members of the armed forces (on a stand-by basis) also are offered by many airlines. Most of the fares have certain restrictions, such as requiring the traveler to make the trip during certain times of the week, principally to avoid those days when traffic is heavy. Discounts change frequently; savings can range from 15 percent to 45 percent over regular coach fare, so check with your travel agent or airline for the exact rates. In San Francisco, charter service via jet-powered helicopters is available to areas in Northern California by *Commodore Helicopter, Spirit Airways* and, from Oakland, *SFO Helicopter.* Charters are also available for aerial photography.

By train. Amtrak's *San Francisco Zephyr,* a new superliner train, provides service to and from Chicago via Denver. Superliner sleepers offer economy bedroom, for two; family bedroom, accommodating two adults and two children; and deluxe bedroom, with sofa and reclining swivel chair. A special bedroom for passengers with handicaps and a traveling companion is available. Daily service to Portland and Seattle north and Los Angeles and San Diego south is provided by the *Coast Starlight.* Connecting with the Coast Starlight in Martinez, Amtrak's *San Joaquin* trains travel through the Central Valley, gateway to three national parks: Yosemite, Kings Canyon, and Sequoia. Year-round buses leave Amtrak's Merced depot for Yosemite Park. During the summer season, Amtrak's Fresno depot buses transport visitors to Sequoia and Kings Canyon National Parks. California's Central Valley provides much of the grapes, raisins, nuts, peaches, and plums grown in the U.S.

See your local travel agent or Amtrak for details on excursion fares; Family A-Fare; and discounts for Senior Citizens and the handicapped. Ask for the "Rail America" West tour book.

One- and two-day tours are offered to Yosemite National Park and a two-day train tour to magnificent Hearst Castle is available on the *Coast Starlight.* There is daily service to Stockton, Merced (Yosemite), Fresno, Bakersfield, and San Joaquin Valley points.

San Francisco-bound passengers board shuttle buses at Amtrak's Oakland depot, 6th and Wood St., for transport to the Trans-Bay Terminal, in San Francisco, at First and Mission Sts.

 TELEPHONES. The area code for all of San Francisco (and Marin County, Berkeley, and Oakland as well) is 415. You do not need to dial the area code if it is the same as the one from which you are dialing. Information (directory assistance) is 555–1212. An operator will assist you on person-to-person, credit-card, and collect calls if you dial "O" first. From outside San Francisco, directory information can be obtained toll-free by dialing (415) 555–1212. Dial (800) 555–1212, directory information for toll-free 800 numbers, to see if there is an 800 number for the business you want to reach.

 HOTELS AND MOTELS. San Francisco is singularly blessed with many distinguished hotels of world renown, as well as charming bed-and-breakfast hideaways, convenient and popular chain motels and other affordable accommodations located throughout the city.

However, confirmed reservations are suggested. Demand for rooms is heavy year-round because of constant convention and business visitors. From May to October, family travel is at its peak. The most common reason for traveling in California is to vacation. This is especially so for the foreign visitors who comprise about 4 percent of the yearly visitor count. And over 70 percent of the vacationers on the latest survey were state residents. San Francisco's world-renowned attractions, especially its renovated cable cars, will continue to attract increasing numbers of tourists.

Hotel rates are based on double occupancy, European Plan. Categories determined by price are: *Super Deluxe,* $100.00 and up; *Deluxe,* $80.00 to $100.00; *Expensive,* $70.00 to $79.00; *Moderate,* $60.00 to $69.00; *Inexpensive,* $50.00 to $59.00; and *Basic Budget,* under $50.00. All rates are subject to a Transient Occupant Tax, currently 9.75 percent. Hotels are listed by location and are in alphabetical order by price category. For a more complete explanation of hotel and motel categories, see Facts At Your Fingertips at the front of this volume.

AIRPORT AREA

Note: All hotels listed offer free shuttle service to San Francisco airport. Hilton Hotel is the only one right at the airport. South of the airport, Burlingame offers a variety of excellent restaurants, including a new Benihana of Tokyo.

Deluxe

Amfac Hotel. 1380 Bayshore Hwy., Burlingame; 347–5444; (800) 622–0838 in California; 800–227–4700 nationwide. Attractive décor; gourmet dining in the *Calcutta Cricket Club.* Indoor pool, movies.

Hyatt Burlingame. 1333 Old Bayshore Hwy., Burlingame; 342–7741; (800) 228–9000. Fine Hyatt hotel, just 1½ miles from airport. Enjoy elegant dining in the award-winning *Hugo's;* lunch stars California-style salads and seafood; *Chasser's* lounge features live entertainment. Special weekend packages.

San Francisco Airport Hilton. The first and only hotel located at the San Francisco airport on U.S. 101; 589–0770; (800) 652–1094 in California. Over 500 rooms; popular group and convention hotel. Spacious grounds, Olympic-size swimming pool. Some rooms designed for the handicapped traveler, plus special phones for the deaf. Fine dining; entertainment nightly.

Expensive

Best Western Grosvenor Airport. 380 South Airport Blvd., South San Francisco; 873–3200; (800) 528–1234 nationwide; (800) 722–7141 in California. 200-room high-rise property, about 20 minutes from downtown San Francisco. In-room luxuries include Thermasol whirlpool, steam baths. Outdoor swimming pool. Family plan. Charming *Brass Elephant* lounge and restaurant.

Clarion Hotel (formerly Airport Plaza). 401 East Millbrae Ave., Millbrae; 692–6363; (800) 632–0513 in California. Attractive family accommodations. Pool, movies. Free continental breakfast. Free parking.

Ramada Inn (Airport). 1250 Old Bayshore Hwy., Burlingame; 347–2381; (800) 228–2828 nationwide. Very attractive. Outdoor pool surrounded by flower beds and rose bushes. Senior citizen discounts. Family plan.

Sheraton Inn-San Francisco Airport. 1177 Airport Blvd., Burlingame; 342–9200; (800) 325–3535 nationwide. About three miles from airport. Indoor/outdoor pool, adjacent jogging course. Barber/beauty shops. Restaurant.

Moderate

Holiday Inn-Airport. 245 South Airport Blvd., South San Francisco; 589–7200. Refurbished; free H.B.O. movies. About five miles from Cow Palace and Candlestick Park. Entertainment nightly; pleasant dining in *Frederic's.* Pets allowed in rooms.

Inexpensive

TraveLodge at San Francisco Airport. 326 South Airport Blvd., South San Francisco; 583–9600; (800) 255–3050 nationwide.

Basic Budget

Super 8 Motel. 111 Mitchell Avenue (Hwy. 101 at South Airport Blvd. Exit), South San Francisco; 877–0770; (800) 843–1991 nationwide. Very good value, attractive décor.

FISHERMAN'S WHARF

Super Deluxe

Holiday Inn. 1300 Columbus; 771–9000; (800) 238–8000 nationwide. Near Ghirardelli Sq., the Cannery and the Wharf. Heated outdoor pool. Electronic games. Fine dining in *Charley's Restaurant* and cafeteria-style café.

Sheraton at Fisherman's Wharf. 2500 Mason; 362–5500; (800) 325–3535 nationwide. Handsome, contemporary, brick-and-redwood design with lush greenery. Outdoor pool. Elegant dining in the *Grand Exhibition;* more modest fare in the *Coffee Brake.*

TraveLodge at the Wharf. 250 Beach; 392–6700; (800) 255–3050 nationwide. Located right on the wharf, convenient to downtown shops and sights. Heated pool; barber shop; gift shop; restaurant and lounge.

Deluxe

Howard Johnson's Motor Lodge. 580 Beach; 775–3800; (800) 654–2000 nationwide; (800) 652–1527 in California. Adjacent to the Anchorage Shopping Plaza; close to Wharf, Ghirardelli Sq. and the Cannery. Free parking in enclosed garage. Nearby restaurants.

Ramada Hotel. 590 Bay; 885–4700; (800) 228–2828 nationwide. Good location; attractive atmosphere. Free parking; tour desk. Suites with refrigerators, non-smoking rooms available.

Moderate

Columbus Motor Inn. 1075 Columbus; 885–1492. Very attractive, locally owned 45-room inn. Walking distance to Wharf; public transportation handy. Very well maintained.

Fisherman's Wharf TraveLodge. 1201 Columbus; 776–7070. Just two dozen rooms. Public transportation to Wharf or downtown at the door. Easy walking distance to North Beach and Chinatown.

NOB HILL

Super Deluxe

Fairmont Hotel and Tower. California and Mason Sts.; 772–5000; (800) 527–4727 nationwide. This elegant hotel has the city's most dazzling public rooms, as well as the most expensive overnight lodging in the country—the eight-floor penthouse suite—with a tile game room, three bedrooms and 16-hour private butler—rents for $2,500 a day. Select shops; choice dining and drinking experiences plus the city's only top-name entertainment showplace, the *Venetian Room,* which is also very expensive.

Huntington. 1075 California; 474–5400; (800) 227–4683 nationwide; (800) 652-1539 in California. The mood is English. Low-profile elegance with emphasis on security and anonymity for its guests. Popular with diplomatic delegations, celebrities and heads of state.

Mark Hopkins. 1 Nob Hill; 392–3434; (800) 327–0200 nationwide. Extensively refurbished. InterContinental's striking landmark. The famed *Top of the Mark* lounge, opened in 1936, attracts nightly crowds. Buffet Brunch Monday through Friday.

Stanford Court. 905 California; 989–3500; (800) 227–4736 nationwide; (800) 622-0957 in California. Considered to be the best-run hotel in the city. "European-type" hostelry. Superb dining in the charming *Fournou's Ovens* and the $1-million, iron-and-glass conservatory. Tea, served daily in the lobby-lounge from 3–5 P.M., includes little sandwiches, petit fours, tea, Irish coffee. Priced by the item.

Moderate

San Francisco Residence Club. 851 California St.; 421–2220. Most rooms share baths and are rented by the month. Rates include breakfast and dinner. This is very popular with foreign visitors. Excellent location from which to walk to Union Sq. or Chinatown. Reservations essential since fewer than ten rooms are set aside for short stays.

CHINATOWN

Deluxe

Holiday Inn–Financial District. 750 Kearny, one block from Chinatown; 433–6600; (800) 238–8000 nationwide. Central location with Embarcadero Center a four-block walk. Chinese motif. Chinese Cultural Center on third floor has changing exhibits. Gift shops. *Eight Immortals* restaurant. Roof-top pool.

UNION SQUARE/DOWNTOWN

Super Deluxe

Campton Place. 340 Stockton (opposite Hyatt Union Square); 781–5555. Elegant ambience; expensive dining presided over by noted young chef, Bradley Ogden.

Four Seasons-Clift. 495 Geary, at Taylor; 775–4700; (800) 828–1188 nationwide. This select spot has become a favorite gathering place for San Franciscans. Outstanding Sunday brunch in the lovely French Room. Exceptional services and amenities. *Fortune* magazine rates this as one of the world's great small hotels.

Hyatt Regency. 5 Embarcadero Center; 788–1234; (800) 228–9000 nationwide. Spectacular atrium lobby, glass elevators. The *Equinox,* revolving roof-top restaurant, offers spectacular views. On Friday evenings (5:30–8:30 P.M.) tea dancing and the music of the big bands fill the lobby; crowded, no cover, but pricey drinks.

Hyatt Union Square. 345 Stockton; 398–1234; (800) 228–9000 nationwide. Prime locale for shopping (I. Magnin, Macy's, Saks, Neiman-Marcus, Gump's), theaters and restaurants. Distinctive design with the sculptured fountain created by Ruth Asawa, local artist, who sought the help of hundreds of children to mold the figures of this historic work.

Pacific Plaza. 501 Post; 441–7100; (800) 227–3184 nationwide; (800) 227–3184 in California. One of the city's most elegant smaller hotels; very popular with corporate accounts. *Donatello's,* the hotel's classic Italian restaurant, attracts a faithful local clientele.

San Francisco Hilton & Tower. 333 O'Farrell; 771–1400. This huge, popular convention and tour-group hotel is a short walk from the Airporter downtown terminal at Taylor and Ellis. It is also near the unsavory people and places of the Tenderloin district; after-dark strolling is discouraged.

Westin St. Francis. Union Square; 397–7000; (800) 228–3000 nationwide. This stately grande dame has hosted many notables, including Queen Elizabeth (in 1983), the Emperor and Empress of Japan and many other heads of state. Impeccable dining at *Victor's;* fascinating people-watching at the Art Deco *Compass Rose* lounge. Smart shops in-house and nearby.

Deluxe

Galleria Park. 191 Sutter; 781–3060. The former 73-year old *Sutter Hotel,* renovated at a cost of about $10 million. Adjacent to the Crocker Galleria shopping complex.

Handlery Motor Inn. 260 O'Farrell; 986–2526; (800) 241–3848 nationwide; (800) 352-6686 in California. Good location; short walk to Union Square. Pool, sauna. Free Parking. Fine for families.

Holiday Inn–Union Square. 480 Sutter; 398–9800; (800) 238–8000 nationwide. Very attractive location, one block from Union Sq. *Sherlock Holmes Esq. Public House,* on the 30th floor, serves weekday buffet luncheon, cocktail lounge offers entertainment. Take in the Holmes memorabilia. On the street level, the *White Elephant,* in the manner of a quiet English country inn, serves seasonal specialties and innovative nouvelle cuisine.

Raphael. 386 Geary; 986–2000; (800) 821–5343 nationwide. Near neighbor to the St. Francis and Union Sq. Delightful, low-key, attentive service. Handy to shopping, theaters, restaurants. *Pam Pam* 24-hour coffee shop excellent for breakfast and informal dining.

Sir Francis Drake. 450 Powell; 392–7755; (800) 223–1818 nationwide; (800) 652–1668 in California. One block from Union Sq. Gracious public rooms. *Starlite Roof* offers nightly dancing and a Sunday champagne brunch. The hotel is famed for its Beefeater-costumed doormen.

Expensive

Bellevue Hotel. 505 Geary, at Taylor; 474–3600; (800) 421–8851 nationwide; (800) 223–9869 in California. Convenient to Union Sq.; ACT Theater. Convention and tour groups frequent this hotel. 24-hour coffee shop; pay garage.

Canterbury/Whitehall. 750 Sutter; 474–6464; (800) 227–4788 nationwide; (800) 652–1614 in California. Attractive accommodations along with *Lehr's Greenhouse* restaurant. Ideal location from which to stroll Sutter St. art galleries, some of the city's finest.

Savoy. 580 Geary; 441–2700; (800) 227–4223 nationwide; (800) 622–0553 in California. Charming smaller hotel, three blocks from Union Sq. Victorian ambience; free continental breakfast.

Moderate

Bedford. 761 Post; 673–6040; (800) 227–5642 nationwide; (800) 652–1889 in California. A small, European-style hotel with an English pub and a lovely dining room. A short walk from Union Sq.

Cartwright. 524 Sutter; 421–2865; (800) 227–3844 nationwide; (800) 652–1858 in California. Very comfortable accommodations just a block from Union Sq.

York. 940 Sutter; 885–6800; (800) 227–3608 nationwide. Attractive restored property. Home of the *Plush Room,* a small cabaret starring big names that have been around for awhile—Eartha Kitt, Vivian Blaine. Popular with San Francisco's gay crowd.

Inexpensive

Andrews. 624 Post; 563–6877; (800) 227–4742 nationwide; (800) 622–0557 in California. Just off Union Sq., the 48-room, renovated "country inn" exudes charm.

Californian. 405 Taylor; 885–2500; (800) 227–3346 nationwide; (800) 622–0961 in California. Excellent location.

Chancellor. 433 Powell; 362–2004. Prime location. Popular with conventions, tour groups and business travelers.

King George. 334 Mason; 751–5050; (800) 227–4240 nationwide. This 140-room, European-style establishment is just off Union Sq., close to the airline terminal and theaters.

Merlin (formerly Pickwick). 85 Fifth Street; 421–7500; (800) 227–3282. Refurbished recently. Convenient to Moscone Center.

Basic Budget

Beresford. 635 Sutter; 673–9900, (800) 227–4048. Excellent location. Popular with overseas guests.

Cecil. 545 Post; 673–3733; (800) 227–3818 nationwide; (800) 652–1535 in California. European-style 150-room hotel just a block from Union Sq.

El Cortez. 550 Geary; 775–5000; (800) 223–5695 nationwide. This Moorish-influenced structure has 173 rooms, most with kitchenettes. Three blocks from Union Sq.; good for families and extended visits.

Mark Twain. 345 Taylor; 673–2332; (800) 227–4074 nationwide; (800) 622–0873 in California. This nine-story, 115-room charmer is on the fringe of the Tenderloin. Small, attractive rooms have pictures of Mark Twain; guests are welcomed with wine and lollipops on their beds—inviting them to "lick their worries."

Oxford. Mason & Market Streets; 775–4600; (800) 221–6509. Inexpensive parking. Family operated.

Victorian. 54 Fourth St.; 777–5354; (800) 227–3804 nationwide. Charming restored oldie, Victorian antiques used as accents.

Yerba Buena. 55 Fifth St.; 543–3130; (800) 227–4673 nationwide. Very attractive, with a nostalgic San Francisco mood.

Y.M.C.A. 166 The Embarcadero; 392–2191. Co-ed. No private baths.

CIVIC CENTER

Expensive

Holiday Inn–Civic Center. 50 Eighth St.; 626–6103; (800) 238–8000 nationwide. Two blocks to Civic Center complex and close to public transportation. Pool, free H.B.O. 25% senior-citizen discount.

San Franciscan. 1231 Market; 626–8000; (800) 227–4747 nationwide; in California, call collect: (415) 626–8000. This 1911 landmark has been completely restored; short walk to Civic Center. Family plan; pets okay. Popular Italian restaurant/lounge.

Moderate

Abigail. 246 McAllister; 861–9728. Small hotel recently renovated.

Argyle. 146 McAllister; 552–7076. European-style accommodations come with equipped kitchens. Excellent for longer stays and family travelers. Close to Civic Center and public transportation. Restaurant.

Atherton. 685 Ellis; 474–5720; (800) 227–3733 nationwide; (800) 792–9861 in California. Attractive 80-room renovated hotel; dining room and lounge.

Best Western Americana. 121 Seventh St, at Mission; 626–0200; (800) 528–1234 nationwide. Courtesy shuttle to and from downtown airline terminal. Children under 12 free. Pool, sauna. Restaurant, lounge.

Best Western Flamingo. 114 Seventh St.; 621–0701; (800) 528–1234 nationwide. 38 units opposite main Post Office and Greyhound bus terminal. Courtesy shuttle to and from downtown air terminal. Small pets only.

San Francisco Downtown TraveLodge. 790 Ellis; 775–7612; (800) 255–3050 nationwide. Centrally located; public transportation at door. Free parking; free continental breakfast. Free transportation from airport.

Inexpensive

Y.M.C.A. Central Branch. 220 Golden Gate; 885–0460. Co-ed.

JAPANTOWN

Deluxe

Westin Mikayo. 1625 Post; 922–3200; (800) 228–3000 nationwide. A $3-million refurbishing was completed in June 1983. Japanese décor, sunken tub, some suites with saunas. Convenient to numerous Japanese shops and restaurants in Nippon complex.

Moderate

Best Western Kyoto Inn. 1800 Sutter; 921–4000; (800) 528–1234. One block from Japan Center and some of the area's fine sushi bars.

VAN NESS AVENUE/DOWNTOWN

(From Geary to Sacramento Streets)

Super Deluxe

Queen Anne Hotel. 1590 Sutter; 441–2828; (800) 227–3970. 49 large, 19th-century guest rooms with authentic antiques. Complimentary breakfast/paper; same-day laundry and dry cleaning. A Victorian landmark.

Deluxe

Cathedral Hill. 1101 Van Ness; 776–8200; (800) 227–4730 nationwide; (800) 622–0855 in California. The former Jack Tar has been completely refurbished at a cost of $7 million. Extremely attractive.

Holiday Inn–Golden Gateway. 1500 Van Ness; 441–4000; (800) 238–8000 nationwide. Walking distance to Civic Center and Performing Arts Center. Pool; restaurant, lounge, entertainment.

Expensive

Grosvenor Inn. 1050 Van Ness, at Geary; 673–4711. Another landmark restoration with Victorian ambience. Free H.B.O. movies; free parking. Complimentary continental breakfast, complimentary cocktail party, 4-6 P.M. Coffee shop. Public transportation at door.

Inexpensive

Carlton. 1075 Sutter; 673–0242; (800) 227–4496 nationwide; (800) 792–0958 in California. Extremely attractive.

Lombard. 1015 Geary; 673–5232; (800) 431–1953 nationwide. Newly remodeled 100-room property.

Rodeway Inn. 895 Geary; 441–8220; (800) 228–2000 nationwide.

LOMBARD/VAN NESS

Expensive

Cable Motor Inn. 1450 Lombard, just off Van Ness; 673–0691. 77 newly redecorated rooms; free parking. Sundeck; some private patios. Restaurant, lounge and deli dining. One block to public transportation. Family plan.

Moderate

De Ville Motel. 2599 Lombard; 346–4664. Well-maintained 40-room motel.

Quality Inn. 2775 Van Ness; 928–5000; (800) 228–5151 nationwide; (800) 268–8990 in California. 140-unit high-rise just four blocks from Fisherman's Wharf.

Inexpensive

Chelsea Motor Inn. 2095 Lombard; 563–5600. Be sure to reserve; these are exceptional accommodations.

Cow Hollow Motor Inn. 2190 Lombard; 921–5800. Opened in 1979; same owners and fine accommodations as the Chelsea Motor Inn, above.

Rancho Lombard Motel. 1501 Lombard at Franklin; 474–3030. 34 attractive rooms; penthouse suites; kitchenettes.

Vagabond Inn. 2550 Van Ness; 776–7500; (800) 854–2700 nationwide; (800) 522–1555 in California. Pool; kitchenettes.

Basic Budget

Redwood Inn Motel. 1530 Lombard; 776–3800. Comfortable units with queen-size beds.

OCEAN BEACH/SAN FRANCISCO ZOO

Basic Budget

Great Highway Motor Inn. 1234 Great Highway; 731–6644; (800) 228–3939 nationwide. 54 rooms. Small pets okay.

Ocean Park Motel. 2690 46th Ave.; 556–7020. City's first motel (1936).

HOSTELS. Hostels are low-cost (fees generally range from $4 to $8) lodgings that offer clean sleeping and eating facilities. They are for people of all ages, with separate dorms for males and females, and kitchens. General housekeeping duties are assigned to each hosteler. Reservations suggested. See section on Youth Hostels in *Facts at Your Fingertips* at the beginning of this book.

San Francisco International Hostel (AYH). Building 240, Fort Mason; 771–7277. $6 per person with hostel pass; $8 per person without hostel pass.

Youth Hostel Centrale. 116 Turk, between Taylor and Jones; 346–7835. Dorm rooms with two twin-size bunkbeds are $8 per night. Private rooms also. All share baths.

 BED-AND-BREAKFAST TREASURES. San Francisco's first new/old inn opened in 1976. The tiny Bed & Breakfast Inn, tucked away off busy Union St., offers just nine delightfully decorated rooms housed in twin ivy-covered Victorian gingerbreads. Today the Bay Area hosts about 40 B&Bs and there are over 150 scattered throughout Northern California.

They do not all have rooms with baths; most lack TV's and telephones. But all offer warm hospitality; luxurious touches of fresh flowers and fruit, eclectic décor featuring brass beds, romantic French country flower-patterned wallpaper and drapery designs; claw-foot tubs, and working fireplaces. Breakfast, either in one's room or in a cozy public room, features fresh orange juice, warm home-baked breads or croissants, choice jams and a variety of hot drinks.

Each inn has been restored by relatively young people; the innkeepers of these *pensiones* are usually the staff. Some serve sherry or champagne in the parlors and join their guests for a relaxing pre or post-dinner chat.

Reserve rooms well in advance. Prices range from about $40.00 single to over $100.00 for double occupancy. Most of the city inns accept American Express, MasterCard or Visa; however, this is not always the case with some of the country inns. Be sure to inquire regarding individual credit card policies when making reservations or when checking into the establishment. B&Bs are usually not for families and certainly not for all travelers.

Super Deluxe to Expensive

Bed & Breakfast Inn. 4 Charlton Court; 921–9784. Opened in 1976, the original is off trendy Union St. Just nine Victorian accommodations.

The Inn at Union Square. 440 Post St.; 956–2544. Georgian elegance just one half block west of Union Sq. The inn adjoins John Howell Rare Books, one of the country's oldest antiquarian dealers.

Stanyan Park Hotel. 750 Stanyan St., across from Golden Gate Park; 751–1000. Renovation of this 36-unit property, declared a San Francisco historic landmark, cost $2 million. Its Victorian charm is reflected in smartly polished brass, crystal chandeliers, walnut armoires, oval mirrors, and four-poster beds.

Expensive to Moderate

Albion House. 135 Gough; 621–0896. A 1906, 9-room charmer.

Hermitage House. 2224 Sacramento St.; 921–5515. Popular with film crews. Ten cozy rooms with fireplaces.

Hotel Edward. 3155 Lombard, at Scott; 921–9776. Circa-1915 European-style pensione; thirty attractive rooms. In the Marina residential district over an Italian bakery.

Mansion. 2220 Sacramento St.; 929–9444. Pacific Heights Queen Anne Victorian. Classical concerts; famed Bufano sculpture garden.

Millefiori Inn. 444 Columbus; 433–9111. North Beach ambience; patio for breakfast.

Nob Hill Inn. 1000 Pine St.; 673–6080. Downtown locale.

Petite Auberge. 863-Bush; 928–6000. French country charm in 26 rooms.

Spreckels Mansion. 737 Buena Vista W.; 861–3008. Parklike area. Jack London was a guest of the original owners.

Union Street Inn. 2229 Union St.; 346–0424. A 9-room European-style *pensione.* "In" shopping and sipping street.

Washington Square Inn. 1660 Stockton St.; 981–4220. Historic North Beach area, one block to Telegraph Hill. Antique-filled.

HOW TO GET AROUND. Airport. Downtown to San Francisco Airport, by cab, averages about $25.00, without tip. The *Airporter,* 24-hour bus service between downtown San Francisco and the airport, is available. The ride averages 20–30 minutes. Buses depart from the new downtown terminal at the corner of Ellis and Taylor Sts., 3 blocks from Union Sq. Departure from the airport is from clearly marked stops. Present fare: $4.00, one way. For information, phone 673–2432. Limousine service to and from the airport is available. Rates vary. Lorrie's Travel & Tours has direct transportation to and from San Francisco hotels, motels and some midtown private residential areas and all airlines at San Francisco International Airport. Fare: $6.50, reservations required. Phone (415) 826–5950, or write 2660 3rd St., San Francisco, CA 94107.

BART, or the Bay Area Rapid Transit, crosses the bay between San Francisco and the East Bay, with stops in Oakland, Berkeley, Concord, Richmond, and Fremont, and Daly City to the south. Air-conditioned aluminum cars move at speeds of up to 80 miles an hour on surface, elevated, and subway track. Tickets are purchased from dispensing machines, change available. In the attractive BART stations, wall maps list destinations and cost. Fares range from 60¢ to $2.15. From downtown San Francisco (there is a station at Powell and Market Sts.) to Oakland City Center is $1.20. A $2.00 excursion ticket buys a three-county tour ride, and visit any of the 34 stations for up to 3 hours, as long as you enter and exit at the same station. BART operates Monday–Saturday from 6:00 A.M. to midnight; on Sunday from 9:00 A.M. to midnight. For information, phone 788-BART.

Cable Cars. "They turn corners almost at right angles; cross other lines and, for all I know, may run up the sides of houses," wrote Rudyard Kipling in 1889. In June 1984, the 109-year old system returned to service after a $58.2-million overhaul. Because the cable cars had been declared a National Historic Landmark in 1964, renovation methods and materials had to be such that Andrew Hallidie's system's historical and traditional qualities were maintained. The Cable Car Barn's exterior was left intact, but the interior was gutted and rebuilt. An underground viewing room was added to the museum so that visitors can observe the huge sheaves—grooved wheels that guide the cables under the street. The rehabilitated "moving" landmark has been designed to withstand another century of use. Fare $1. The Powell-Mason (#59) and the Powell-Hyde (#60) terminate at Fisherman's Wharf. The California (#61) runs east-west.

San Francisco Municipal Railway System. "Muni's" system includes *motor* and *trolley buses, surface street cars,* the new Muni Metro *below-surface street-cars,* as well as the popular *cable cars.* Each car is numbered, destinations clearly marked. 24-hour service. Fares are 60¢ with free transfers available; good in any direction for 1½ hours. Exact change required—drivers carry no change. On Sundays or certain holidays, Muni offers a $1.00 pass good for unlimited travel all day on all routes; passes may be purchased from conductors on cable cars. For 24-hour information on routes and services, phone 674-MUNI, or check the Yellow Pages. Visit the Redwood Empire Association Visitors' Information Center, #1 Market Plaza, for their free *How to Get There from Here* information sheet. MUNI's fares are 60¢, with free transfers good in any direction for 1½ hours.

Here are some Muni routes of especial use to visitors: *(The numbers refer to surface buses unless otherwise stated.)*

Castro. #24 Divisadero from Market and Powell; Muni Metro to Market.

Chinatown. #30 Stockton, from Stockton and Sutter.

Civic Center. #5 west on Market to Van Ness Ave.

Clement Street. #55 Sacramento to 6th and Clement.

Cliff House/Ocean Beach. #38 Geary to 48th Ave. and Point Lobos.

Exploratorium/Palace of Fine Arts/Marina. #30 Stockton from 3rd and Market.

Golden Gate Bridge/Fort Point. #30 Stockton from 3rd and Market, transfer to #28 at Chestnut and Fillmore.

Golden Gate Park. #38 Geary from Union Square; transfer to #10 Monterey.

Japantown. #38 Geary to Laguna St., from Union Sq.

North Beach. #30 Stockton, from Stockton and Sutter.

Northern Waterfront. #19 from 9th and Market to Beach St.; #32 north bound along the Embarcadero to Fisherman's Wharf.

Nob Hill. #55 Sacramento; California Cable Car line.

Pacific Heights. #3 Jackson on Sutter St.

Presidio. #3 Jackson on Sutter St.

Russian Hill. #30 Stockton from Stockton and Sutter.

Telegraph Hill. #30 Stockton from Stockton and Sutter, transfer to #39 Coit, at Union and Stockton (Washington Square).

Twin Peaks. Muni Metro K, L, M west to Castro, transfer to #37 Corbett bus. Get off at Crestline. (NOTE: This route, "Burnett" goes through the Haight and Ashbury districts.)

Haight-Sunset Scenic Route. #72/from 5th and Market goes through the Western Addition, along Golden Gate Park to Sunset Blvd., to Lake Merced, Stonestown shopping mall and San Francisco State University. Daily service during business hours.

A.C. Transit (Alameda–Contra Costa Transit) buses depart from the Trans Bay Terminal, 1st and Mission Sts., for East Bay communities. Over 7,000 A.C. Transit bus stops are marked with signs indicating the line number of all buses making that stop and a brief description of each route's intermediate and final destinations. For information phone 839–2882.

Golden Gate Transit (332–6600) provides year-round daily ferry service to Sausalito and Larkspur. Depart from the Ferry Building at the foot of Market St. Adult fare between San Francisco and Sausalito is $2.75 weekdays; $3.00 weekends and holidays. 6–12 yrs.—half-fare; children 5 or under, with adult—free. Fare to Larkspur is $2.20 weekdays; $3.15 weekends and holidays. **Red and White** (546–2810/2815) offers ferries to Tiburon (leaving from Pier 43½ and the Ferry Bldg.; round trip, $6.00); Sausalito (leaving from Pier 41; Fisherman's Wharf; $6.00); and Angel Island (leaving from Pier 43½; $6.00). GGT also provides bus service, via the Golden Gate Bridge, to communities in Marin and Sonoma counties. Operates daily, fares vary between 35¢ and $2.25.

The Greater Bay Area has seven mass-transit systems. They offer nine ways to get from here to there, employing five modes of travel. The Regional Transit Association has a new map showing where the systems interface. Its aim is to acquaint the public with the RTA's systems availability for use not only during commuting hours, but at off-peak times and weekends. Following is a sample Sunday tour: take Muni bus to Golden Gate Bridge, board GG Transit bus to Sausalito, stroll a bit, board ferry for ride back to San Francisco. Then BART under the bay to Fremont, then board Santa Clara County Transit to San Jose, after a brief layover, board the CalTrans train back to San Francisco, return to hotel or home by Muni Metro, bus, or cable car. Cost per person about $10.00, the time, 6 or more hours, depending on length of stays in Sausalito and San Jose. And no hassle with Sunday drivers on this 110-mile excursion.

The new *Regional Transit Guide* is available for $2.00 at local bookstores or by mailing $3.00 (to cover postage and tax) to: Metropolitan Transportation Commission, Public Information Office, Hotel Claremont, Berkeley, CA 94705. In addition to transit maps for downtown San Francisco, Oakland and Berkeley, the guide has listings of popular Bay Area destinations and the transit lines that serve them.

Sam Trans, at 1st and Mission, provides bus service to San Mateo County, south of San Francisco. For information phone 761–7000.

Southern Pacific commuter trains operate from their 4th and Townsend Sts. depot south to San Jose and other peninsula communities. Daily service. For information, phone 495–4546.

Taxi Service. Rates are high in the city, though most rides are relatively short. It is almost impossible to hail a passing cab. Either phone, or use the nearest hotel taxi stand, midtown. Weekends are especially difficult. Check the Yellow Pages for numbers of various services.

Walking. The best way to see this compact city is afoot. Many of the historic or sightseeing districts are easy walks from midtown or from available public transit. However, as mentioned earlier in the *Facts at Your Fingertips* section, there are certain neighborhoods that should be avoided. It is not safe, nor convenient, to attempt to walk from the City Hall–Civic Center complex to Golden Gate Park, as some tourist maps appear to indicate. The Western Addition has been the scene of continual assaults on both residents and visitors. Avoid the area roughly bounded by Geary St. to the north, Hayes St. to the south, Gough St. on the east and Steiner St. on the west. Use a bit of caution and have a memorable visit to this wonderful city. Walking tours are detailed in information available from the *Redwood Empire Association Visitor's Information Center* and the *San Francisco Visitor and Convention Bureau.* Dress comfortably; have a sweater or jacket for late afternoon winds and fog.

By Car. If possible, avoid using a car in the downtown areas of this easy-to-walk city. On certain streets, parking is forbidden during rush hours. Look for the warning signs; illegally parked cars are towed away. Parking lots are expensive, usually quite busy with normal daily traffic. Parking metered spaces are available, but offer limited time use. In a city boasting at least 40 hills, be sure brakes are set and wheels turned into the curb to prevent rolling. Cable cars and pedestrians always have the right of way. Be sure to have your car's brakes checked before driving in San Francisco. Curbs painted different colors designate parking restrictions: red for no parking, green for limited period parking, and blue for use by handicapped drivers.

Rental Cars. Most major car rental agencies, including *Avis, Budget, Rent-A-Car, Econo-Car, Hertz* and *National,* service the airport and many rent vans as well as cars. Reservations are usually necessary. It is usually cheaper to rent *at* the airport. Check your local telephone directory for toll-free reservation numbers.

RENTAL RECREATIONAL VEHICLES AND CAMPERS. Many vacationers are renting fully self-contained motor homes for short and long trips through

California. *Chase Family Motor Homes,* 545 Airport Blvd. (P.O. Box 391), South San Francisco, CA 94080 ([415] 589–6383) has rentals that run from economy, compact vehicles to super-luxury coaches with color TV, microwave ovens and designer décor. Rather pricey: $495–$1200 weekly. *U-Haul RV Rentals.* 1575 Bayshore Blvd. San Francisco, (415) 467–3830, has motor homes and travel trailers available for a day, weekend, week or month. 24-hour emergency road service.

 TOURIST INFORMATION. The *San Francisco Convention and Visitors Bureau* publishes a series of booklets and maps on San Francisco, which are free. They also publish a general information folder in four foreign languages—French, German, Spanish, and Japanese. First stop for tourists should be their Visitor Information Center, lower level, Hallidie Plaza, Powell and Market Sts. This is at the cable-car turnaround and is also the Powell St. entrance to BART. Open daily except Thanksgiving, Christmas and New Year's Day. Written requests for information should be addressed to the bureau's office: 201 3rd St., San Francisco, CA 94105, (415) 974–6900. Their 24-hour telephone-information service, 391–2000, provides a recorded message summarizing the day's events, plus suggestions on what to do and see in the city.

The *Redwood Empire Association,* located at One Market Plaza, 10th floor, San Francisco, CA 94105, publishes an annual, comprehensive guide on the Redwood Empire as well as San Francisco. Services are free. The Redwood Empire stretches more than four hundred miles from San Francisco to the southern Oregon county of Josephine. The knowledgeable staff will help plan itineraries and suggest current events of interest. If mailing for their *Redwood Empire Visitors Guide,* please enclose $1.00. Phone (415) 543–8334. Open Monday through Friday, 9:00 A.M.–4:30 P.M.

Visitor Service Representatives are on duty in the International Arrival Area, at San Francisco International Airport. They will assist visitors in clearing Customs, assist in language difficulties, and provide tourist information.

The *International Visitors Center,* 312 Sutter St., 4th Fl., San Francisco, CA 94108, 986–1388, is open Monday through Friday from 9:00 A.M. to 5:00 P.M. This private voluntary organization is the Bay Area host organization for the "Meet Americans at Home" program. Arrangements can be made for international visitors to spend an afternoon or evening in the home of one of its members. Requests must be made in person, at least 48 hours in advance. Foreign visitors are invited to visit their headquarters while in San Francisco.

Foreign Currency Exchange: *Bank of America,* 315 Montgomery St., San Francisco, CA 94104, 622–2451, is open Monday through Friday from 10:00 A.M.–3:00 P.M. Their office at the South Terminal, San Francisco International Airport, is open seven days, from 7:00 A.M. to 11:00 P.M. In addition, a Bank of America Day and Night Office is located at Powell and Market Sts., opposite Hallidie Plaza, 622–4182. This centrally located service is open Monday through Friday from 10:00 A.M. to 7:00 P.M. *Deak-Perera & Co. of California* have an office at 100 Grant, near Union Square, open Monday to Friday from

9:00 A.M. to 5:00 P.M. and on Saturday from 9:30 A.M. to 2:30 P.M. They also have a branch at the South Terminal, San Francisco International Airport, open seven days, from 7:30 A.M. to 11:00 P.M. *Macy's* on Union Square has a Cashier's Office, on the 4th floor; Monday through Friday, 9:30 A.M.–9:00 P.M.; Saturday 9:30 A.M.–6:00 P.M.; and Sunday, noon–5:00 P.M.

Service Clubs. *Rotary* meets Tuesday, noon at the Sheraton-Palace Hotel, 546–0644; *Kiwanis* has four weekly noon meetings, 362–4197. Phone 771–7070 for information on *Lions* meeting times and places; 776–0625 for information the *Business and Professional Women's Club.* Information on *Soroptimist International* is available at their office at 55 Sutter St., Suite 194, or phone 543–4487.

 SEASONAL EVENTS. January. The International Boat Show at Moscone Center attracts armchair athletes as well as seasoned sports enthusiasts. Later in the month, at the Cow Palace, canine fanciers flock to the Golden Gate Kennel Club Dog Show.

January or **February** heralds Chinese New Year with an elaborate nighttime parade, attended by thousands of Bay Area Chinese-Americans, as well as visitors, which opens a week-long family festival season. Sample *dim sum* luncheon in one of the many Chinatown restaurants, if schedule and crowds permit.

March is a bonny month, with the *St. Patrick's Day Parade,* which takes place on the Sunday closest to March 17. Famed *Buena Vista* no longer can accommodate the Irish-coffee fans, but the whole town offers corned beef, cabbage, the aforementioned liquid refreshment, plus green carnations and a lot of blarney!

April swings in with the lovely *Cherry Blossom Festival* in Japantown; the pink-and-white dazzle of cherry blossoms in Golden Gate Park, and the attendant flowering of the thousands of rhododendrons throughout the city. There are *Easter Sunrise Services* at Mt. Davidson, elevation 938 feet, the highest peak in the city. Since 1923, thousands of pilgrims have attended this interdenominational gathering. The *International Film Festival,* formerly held in autumn, is now a springtime delight for Bay Area film buffs and visitors. The two-week Film Festival draws international entries and personalities. Check the pink "Datebook" section of the *Sunday Examiner and Chronicle* for the most current information.

May San Francisco Bay to Breakers Race.

June busts out all over—early in the month the trendy *Union Street Spring Festival and Crafts Fair* lures with fancy food, portables, fashions, and furnishings. Later in the month, the bustling *Upper Grant Avenue Street Fair* is more of the "'60s Haight look." June 29, the locals celebrate *San Francisco's Birthday.*

July pops off with the 4th *Fireworks* at the waterfront. The same weekend stars the *Polk Street Fair,* a parade of the straights, gays, and bisexual personalities drawn to the permissive city.

August's summery mood is captured at the *San Francisco County Fair Flower Show,* in Golden Gate Park.

September shines with the weekend *Japanese Fall Festival* (Aki Matsuri) in Japantown.

October focus on North Beach, with the *Blessing of the Fishing Fleet,* at the Church of Sts. Peter and Paul, and at Fisherman's Wharf. Soon after, North Beach is the site of much merriment at the *Columbus Day Parade;* local dining spots are even more crowded than usual. Late in the month or in **November,** the Cow Palace again offers a whopper—the *Grand National Livestock Exposition, Rodeo and Horse Show.* By Thanksgiving, attention is turning to Yuletime.

December is a sound and light affair. Union Square's elegantly decorated shops glow with festive displays. Nob Hill hostelries attract thousands of Bay Area residents as well as holiday visitors to their Yule celebrations.

 FREE EVENTS. San Francisco has a year-long calendar of street fairs and festivals—and all free. Fun gets off to a super start with the annual *Chinese New Year*—nine days of fireworks, celebration, and the colorful and crowded Golden Dragon Parade, climaxing the calendar. April stars the charming *Nihonmachi (Japantown) Cherry Blossom Festival.* Ethnic musical and dance programs, a parade, judo, karate, kendo (Japanese fencing), and ikebana (flower arranging) exhibits mix old and new Japanese customs and traditions. June is highlighted by both the *Union Street Spring Festival* and the *Upper Grant Avenue Street Fair.* Union St.'s classy boutiques and chic eateries may dent the pocketbook, but there's much to enjoy by merely looking. The Upper Grant Avenue Street Fair is a good deal more pedestrian in the myriad arts and crafts offerings each Father's Day weekend. The lively *Polk Street Fair,* held on the weekend closest to the Fourth of July, features dozens of arts and crafts booths, and a merry and mixed audience of gay and straight lookers. Japantown in July offers a double bill—the *Tanabata/Bon Odori Festival.* Dancing, flower-arranging demonstrations, and calligraphy displays are part of the festivities. And there's the biggie on the Fourth of July: the all-day family entertainment at Crissy Field, in the Presidio, topped by the annual fireworks display exploding over the Bay. In late September, Japantown hosts its *Fall Festival (Aki Matsuri)* The city's growing gay-oriented community stages a *Castro Street Fair,* usually in late August. Great for people-watchers, if the dress or antics of the participants don't offend.

Parades are very much a part of all the above special celebrations, plus the annual *St. Patrick's Day* turn-out and the spectacular *Columbus Day Parade.* There are bocce ball tournaments, bike races, as well as the traditional Columbus landing pageant, coronation of Queen Isabella, and the blessing of the fleet at Fisherman's Wharf. The first-ever *Santa Claus Parade,* with 35 units including Santa atop a Wells Fargo stagecoach and Mrs. Claus traveling in an antique fire engine, was held in early December, 1981, on Market St. Sponsors included the Downtown Association and stores like Emporium-Capwell would like the event to grow over the years into something like Macy's parade in Manhattan.

Christmas is very special in the city by the Bay. Thanksgiving week, the Embarcadero Center's four high-rise shopping, dining and office buildings are lavishly decorated with poinsettia shrubs. Colored lights festoon downtown landmarks as well as sailboats and ships of all sizes docked along the waterfront. Extravagant holiday-themed decorations thrill visitors and locals at the Hyatt Regency Hotel, the St. Francis, Mark Hopkins, and Fairmont Hotels. Free entertainment at Union Square and other parts of the city add to the all-out holiday spirit. There may not be the traditional snow and cold of Eastern cities but there is lots to recall the meaning of Christmas.

Plan to spend some time in San Francisco's many museums. Free at all times is the *Cable Car Museum,* Washington and Mason Sts.; the *Mexican Museum* at its new home at Fort Mason; *National Maritime Museum,* Hyde St. Pier and Aquatic Park; *Old Mint,* 5th and Mission Sts.; *Presidio Army Museum,* Lincoln Blvd. and Funston Ave.; *Navy/Marine Corps Museum,* Building One, Treasure Island (reached via San Francisco–Oakland Bay Bridge by auto or public transportation); *San Francisco Fire Department Museum,* 655 Presidio Ave. at Bush St.; *Wells Fargo History Room,* Wells Fargo Bank, 420 Montgomery St., at California St.; *Energy Expo,* Pacific Gas and Electric Company, 77 Beale St.; *World of Economics,* Federal Reserve Bank, 101 Market St.; *Merchants-Exchange Trading Hall,* The Chartered Bank of London, 465 California St.; "A World of Oil," Standard Oil Company of California, 555 Market St.; *Society of California Pioneers,* Pioneer Hall, 456 McAllister St., Civic Center; *Fort Point National Historic Site,* Presidio of San Francisco; *Chinese Cultural Center,* 750 Kearny St., in the Holiday Inn.

The first Wednesday of the month is free-admission day to the *M. H. de Young Memorial Museum, the Asian Art Museum, the California Palace of the Legion of Honor.* The *San Francisco Art Institute,* 800 Chestnut St., offers free guided tours, Tuesday through Saturday, 10:00 A.M.–5:00 P.M. Don't miss the Diego Rivera mural.

The *San Francisco Museum of Modern Art* has free admission on Thursday evenings, 6:00 P.M.–10:00 P.M.; located in the War Memorial Veterans Bldg., Van Ness Ave. and McAllister St. (Civic Center).

First Wednesday of the month is free admission to the *California Academy of Sciences,* Golden Gate Park.

A varied presentation of music, opera, and dance are featured each summer in a series of free Sunday-afternoon concerts at Stern Grove, Sloat Blvd. and 19th Ave. Concerts start at 2:00 P.M.; come early and tote a picnic to this outdoor amphitheater. The San Francisco Opera, the Symphony, and Ballet companies perform during the festival. The season runs from late June through August.

The city celebrates the Fourth of July musically with a free annual concert of Turk Murphy's Band (based at Earthquake McGoon's) at Fort Point, at the base of the Golden Gate Bridge tower.

The Bank of America sponsors free noon concerts in their Giannini Auditorium several times a week with live entertainment that has included Brown Bag Opera, the San Francisco Chamber Orchestra and even Russian rock groups.

The Embarcadero Center, along with Levi Strauss, whose headquarters are in San Francisco, have cosponsored all kinds of musical programs, most of them around noontime on weekdays. The plaza of the Crown Zellerbach company is often the scene of noonday entertainment surprises, including Dixieland groups and ballet troupes.

The all-French *California Palace of the Legion of Honor* has Sunday-afternoon chamber music concerts in their Little Theater, 2:00 P.M.; and an organ recital Saturday and Sunday afternoons at 4:00 P.M.

There are frequent free musical events throughout the area. We suggest the reader consult the *Datebook* section of the Sunday San Francisco *Chronicle* or phone 391–2000 for a recording of the day's events.

Pier 39, Ghirardelli Square, and Union Square all offer a variety of free entertainment.

Walking is a great way to discover San Francisco. A series of free walking tours of Golden Gate Park every weekend, May through October, concentrate on the plant life and history of the park. Phone 221–1310 for current information. Free guided plant walks are offered daily at the Strybing Arboretum, 9th Ave. and Lincoln Way, Golden Gate Park. Phone 661–1316 for details. One-hour free City Walking Tours are offered year-round on Saturday. There is a noon City Hall tour, Thursday each week. Phone City Guides, 558–3770, for updated schedules.

TOURS. Bay Cruises. From Pier 39, the *Blue-and-Gold Fleet* has daily 1¼-hour narrated cruises. Frequent departures from Pier 39's West Marina; validated parking. Phone 781–7877 for further information. Their three 85-foot triple-deck tour boats provide one of the most relaxing and enjoyable ways to survey the San Francisco skyline and explore the bay. The *Red-and-White Fleet's* seven enclosed vessels offer daily 1¼-hour narrated cruises year-round (weather permitting). From June to October, every Friday night, their 2½-hour "Bar-B-Que Cruise" includes dinner, dancing, and entertainment. Also, every Sunday from June through October, a 1½-hour "Champagne Brunch Cruise" is available. Departures from Pier 41 at Fisherman's Wharf. Very popular, reservations suggested, is their 2½-hour "Alcatraz Tour." This includes the boat transportation and a guided tour of the famous former federal prison and grounds. Walking shoes, head scarf, and binoculars suggested. Departures from Pier 41, Fisherman's Wharf. Phone 546–2815 for all cruises listed except Alcatraz Tour, for which phone 546–2805. Red-and-White has ferry service to Angel Island, across the Bay in Marin County, every day from the first Saturday in June through Labor Day; otherwise only on weekends and holidays except Thanksgiving, Christmas, and New Year's Day. Departs from Pier 43½. $6.00 round-trip for adults. There are also trips to Tiburon (leaving from Pier 43½ and the Ferry Bldg.; $6.00) and Sausalito (leaving from Pier 41, Fisherman's Wharf; $6.00). (Strictly speaking, these Red-and-White trips and the Golden Gate Transit trips from the Ferry Bldg. to Sausalito and Larkspur—see "How to Get Around"—are not "tours," but can be as pleasant as a tour, often less crowded, lacking only a guide.)

Two-night bicycle trips through the Napa or Sonoma valleys are offered by *Backroads Bicycle Touring Co.*, P.O. Box 5534, Berkeley, CA 94705; 652–0786.

The fee includes a support van, two tour leaders, all meals, and accommodations, BYOB or rent one (about $37.00). These are deluxe trips, include excellent lodging, fine food, and stops at some of the famous wineries. Tour groups range from 15 to 24; fee, $188–243 per person. They also offer 3-day trips to the Russian River or Gold Country; fee, around $299.

City Tours. *Gray Line* offers a variety of tours, from a *deluxe* 3-hour comprehensive view to an all-day city, Sausalito, Muir Woods, and Bay Cruise excursion. Half-day trips to Muir Woods and the famous giant redwoods in the 424-acre National Monument are very popular. These operate daily. From November through April, there are tri-weekly day-long excursions to the famed Napa and Sonoma Valleys. Special stops are made at two wineries, and a tasty picnic box lunch is included. Daily tours are scheduled from May through October, except Sundays. Reservations are a must. Another scenic route is south to Monterey, and includes charming Carmel and a picturesque drive thru privately owned Del Monte Forest. Though a long day, there is a leisurely lunch at Monterey's Cannery Row and shopping/strolling time in Carmel. Daily May through October; three times weekly other months. For information on all Gray Line tours phone 771–4000 or see the Gray Line agent in your hotel or motel.

The Great Pacific Tour, 929–1700, uses 13-passenger vans for its daily 3½-hour city tour. If required, bilingual guides may be requested. Daily 3½-hour tours to Muir Woods and Sausalito are available.

A Night Tour of Chinatown is offered every evening year-round by *Ding How Tours;* 981–8399. About 3 hours; with or without dinner; walking shoes are recommended.

Holiday Tours, 986–6060, offers San Francisco by night, with either a Chinese banquet or seafood-and-wine evening on Pier 39. Monday and Wednesday evenings Holiday Tours offers a Sunset dinner cruise to Tiburon, return drive to the city, with a nightcap at the 52-floor Bank of America's Carnelian Room.

Other Tours. Helicopter Tours: *Commodore Helicopter Tours,* Pier 43, Fisherman's Wharf, offers a 4-minute Bay tour, views of Alcatraz, the city's skyline, Bay and Golden Gate Bridges; 981–4832. *Helicop Tours* offers five spectacular flights above the city and the Bay Area from 20 to over 100 miles, from the China Basin Heliport, ½ mile south of the Oakland Bay Bridge and 3 miles from Fisherman's Wharf. Phone 495–3333 for rates and reservations. Flights daily (weather permitting) from 10:00 A.M. to sunset.

TOURS TO OTHER AREAS

California White Water Rafting. If time is limited, one-day trips are offered spring and summer. Rates: $49.00–90.00 For reservations, phone *White Water West,* 548–0782.

Point Reyes National Seashore. From May to October, a cycling/camping weekend experience. Explore this isolated area of Marin County. Enjoy an oyster bake on the beach. Contact: Backroads, P.O. Box 5534, Berkeley, CA 94705; (415) 652–0786.

Hearst Castle, *California Parlor Car Tours* offers "Three Day Hearst Castle-Monterey Circle Tour", phone 474–7500. *Express Tours,* "Hearst Castle Overnighter," is a 2-day/1-night tour; 621–7738 or 621–7652.

Lake Tahoe. *Express Tours Unlimited:* "Tahoe-in-a-Day" is approximately 12 hours and includes a visit to a gambling casino and a sightseeing boat cruise. Phone 621–7738 for rates and schedules. A new tour is "Reno-in-a-Day."

Monterey/Carmel. *Gray Line's* approximately 11-hour tour includes lunch, drive through world-famous 17-Mile Drive, and a wine-tasting stop. Reservations are required; phone 771–4000. *Lorrie's Travel and Tours* vans depart daily, April–October, for about ten hours; lunch is included. Phone 885–6600 for rates and reservations. *The Great Pacific Tour Co.* offers tours, three days a week; lunch is included. Hotel pick-up. 929–1700.

Sacramento Delta Cruise. From April to November, one-way cruising between San Francisco and Sacramento, on the bay and delta. Return by bus. Reservations; phone (916) 372–3690.

Wilderness Hiking (Yosemite, the King Range). Accompanied by naturalists; llamas used to pack supplies. Contact: *Mama's Llamas,* Box 655, El Dorado, CA 95623; (916) 622–2566.

Wine Country. *Gray Line* operates daily a Napa Valley tour, approximately 9 hours, lunch included. Stop for tour and tasting at two of the local wineries. *The Great Pacific Tour Co.* tour to Napa and Sonoma valleys includes lunch, wine, and champagne tasting. Tuesday through Sunday, about 8 hours; 929–1700. See also *Wine Country* section later in the book.

Yosemite. *California Parlor Car Tours* offers 1- to 3-day tours; phone 474–7500 for details. *Express Tours Unlimited* offers a 1-day outstanding tour. Phone 621–7738. *Quality Tours* offers a 13-hour multilingual tour: French, Spanish, Japanese, German, Italian in mini-vans. Phone 788–6838.

SPECIAL-INTEREST SIGHTSEEING. City Guides. Volunteers conduct these free tours; no reservations. Appear at the starting point and look for a guide wearing the "City Guide" badge. Phone 558–3770 for updated information. Here are the tours:

City Hall. Thursdays, noon. Leaves from San Francisco Room, 3rd fl., Main Library, 200 Larkin.

Coit Tower. Saturday, 11:00 A.M. Leaves from reception desk of the tower on Telegraph Hill.

Fire Department Museum. Thursdays through Sundays from 1:00 to 4:00 P.M. 655 Presidio Ave.

Gold Rush City. Every Wednesday and Sunday, noon. Leaves from Trans America Bldg., Clay St. lobby, 600 Montgomery.

Historic Market Street. Saturday, 2:00 P.M. Leaves from One Market Plaza.

Moscone Center. Saturday, 1:00 P.M. Entrance on Howard, between 3rd and 4th.

North Beach. Saturday, 10:00 A.M. Leaves from the steps of Sts. Peter and Paul Church, 666 Filbert St.

Pacific Heights Victorians. 1st and 3rd Saturday of each month at 10:00 A.M. and 2:00 P.M.; leaves from Mary Ellen Pleasant Park, 1801 Bush St., at Octavia St.

Presidio Army Museum. Saturday and Sunday at 1:00 P.M. Building 1 inside the Presidio at the corner of Lincoln Way and Funston Ave.

These tours above are sponsored by the Friends of the San Francisco Public Library. In May and October, City Guides conduct neighborhood walks on Saturdays. Tours include Noe Valley, Nob Hill, inner Mission, Bernal Heights, Glen Park, Eureka Valley, and Crocker-Amazon.

The **Foundation for San Francisco's Architectural Heritage** offers two 45-minute historic downtown tours, Thursday, noon; $1.00. Phone 441–3046.

Haas-Lilienthal House: 45-minute tour, Wednesdays, noon to 4:00 P.M.; Sundays, 11:00 A.M.–4:30 P.M. No reservations; adults, $3.00; seniors and children, $1.00. 2007 Franklin St.

Victorian and Edwardian Pacific Heights: Sundays 12:30 P.M. 2-hour tour begins and ends at Haas-Lilienthal House. One-mile route with 12 stops. No reservations; $3.00. Phone 441–3046.

Don Herron does 3-hour literary walks. No reservations; Adults, $4.00, Seniors, $1.50. Phone 564–7021 for updated information.

Dashiell Hammett walks start Sunday noon from the steps of the main library, 200 Larkin.

Two other walks cover other areas in the city. One starts at noon Saturdays at Coit Tower, goes through Telegraph Hill, North Beach, the Financial District, and Union Square. The other starts at noon at the southwest corner of Sacramento and Mason Streets and covers Nob Hill, Russian Hill, and Pacific Heights. Phone 564–7021 for details.

Golden Gate Park. The Friends of Recreation and Parks have tours throughout the year. Phone 221–1310 for current tours.

Japanese Tea Garden. Saturday, 10:00 and 11:00 A.M.; Sunday, 2:00 and 3:00 P.M. Meet inside main gate of Japanese Tea Garden. Tour free, plus small entrance fee to garden.

De Young Memorial Museum offers free docent tours, scheduled by the subject matter, Wednesday through Sunday. Phone 387–5922 for details. Admission fee.

Asian Art Museum offers free docent tours daily. Admission fee. 558–2993.

Other cultural tours include: *Lincoln Park.* California Palace of the Legion of Honor. 2:00 P.M. docent tours, Wednesday through Sunday; 752–5561. Admission fee.

Civic Center. Museum of Modern Art: Free docent tours, Tuesday through Sunday, 1:15 P.M. leaves from 4th fl. Van Ness Ave. and McAllister St.; 863–8800. Admission fee.

Performing Arts Center tours of the new Louise M. Davies Symphony Hall, Herbst Theater, and War Memorial Opera House. Mondays (except holidays) on the hour and half-hour from 10:00 A.M. to 2:30 P.M. 552–8000. Adults, $3.00; seniors and students, $2.00.

Mexican Museum has guided walks through the city's historic Mission district. For information and time schedule, call 441-0404. Adults, $3.00, seniors and students, $1.00.

Sutro Heights. A scenic two-hour walk, overlooking Ocean Beach. Sunday 11:00–1:00; meet at lion statues, 48th Ave. & Pt. Lobos Dr. Phone 556–8642.

African-American Historical and Cultural Society offers tours at Bldg. "C" at Fort Mason. Adults 50¢, children 25¢.

Whittier Mansion has California Historical Society docent tours at 1:30 P.M. and 3 P.M. on Wednesday, Saturday, and Sunday. 2090 Jackson St. 567–1848. Adults, $2, seniors and students, $1.00.

The **Chinese Cultural Foundation** of San Francisco offers two walks in Chinatown:

Heritage Walk: Saturday, 2:00 P.M. Adults, $6.00; children under 12, $2.00.

Culinary Walk: Stroll through the markets and food shops. Enjoy a *dim sum* lunch. 986–1822. Adults, $12.00, children, $6.00. Reservations necessary.

 PARKS. Golden Gate Park, the world's largest man-made park, offers 1,017 acres of woods and meadows, lakes and streams, flowers and trees. Visitors who see only the portion of the landscape driving through miss half of the wonders of John McLaren's masterpark. The Scottish gardener began work at the park in 1887. He planted the principal "shrub"—really the Australian "tea tree"—as well as beach grass, lupine, and *Acacia longifolia* in the dunes which made up most of the allotted land. Uncle John died in 1943, at the age of ninety-six, and was on the job until a few months before his death. The *Japanese Tea Garden* is easily the park's most popular natural feature. Open daily, there is a small admission charge, except on Monday's when it's free. It's famous for its pink-and-white cherry blossoms on parade each spring; the busy Tea House; and the photogenic Moon Bridge set amid exotic landscaping. A short stroll from the tea garden is the free *Garden of Shakespeare's Flowers.* Two hundred flowers mentioned by the Bard, as well as bronze-engraved panels with floral quotations of his, are set throughout the area. Near the Fell St. park entrance, the glass and wood *Victorian Conservatory* is an eye-catcher. Outside, a huge floral "bulletin board" carries seasonal messages in flowers. Patterned after London's Kew Gardens, its interior is a tropical plant paradise. Free; open daily. Nearby are colorful Fuchsia, Dahlia, Camellia gardens, and the 20-acre McLaren Memorial Rhododendron Dell. Rhododendrons were McLaren's favorite flower. The blooms are at their peak in spring and early summer. *Strybing Arboretum* specializes in plants from areas with climates similar to the Bay Area, such as the west coast of Australia, South Africa, and the Mediterranean. There are many gardens inside the grounds, with 6,000 plants of different species in seasonal bloom. Free; tours are offered, but check for schedule; 558–3706. (Also in the Park are the *de Young* and *Asian Art Museums* and the *California Academy of Sciences—see Museums—*and sports facilities—see *Participant Sports.*)

Some of the largest and best-formed Monterey cypresses line the fairways at **Lincoln Park's** golf course, providing much needed windbreaks in the breezy area. This park affords smashing views of the Golden Gate and its 200-foot cliffs, as well as being the setting for the *California Palace of the Legion of Honor,* a museum devoted to French art.

Pine Lake Park, along with open space for picnicking, lawn bowling, and croquet, a natural amphitheater, **Sigmund Stern Grove,** for summer concerts, including a jazz festival, in a setting of redwood, fir, and eucalyptus trees.

With over 3,500 city acres given over to parks and people-space, not all the areas are large and heavily utilized. Chinatown's **Portsmouth Square,** the city's first plaza, is an early-morn tai chi exercise spot. The stunning **Palace of Fine Arts** rotunda (*not* a museum; it houses the Exploratorium), at Marina and Lyon Sts., is a quiet haven for a picnic or loafing around its swan-filled lagoon.

Across the Bay, Oakland's **Lakeside Park,** just off Grand Ave. at the north end of Lake Merritt, has some unusual gardens including a cactus and succulent garden, a Polynesian garden, a Japanese garden, a herb and fragrance garden, and a soon-to-be completed palm garden.

ZOOS. The time was 1889; the place—Golden Gate Park. The beginning of the **San Francisco Zoo** was the arrival of one inhabitant, a grizzly bear named Monarch, a gift of the San Francisco *Examiner.* Not until 1940 was the major portion of the present zoo completed, at its current site just northwest of Lake Merced. Presently, of the 1,000 animals, over 130 have been designated as endangered species. Among the protected are: snow leopard, black rhinoceros, red panda, grizzly bear, bengal tiger, chimpanzee, Asian elephant and jaguar. Very new is Gorilla World, a $2-million exhibit almost an acre in size, the world's largest and most natural gorilla habitat. The circular outer area is carpeted with African kikiyu grass, while trees, shrubs and waterfalls create communal play areas. Eight separate landscaped sites allow visitors to view the gorillas as if in the bush. Over 450 volunteers care for the animals and help educate the public in wildlife conservation. Zoo docents provide hundreds of tours for the over 650,000 annual visitors. In 1980, the first year of a successful fund-raising program, Adopt An Animal, netted over $70,000 to be used in animal habitat improvements. Zoo parents range from less than one year to over ninety. Some live in faraway places like Singapore and Moscow. Pick an animal for yourself or a friend. The price: from $15 to $5,000 or more. The "adoption fee" contribution for one year is tax-deductible. A llama costs $15.00; a Mandarin duck, $45.00; the $200 fee fetches a snowy owl, and a corporate $5,000 bags a rare polar bear. The zoo family consumes about 400 tons of feed annually.

The **Children's Zoo** houses over 300 mammals, reptiles, birds, and amphibians. The mini-zoo has a summer Nature Trail, the Baby Animal Nursery, and was the first Insect Zoo in California; there are only three in the United States. For a 4-mile safari through the park, board the Zebra Zephyr. The twenty-minute tram tour costs $1.00 for adults; 50¢ for children and seniors. Another great 50¢ ride is astride one of the 52 hand-carved menagerie animals on the

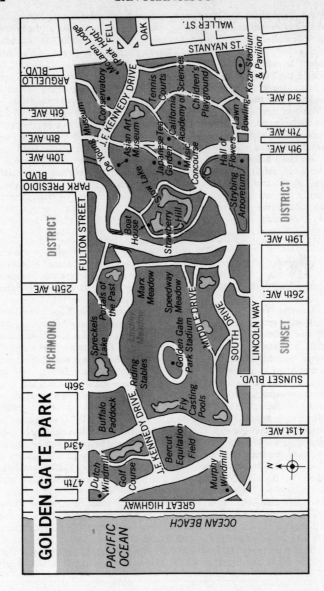

recently restored Dentzel Carrousel. (This was one of the last machines constructed by Dentzel in 1921. America's first carrousel shop opened in 1867 in Philadelphia by German immigrant Gustav Dentzel. His handsome, proud beauties are known as the Philadelphia-Style and lack the flamboyant "glass" jewels typical of the Coney Island carvings. The Philadelphia Toboggan Company first manufactured sleds, but around 1903 began to make delicately carved carrousels, rather similar to Dentzel's work. They also omitted jewels, and a handsome PTC carrousel is featured at Marriott's Great America.)

The zoo is open daily, 10:00 A.M.–5:00 P.M. Admission: adults, $2.50; children 15 years and under, admitted free with adult; without adult, $2.50. Senior Citizens, 50¢. Children's Zoo admission: adults and children, 75¢. The location is at Sloat Blvd. at the Pacific Ocean, near Lake Merced.

The **Oakland Zoo** is located in 500-acre Knowland Park. The African Veldt features some of the more than 200 birds, mammals, and reptiles in the park, living together in a natural habitat. The Jungle Lift 1,250-foot chair lift overlooks the African Veldt where animals graze. A train ride encircles the zoo. Small fees for both rides. The Baby Zoo allows youngsters to feed or touch nearly 200 animals; entrance fees. Open daily; 98th Ave. and Golf Links Rd., Oakland. Admission: pedestrians free; parking fee, $2.50 per car. Baby Zoo: adults, $1.00; children, 75¢.

GARDENS. Berkeley's *East Bay Regional Park District Botanical Garden* is a tribute to native California plants. Nearly 1,600 species, from both Northern and Southern California, are planted on 6½ acres. This project began in 1940 by forester James Roof. Native wildflowers star in late spring. Open daily, free. The *University of California's Botanical Garden* is a 33-acre site located in Strawberry Canyon; its near-neighbor is the Lawrence Hall of Science. The emphasis here is on desert plants gathered round-the-world. Open daily, except Christmas; free. Berkeley's *Rose Gardens,* perched in the hills between Bay View Pl. and Eunice St., are open daylight hours daily and are free. Combine a spectacular view of San Francisco Bay with 3,000 rosebushes in a five-tier terraced planting, plus trials and additional flowering shrubs, trees, and evergreens.

The *Marin Art and Garden Center* north of San Francisco in Ross, at Sir Francis Drake Blvd. and Laurel Grove Ave., is a ten-acre estate maintained by volunteers. In addition to the garden, there is an art gallery and shops. Free; phone (415) 454–5597 for information. The gallery open weekends from 1:00 to 4:00 P.M. Shops: Monday, 10:00 A.M.–4:00 P.M.; Tuesday–Friday, 11:00 A.M. –4:00 P.M.

About 50 miles north of San Francisco in Santa Rosa is *Luther Burbank Memorial Gardens and Home.* The great naturalist died in 1926 and is buried at the foot of a 118-foot Cedar of Lebanon, which he planted and used frequently as a spot to relax and visit with friends. Open daily 8:00 A.M.–5:00 P.M., free. There is a small fee to tour Burbank House, open Tuesday–Sunday, noon–3:30 P.M. March through October. His experimental work made him famous at the time as "the Edison and Ford of horticulture." Each spring there is a Luther Burbank Rose Festival here.

Thirty miles south of San Francisco, *Filoli,* a magnificent 1916 43-room brick mansion patterned after an English country house designed by Christopher Wren, is open to the public. Administered by the National Trust for Historic Preservation, Filoli features tours offered by knowledgeable docents, and which take about 2 hours. Sixteen acres of enclosed gardens include plantings from the Middle Ages, such as the Rose of Lancaster. The estate is open from February until November. Tours, including both the house and garden, are $6.00 per person. Reservations only; (415) 364–2880. Canada Rd., Woodside, CA 94062.

In Menlo Park, also about 32 miles south of San Francisco, is *Sunset Gardens.* The 10-acre showplace is the headquarters of Lane Publishing Co., publisher of *Sunset* magazine. Free tours of the gardens, test kitchens, and offices are conducted weekdays. Trees, shrubs, and flowers represent various areas of the Pacific coast. Also in Menlo Park is the *Allied Arts Guild,* at Arbor Rd. Open Monday–Saturday, free. This 3.5-acre Spanish Colonial estate contains a complex of shops operated by the Woodside-Atherton Auxiliary of Stanford's Children's Hospital as a charity. The charming gardens are similar to those found in Granada.

Fifty miles south of San Francisco, the charming town of Saratoga nestles in the Santa Cruz Mountains foothills. *Hakone Gardens,* 21000 Big Basin Wy., is a 15-acre city-owned retreat with authentic Japanese structures, including a teahouse, waterfalls, flowering trees, and wisteria. Free. Open Monday–Friday, 10:00 A.M.–5:00 P.M. Weekends, 11:00 A.M.–5 P.M.

While in Saratoga, visit *Villa Montalvo Arboretum.* This 175-acre estate was built by the late U.S. Senator and San Francisco Mayor James D. Phelan as a summer retreat. He imported plants from all over the world to beautify the grounds surrounding the nineteen-room residence. The formal gardens provide an attractive setting for year-round musical events and live theater. Formal gardens and foothill trails are open daily, 8:00 A.M.–5:00 P.M. Art galleries open Tuesday–Sunday, 1:00 P.M.–4:00 P.M. Small fee. Phone (408) 867–3586.

 BEACHES. Many first-time visitors are dismayed by Northern California's summertime coastal fog. Locals often head for a day of sun and fun at a favorite beach only to find it socked in, though a few miles away blue skies prevail. In summer, damp air blows off the ocean toward land. As it nears the coast, it meets the "California Current," a blast of cold air, and its moisture condenses as fog. For a beach outing in San Francisco, try *Baker* and *Phelan Beaches.* Baker Beach is not recommended for swimming; be watchful of larger-than-usual waves. Weather is typical for the bay shoreline: summer fog; usually breezy and occasionally warm. Picnic tables, grills, trails, and a day-camp area are available. The mile-long shoreline is great for jogging, fishing, and for the children's sand castles. From April to October, Phelan Beach, a smaller cove, offers a lifeguard, gentler water, changing rooms, and showers for all the family. *Ocean Beach* stretches along the western (ocean) side of San Francisco, south of Cliff House. It's a beautiful, wide beach, good for walking, running, or lying in the sun—but not for swimming.

The Marin Headlands beaches are not safe for swimming. The cliffs are steep and unstable, making falls a constant danger. However, the Marin coast offers two beaches for picnics and sunning: *Muir* and *Stinson Beaches.* Swimming is recommended only at Stinson Beach, and only from late May to mid-September, when lifeguard services are provided. If possible, visit these areas during the week; both beaches are very crowded on weekends.

Along the northern shores of the state, lucky and knowledgeable strollers pick up a varied assortment of ocean treasures: glossy agates and jade pebbles, sea-sculptured roots and branches and, rarely, glass floats—special mementos from the sea and sand.

BABYSITTING SERVICES. Traveling with children to San Francisco can be fun for the whole family. When museum trekking, strolling the zoo, Pier 39, Fisherman's Wharf, or any of a dozen other children-oriented activities pall, there is no problem for Mom and Dad. The city offers two outstanding state licensed and bonded babysitters agencies. *The Bay Area Baby Sitters Agency,* 755–0500, 8:00 A.M.–7:00 P.M., has for over thirty years offered sitters—around the clock if necessary. Rates are $2.75 an hour, with a 4-hour minimum, plus transportation charges. *Bristol-Haran,* 1724 Sacramento, San Francisco, 775–9100, is also state licensed and bonded. Rates are $3.00 an hour, with a 4-hour minimum, transportation charges are $4.00 until 10:00 P.M.; $7.00 per cab, after 10:00 P.M. This twenty-year-old firm employs no teenage sitters; it will also provide personnel to sit with elderly persons or dogs. Many hotels and motels also list babysitters.

CHILDREN'S ACTIVITIES. A visit to the *Golden Gate National Recreation Area* (GGNRA) offers countless ways to entertain and educate youngsters. This nearby national park covers 39,000 acres of continuous parkland extending along both the San Francisco and Marin County shorelines. It contains many of the area's well-known attractions: Ocean Beach, and Cliff House with its view of the Seal Rocks and the marine mammals who dwell there. Be sure to have a set of binoculars, also to inspect the variety of marine birds. *Aquatic Park* offers fishing, kite-flying, a few spots to picnic and the Maritime Museum. Self-guided tours of the West Coast's largest museum for maritime history, with its model ships, historic photographs, and all-things nautical is a perfect primer for touring three nearby vessels. Berthed at the Hyde Street Pier are: the *C. A. Thayer,* a three-masted lumber schooner: the steam-driven passenger and cargo-carrying *Wapama,* and the ferryboat, *Eureka.* Open daily, 10:00 A.M.–5:00 P.M., free. The *Balclutha,* a square-rigged 1880 Cape Horn sailing ship, is docked at Pier 43, Fisherman's Wharf. Admission charge; open daily, 10:00 A.M. to 10:00 P.M.

Alcatraz is also part of the GGNRA, and the 30-minute ferry ride there offers spectacular views of the Bay and the city. The 1.5-mile conducted tour may be too difficult for small children, however. Angel Island, by contrast, is fun for all ages. In addition to picnic sites there are playing fields for softball and volleyball. A hike around the island would take about 2½ hours, and bicycles can be used on the fire road which encircles the island. Access to this park is either by ferry or private boat.

Another GGNRA gem is the *Fort Point Historic Site.* Located just under the Golden Gate Bridge, these brick forts were built during the 1800s to defend the coastline. Today, park rangers explain the fort's history, give cannon drill demonstrations, and local elementary schoolchildren are offered an Environmental Living Program which takes them back to a soldier's life in the 1860s. It is usually windy and foggy as well as cold inside the brick walls of the fort, so dress warmly and wear proper footgear. Open daily; free.

Fun of another sort beckons at *Pier 39.* From the gaudy Palace of Fine Arts, at the entrance, with its double-decker Venetian carrousel, to the free daily high-diving exhibitions, the Pier is a dawn-to-dusk attraction. Open daily, convenient, inexpensive parking. Shops, restaurants, and the Blue-and-Gold Fleet Bay Cruises call this home port.

Golden Gate Park is made for kids, with miles of trails for biking or roller skating, plus tennis courts, riding stables, the Steinhart Aquarium—with daily dolphin-feeding shows—and the Morrison Planetarium, with varied sky shows.

There is plenty to occupy the young at the *San Francisco Zoo,* with its new Gorilla World and the ever-popular Children's Zoo. For more information see the *Zoo* section above.

Investigate the *Exploratorium,* a museum of touching, hearing, and seeing "exhibits to be manipulated, tinkered with, or activated by the touch of a button." In the Palace of Fine Arts at the eastern end of the Presidio. Admission charge; open weekends, noon to 5:00 P.M.; Wednesday through Friday, from 1:00 to 5:00 P.M.; Wednesday evenings from 7:00 to 9:30 P.M. Palace of Fine Arts, 3601 Lyon St.

The *Cable Car Museum,* Washington and Mason Sts., to the delight of local cable car fans and interested visitors, reopened in June 1984 after extensive rehabilitation. The 1887 red brick walls of the barn have been preserved and reinforced to meet current earthquake resistance standards. In addition to the informative exhibits and cable car memorabilia, a new underground viewing room will allow visitors to observe the huge sheaves that guide the cable cars. All three cable car lines, #59 and #60 to Fisherman's Wharf and #61, which runs up to Nob Hill and east to Van Ness Ave., are now greeting passengers. The fare for a ride bound to please any child is $1.00; children 5–17 years 25¢; seniors 5¢.

The new *California Marine Mammal Center,* Marin Headlands, GGNRA, Fort Cronkhite, operates a free museum and bookstore, open daily 10:00 A.M. –4:00 P.M. The center is devoted to the rescue, emergency care, long-term treatment and research of pinnipeds (web-footed sea mammals), seals, sea lions, sea otters and walrus. It also rescues dolphins, porpoises and small whales, which are taken to Marine World/Africa U.S.A., south of San Francisco, for care. The center presently cares for 30 to 40 animals at a time.

For more than a quarter century, from 1882 to 1908, San Francisco was the whaling capital of the world. More whalers set out each year than the numbers sailing out of famed New Bedford. The prize was "whalebone," used in women's hoop skirts and corsets, and whale oil, no longer necessary after the invention of kerosene. Today, "there she blows" is the excited cry of passengers on one of the whale-hunt boats cruising to the whale migrating lanes for a closer look at the *California gray whales,* during their annual migration to the bays and lagoons of Baja California. These baleen whales grow to approximately 40 feet in length and reach a weight of 35 to 40 tòns. From mid-December to the end of April, as they travel close to land on their way south, they are viewable from many places along the Northern California coast. Bodega Head, Point Reyes, Gualala Head, and Pigeon Point are favorite lookout points. Contact the Oceanic Society, Fort Mason, 441–1104, for information on whale-watching cruises.

In the Bay Area, old-time railroading is alive and well . . . in miniature. Berkeley's Tilden Park's *Redwood Valley Railway* offers a 12-minute ride through the woods. The oil-burner engine is a replica of an 1895 classic. Phone 841–0518. The Oakland Zoo's 24-inch-gauge *Jupiter* steam-type train makes a 10-minute run through the zoo, daily. Meanwhile, off Rte. 9 at Felton, in Santa Cruz County, the *Roaring Camp and Big Trees Narrow Gauge Railroad* passes directly through the first grove of coastal redwoods to be preserved for posterity, in 1867. Passengers board steam trains that date back to the 1880s and '90s for the hour-long excursion to Bear Mountain over the steepest railroad grades in North America. At the summit, one may detrain to picnic or hike and then return to Roaring Camp on a later train. And about a 3-hour drive north of San Francisco at Willits, the world-famous "Skunk" trains offer an exciting outing through Northern California's Redwoods. Phone (707) 964–6371.

In Santa Clara, 45 miles south of the city, *Marriott's Great America* theme park (off U.S. 101) is open daily from Memorial Day to Labor Day. The 100-acre park has entertained over ten million guests since its debut in 1976. It features five eras of America's past brought to life; rock bands and video adventures; 30 thrilling rides, including the *Edge,* a 2½-second free-fall ride; plus boutiques and craft shops, and dozens of snack bars and restaurants. A giant-screen film, "Behold Hawaii," is new in 1984. Phone (408) 988–1800.

Daily tours are offered at San Jose's *Winchester Mystery House,* 525 S. Winchester Blvd. (Rte. 280 at Rte. 17). This $5-million, 160-room Victorian mansion was built by Sarah Winchester and was under construction 24 hours a day for 38 years. Occult signs and numbers are widely used throughout the house, evidencing Sarah's belief in the spiritualist to whom she turned for advice. Secret passageways, trapdoors, secret storerooms, even a seance room fascinate visitors. The extensive Victorian garden includes many rare plants, 100-year-old rosebushes, ferns, feather, fan date palms, and trees from around the world. Two different tours are available: the house interior, and the grounds. Both tours include the historic Winchester Rifle and Wax Museum. Phone (408) 247–2101.

Santa Cruz is a lively family-style seaside resort at the northern tip of Monterey Bay. About 1½ hours' drive from San Francisco, its beach and boardwalk attracts throngs. Built in 1906, the *Boardwalk* charges no admission. Its giant rollercoaster and ferris wheel highlight a real boardwalk filled with games of chance, interesting shops, and rides of every description.

 PARTICIPANT SPORTS. Joggers, bicyclists and aficionados of virtually all sports can find their favorite activities in the Bay Area or within driving distance. Golden Gate Park in San Francisco has numerous paths for runners and cyclists. Lake Merced in San Francisco and Lake Merritt in Oakland are among the most popular areas for joggers.

For information on **running races, tennis tournaments, bicycle races,** and other participant sports, check the monthly issues of *City Sports* Magazine, which is available free at sporting goods stores, tennis centers, and other recreational sites. City Sports' phone is 788–2611.

Two bike routes are maintained by the San Francisco Recreation and Park Department, which is headquartered in McLaren Lodge, Fell and Stanyan Sts., at the eastern edge of Golden Gate Park; 558–3706. One route goes through Golden Gate Park to Lake Merced, the other from the south end of the city to the Golden Gate Bridge and beyond. Many shops along Stanyan St. rent bikes.

Stow Lake in Golden Gate Park has **rowboat** and **pedalboat** rentals. The lake is open for boating, 8:30 to 4:00 each day. San Francisco Bay offers year-round **sailing.** However, tricky currents make the bay hazardous for inexperienced navigators. Boat rentals and charters are available throughout the Bay Area and are listed under Boat Rentals in the S.F. Yellow Pages. Sailing information can be obtained at the Eagle Cafe on San Francisco's Pier 39.

Numerous **fishing** boats leave from San Francisco, Sausalito, Berkeley, Emeryville and Pt. San Pablo. They go for salmon outside the Bay or striped bass and giant sturgeon within the Bay. Inexpensive temporary licenses are available on the charters. In San Francisco, proper, lines can be cast from San Francisco Municipal Pier, Fisherman's Wharf or Aquatic Park. Trout fishing is available at Lake Merced. Licenses are available at sporting goods stores. The cost of fishing licenses ranges from $3.50 for one-day to $13.50 for a complete state license. Some selected sportfishing charters are:

Capt. Phil. Fisherman's Wharf; 583–9782; call up to 10 P.M.; Leaves daily at 6 A.M.

Captain Ron's Pacific Charters. Fisherman's Wharf; 771–2800.

M & M Sport Fishing. Fisherman's Wharf; 285–2000.

Muny Bait & Sport Shop, 3098 Polk Street, across from Ghirardelli Square. 673–9815 or 441–9901. Leaves daily from Fisherman's Wharf.

New Florie S, Fisherman's Wharf; 878–4644 daily.

Wacky Jacky, Fisherman's Wharf; 586–9800. Write: Jacky Douglas (woman skipper) at 473 Bella Vista Way, San Francisco, CA 94127.

San Francisco has four public **golf** courses: Harding Park, an 18-hole, par-72 course, Lake Merced Blvd. and Skyline Blvd; Lincoln Park, 18 holes, par 69,

34th and Clement; Golden Gate Park, a "pitch-and-putt" 9-holer at 47th and Fulton; McLaren Park, a full-size 9-holer, Sunnydale, between Brookdale and Persia. Another municipal course, Sharp Park, is located outside the city south in Pacifica. Nearby there are San Mateo Municipal, Alameda Municipal (36 holes), and in Oakland, Lake Chabot and Lew Galbraith. Among the private courses in San Francisco are the famed Olympic Club, site of the 1955 and 1966 U.S. Opens and 1981 U.S. Amateur, and the San Francisco Golf Club and Lake Merced Country Club. Within a 60-mile radius of San Francisco there are more than 50 golf courses.

Equestrian centers are available throughout the Bay Area. In the city you can ride and rent horses at Golden Gate Park Stables, John F. Kennedy Drive and 36th Ave.; 668–7360. Other stables: St. Francis Riding Academy, 2152 Skyline, Daly City, 755–6400; Palo Mar Stables, 2116 Skyline, Daly City, 755–9973; Chabot Equestrian, 14600 Skyline, Oakland, 569–4428.

The San Francisco Recreation and Park Department maintains more than 100 **tennis** courts, 21 of them in Golden Gate Park. For information, call McLaren Lodge; 558–3706. There are many other private and public courts in the area. A few: San Francisco Tennis Club (indoor and outdoor courts), 5th and Brannan, 777–9000; Golden Gateway, 370 Drumm, 433–2936; Golden Gate Fields Tennis Club, 1100 Eastshore Hwy., Albany (at Golden Gate Fields racetrack), 526–5745; Oakland Hills Tennis Club, 5475 Redwood Rd., Oakland, 531–3700.

SPECTATOR SPORTS. The Bay Area offers a vast selection of sporting events. In spring and summer, the San Francisco Giants **baseball** team plays at Candlestick Park, while the Oakland A's baseball team and Oakland Invaders **football** team share the Oakland Coliseum. (At press time the Raiders look to be staying in L.A., though there is the possibility that they may end up in Oakland.) These games rarely sell out, and game-day tickets are usually available at the stadiums. Call 638–0500 or 638–4900 for Coliseum information. In fall and winter, the San Francisco 49ers football team often sells out at Candlestick. For 49er ticket information call 468–2249. Major college football is played at the University of California in Berkeley, Stanford in Palo Alto and San Jose State. The Golden State Warriors play NBA **basketball** at the Oakland Coliseum Arena from October through April. Depending on the season, there is **horse racing** at either Golden Gate Fields in Albany or Bay Meadows in San Mateo; check local newspapers for post time and place. For **rodeo** fans, the Grand National Rodeo and Livestock Show is held each October at the Cow Palace, just south of the city limits, in Daly City. Call 469–6065 for Cow Palace ticket information. The Cow Palace is also the site of the Transamerica men's **tennis** championships in October, while the Virginia Slims women's tennis tour visits the Oakland Coliseum Arena in January. There are also frequent **yacht races** on the bay and **motor sports** events at various locations. Again, check local papers for details.

HISTORIC SITES AND HOUSES. Mission Dolores. 16th and Dolores Sts., Mission District. Perhaps the oldest building in the city. Originally named Mission San Francis de Asis by founder Father Francisco Palou in 1776, it became known as Mission Dolores, after a nearby lake on whose shores Father Palou had said Mass on June 29, 1776. The structure has survived three major quakes, with major renovation done in 1920 by Willis Polk. It is an excellent example of the late Baroque church style popular in Mexico. Both the handsome carved wood retablos (altar screens) and church bells, dated 1792 and 1797, were imported from Mexico.

The Presidio. Lincoln Blvd. and Funston Ave. Established in 1776 by the Spaniards. The 1,500-acre green-belt now headquarters the United States Sixth Army. Its adobe Officer's Club, restored in 1934, is considered the city's second-oldest building. As part of the Golden Gate Recreational Area as well as a military reserve, the northeast corner is open to the public for drives through redwood and eucalyptus groves to Bakers Beach on the ocean, and to Crissy Field, once the city's airport. Fort Point, at the foot of Golden Gate Bridge, is a Civil War era brick fortress. Rangers explain the site's strategic importance and history. Open daily 10:00 A.M. to 5:00 P.M.

Portsmouth Square. In Chinatown, it was the city's first plaza. This historic mini-park witnessed the raising of Old Glory in 1846 by Captain John B. Montgomery and his Marines. Today, youngsters and old-timers sun and play as visitors scan the historic marker and flip through their guidebooks.

San Francisco's lusty Barbary Coast of the 1860s shows a proper and prosperous face as **Jackson Square.** Present-day denizens include shops, excellent restaurants, and design centers. Actually not a square, these charming brick-faced buildings cover several blocks, bounded by Pacific, Sansome, Washington Sts. and Columbus Ave.

Contemporary history was made on June 25, 1945, on the stage of the **War Memorial Opera House** in the Civic Center complex. It was here that President Truman and others signed the original United Nations Charter. Currently, the Opera House is home to both the San Francisco Opera and Ballet companies.

HISTORIC HOUSES

San Francisco

The California Historical Society's *Whittier Mansion,* 2090 Jackson. Admission fees of $2.00 for adults; $1.00 for seniors, students, and children, include a tour of house, exhibiting art, china, and furnishings. Hours, Wednesday, Saturday, and Sunday, from 1:00 P.M. to 5:00 P.M. Tours, 1:00 P.M., 2:00 P.M., 3:00 P.M., 4:00 P.M. 567–1848.

The *Haas-Lilienthal House,* 2007 Franklin St., is a famed Victorian. Admission: adults, $3.00, seniors and students, $1.00. Docent tours. Maintained by the Foundation for Architectural Heritage. Open Wednesday, noon–4:00 P.M. Sunday, 11:00 A.M.–4:30 P.M.; 441–3004.

The *Octagon House,* 2645 Gough St., is one of the two remaining octagons in the city. Admission by donation. Operated by the National Society of Colonial Dames of America. Open the second and fourth Thursdays of the month from 1:00 P.M. to 3:45 P.M.; except holidays; 885–9796.

Nearby Historic Houses

Filoli, Canada Road, Woodside. About 30 miles south of San Francisco; the National Trust for Historic Preservation maintains this lavish 16-acre estate with its country house and gardens. Admission fee; $6.00; under 12 not admitted. Tours April–July: 9:30 A.M., 11:00 A.M., 1:00 P.M.; other months 10:00 A.M. and 1:00 P.M. Closed Dec. and Jan. Reservations required; (415) 366–4640 or 364–2880.

  MUSEUMS. The magic of San Francisco, its character, its variety and versatility, are all reflected in the city's museums. Not only have the museums achieved national and international recognition for their outstanding permanent collections and traveling exhibits, but also they have achieved world fame for their special ambiance.

People who love museums agree that San Francisco's should not be missed; visitors with an obligatory "as long as I'm here, I ought to go" feeling soon realize that visiting San Francisco's museums is fun as well as educational.

One reason museum-hopping in San Francisco and the Bay Area is a delight is that their settings and buildings are unusual and beautiful. Trips to museums offer opportunities to see exciting vistas and views of the city, take nearby side trips, or enjoy outdoor fun like biking, picnicking, or jogging.

For example, the Bay Area's most famous museums, the de Young and The Asian—as well as the California Academy of Sciences—are all located in the spectacularly beautiful Golden Gate Park.

The Palace of Fine Arts, on the Northern Waterfont at the eastern edge of the Presidio, is *not* a museum of fine arts at all; it houses the Exploratorium, world-famous for its programs, exhibits, "hands-on" activities and outstanding staff. See the *Children's Activities* section above.

M. H. de Young Memorial Museum. The central court of the M. H. de Young Museum—one of America's most popular museums—has a portal of a twelfth-century Spanish monastery, and the sixty-four galleries that surround it contain examples of the art and culture of the Western world from the time of ancient Egypt to the twentieth century. There is also sophisticated gallery space in the East Wing, used for major international exhibitions. The museum contains collections of paintings, sculpture, stained glass, furniture, and decorative arts. Among the masterpieces are Rubens' "The Tribute Money" and El Greco's "St. John, the Baptist." Another famous El Greco depicts the saint for whom San Francisco was named in "St. Francis Venerating the Crucifix." There are period rooms dating to the fifteenth century and collections of art dating from the fourteenth century. Some masters to watch for are Fra Angelico, Titian, Pieter de Hooch, Goya, Rembrandt, Hals, Van Dyck, Rubens, Gainsborough, and Reynolds. A collection of more than 100 American paintings includes Copley, Bingham, West, Eakins, Sargent, Homer, Bierstadt, Church, and Harnett. There is a large, specially designed gallery of Oceania, Africa, and the Americas that has audio recordings. The Café de Young, which opens onto the Oakes Garden, has a complete menu of light refreshments served until 4:00 P.M. Museum hours are Wednesday through Sunday, 10:00 A.M. to 5:00 P.M. Admission: adults, aged 18 through 64, $2.00, juniors, 12 through 17, 50¢; seniors, 65 and over, 50¢. First Wednesday of each month, free to all. For special docent tours, call 750–3638; daily tours 1:30 P.M. and 2:30 P.M.; phone 221–4811. (One admission ticket admits you to The Asian Art, de Young, and Legion of Honor museum on the same day.)

Asian Art Museum. Located in galleries that adjoin the de Young, it is also world famous. It is the only museum in the United States devoted exclusively to the arts of Asia. Here, in the Avery Brundage Collection, are more than 10,000 sculptures, paintings, and ceramics that illustrate major periods of Asian Art. Very special are the Magnin Jade Room and the Leventritt Collection of blue-and-white Chinese porcelain. On the second floor are collections from Iran, Turkey, Syria, Afghanistan, India, Tibet, Nepal, Pakistan, Korea, Japan, and Southeast Asia. Open daily, 10:00 A.M. to 5:00 P.M. Docent tours daily. Admission collected when entering de Young. 558–2993.

The Asian Art Museum maintains a branch in the Japan Extension Center located on the Webster Street Bridge. It is open 10:00 A.M. to 10:00 P.M. 7 days a week. Objects are rotated 3 times a year; information about the art on display is provided in bilingual (Japanese/English) labels. Information on this walk-by gallery and the current exhibits can be obtained from 558–2993.

California Academy of Sciences. A dynamic museum that hosts almost 2 million people each year; this number equals those who visit New York's American Museum of Natural History. Now more than a century and a quarter old, the California Academy of Sciences is located across the Music Concourse from the de Young and the Asian Museum in Golden Gate Park; it is one of the top five natural history museums in the United States and is the only one in the country with both an aquarium and a planetarium. Never staid, it is a busy, fascinating place that is popular with the public as well as respected in the academic and scientific communities. Throngs of citizens enjoy its Steinhart Aquarium and its unusual 100,000-gallon Fish Roundabout; there's no other exhibit tank in the nation like this carrousel-type tank where fish swim around you. The Academy of Sciences' Morrison Planetarium has both daytime programs and evening shows as well as a light show called "The Light Fantastic." Weekday planetarium shows at 2 P.M. and summer evenings on Wednesday and Thursday. Saturday and Sunday programs are at 11:00 A.M., 12:30 P.M., 2:00 P.M. and 3:30 P.M. Fees: $2.00 for adults, 75¢ for seniors and students under 17. The Academy also offers special exhibits. Besides, there's the Wattis Hall of Man, still growing in its exhibits of vanishing cultures. The Academy is open daily 10:00 A.M. to 5:00 P.M. in the winter, to 7:00 P.M. in summer. Phone: 752–8268. Fees are $2.00 for adults, $1.00 for 12–17 year olds and seniors, 75¢ for children 6–11, free for children under 6. First Wednesday of each month is free to all.

MUSEUMS 93

The admission fee to "light fantastic" and rock laser shows is $4.50 for adults, $2.50 for seniors and children 6–12. Matinees: $3.50 for adults, $2.50 for seniors and children 13 and under. Tickets through Ticketron, BASS and at door. The laser shows are offered Thursday–Sunday evenings; matinees on Saturdays and Sundays. Phone 221–0168. For information on all shows and exhibits, phone 221–4214. There is a pleasant cafeteria on the ground floor; it is open daily.

Palace of the Legion of Honor. Noted for its focus on the art and culture of France, the California Palace of the Legion of Honor has a startling site in Lincoln Park near Land's End. There is a wonderful view of the Golden Gate and the city from nearby. The building itself—designed after Napoleon's eighteenth-century palace, the Palais de la Legion d'Honneur—is architecturally exciting and is surrounded by four massive sculptures: Rodin's "Thinker" and "Three Shades" and Anna Hyatt Huntington's "Joan of Arc" and "El Cid." Not only are the collections of French art noteworthy, but the museum's collection of the sculpture of Auguste Rodin is one of the United States' most famous. Exhibits include furniture, porcelain, paintings, tapestries, and decorative arts. Represented are Boucher, Fragonard, Largillière, Corot, Gerôme, Manet, Claude, Poussin, de la Tour, Degas, and Cassatt. The Louis XVI Room is a "must-see." The Achenbach print collection contains more than 100,000 items and is considered the most important print collection west of Chicago. Hours are Wednesday through Sunday, 10:00 A.M. to 5:00 P.M., with docent tours. Fees are linked with the de Young and the Asian Museum. One ticket covers all three museums on the same day. The Café Chanticleer at the Palace of the Legion of Honor offers light lunches, served indoors or al fresco. 221–4811.

The Museum of Modern Art's galleries are located in the Veterans' Building in the Civic Center at Van Ness and McAllister. The museum boasts collections that include outstanding permanent exhibits as well as regional and local exhibits. Traveling exhibits feature national and international works in painting, sculpture, graphics, and photography. Important holdings include works of Henri Matisse, Paul Klee, Alexander Calder, Josef Albers, Grant Wood, Robert Motherwell, and Clyfford Still. Hours are Tuesday through Friday, 10:00 A.M. to 6:00 P.M.; Saturdays and Sundays, 10:00 A.M. to 5:00 P.M.; Thursdays, 10:00 A.M. to 10:00 P.M. Admission is $3.00 for adults; 1.50 for seniors and youth 6–16. Children 5 and under are free. It is free to all on Thursday evenings from 6:00 to 10:00 P.M. 863–8800.

OTHER MUSEUMS

At the **Chinese Culture Center,** 750 Kearny St., 3rd fl. of the Holiday Inn in the Financial District, there's a museum that rotates exhibits frequently; displays focus on Chinese art and culture. Hours are Tuesday through Saturday, 10:00 A.M. to 4:00 P.M. Free. 986–1822. Another Chinese museum is maintained by the **Chinese Historical Society of America** at 17 Adler Pl., near Pacific. Artifacts, art, photographs, documents, and memorabilia focus on the role of Chinese in the Gold Rush era. Hours are Tuesday through Saturday, 1:00 P.M. to 5:00 P.M. Donations welcomed. 391–1188.

The **Museo Italio Americano** has permanent exhibitions of works of nineteenth- and twentieth-century Italian-American artists. Exhibits include paintings, sculpture, etchings, and photographs. Regular special exhibits, lectures, films. Hours are 9:00 A.M. to 5:00 P.M., Monday through Saturday. 678 Green St. 398–2660. Admission: free.

San Francisco African/American Historical and Cultural Society maintains the only **Black Museum** west of Chicago. The permanent collection includes "Black California" and "Black Civil War History." Temporary exhibits focus on living California Black artists. Hours are Tuesday through Saturday, noon to 5:00 P.M. Admission is free, but there is a 50¢ per person fee for guided tours, which can be arranged by appointment. Fort Mason, Bldg. C, 441–0640.

The **Mexican Museum** is unique in the United States, with a permanent collection that includes pre-Hispanic ceramic figures from Jalisco and Colima as well as folk art, lacquerware, and masks. Works of contemporary Mexican and Chicano artists are also included. Fort Mason, Bldg. D, Laguna at Marina Blvd. Open Wednesday through Sunday, noon to 5:00 P.M. Thursdays until 8:00 P.M. Free. 441–0404. Mural tours in the Mission District on second Saturday of every month. Trips begin at 1885 Folsom Street at 10:00 A.M. and the fee is $3.00 per person with special rates of $1.00 for seniors and students.

In a graceful, old-world setting is an exciting new-world, hands-on museum, the **Exploratorium.** Built for the 1915 Panama-Pacific Exposition, the baroque Palace of Fine Arts is a San Francisco showplace that was designed by the renowned Bernard Maybeck and that was restored in the 1940s. This building of Roman Classical design, flanked by huge Corinthian columns and colonnades, is the setting for the lively, ever-growing science museum. The museum includes more than 450 participatory science and art exhibits on light, sound, vision, hearing, touch, smell, electricity, motion, mathematics, and patterns. It has become a model for dozens of new science museums throughout the world. You are invited to picnic by the Lagoon and enjoy the Rotunda while you are at the Exploratorium. Open Wednesdays through Fridays from 1:00 P.M. to 5:00 P.M. and also on Wednesday evenings from 7:00 P.M. to 9:30 P.M. Saturday and Sunday hours are from 11:00 A.M. to 5:00 P.M.; summer hours: Wednesday through Sunday, 11:00 A.M. to 5:00 P.M., and Wednesday evenings. Fees: $3.00 for a 6-month adult pass; $1.50 one-time fee for seniors; 17 and under free. Lyon St. and Marina Blvd. 563–7337.

Less than 30 miles from San Francisco, in a beautiful setting, are the *Stanford Art Museum* and *Stanford Art Gallery,* both including treasures from antiquity through the twentieth century. Some of the museum's Rodin sculptures were recently installed in a new garden. Museum hours: Tuesday–Friday, 10:00 A.M.–5:00 P.M.; Saturday and Sunday, 1:00 P.M.–5:00 P.M. Tours available. Gallery phone: 497–2842: Museum: 497–4177.

SPECIAL-INTEREST MUSEUMS

Old Mint, 5th and Mission Sts. Free. The architecturally famous 1874 building is a National Historic Landmark. Carefully restored rooms, ore and mineral exhibits; a collection of gold bars valued at $10 million. Open Tuesdays through Saturdays, 10:00 A.M.–4:00 P.M., 974–0788.

Navy and Marine Corps Museum, Building One, Treasure Island. Free. Features artifacts, memorabilia, and historical exhibits of both services. Open daily, 10:00 A.M.–3:30 P.M. 765–6182.

National Maritime Museum. Aquatic Park, at the foot of Polk St. Free. Features ship models and memorabilia of San Francisco's maritime history. Open daily: 10:00 A.M.–5:00 P.M. 556–8177. The following historic ships can also be visited: the **Balclutha,** a British square-rigger berthed at Pier 43. 9:00 A.M. to 6:00 P.M. weekdays, to 10:00 P.M., Friday, Saturday, Sunday. Fees: $2.00 for adult, $1.00 for 12–18 and seniors, 25¢ for 6–11, under 6 free. 982–1886. The **Pampanito** is a WWII submarine at Pier 45, Fisherman's Wharf. 9:00 A.M. to 6:00 P.M. weekdays; to 10:00 P.M. Fridays, Saturdays and Sundays. Fees: $3.00 for adult, $2.00 for 12–18, $1.00 for 6–11 and seniors, under 6 free. 441–5819. Also, near the Maritime Museum is the National Park Service's **Hyde Street Pier.** Docked there are: the *C. A. Thayer,* a three-masted schooner; the *Eureka,* a side-wheel ferry; the *Alma,* a scow schooner; the *Hercules,* steam tug; and the *Eppleton Hall,* a sidewheeler tug. Hours: 10:00 A.M.–5:00 P.M. Free. Programs on weekends. Extended summer hours. 556–6435.

Presidio Army Museum. Presidio of San Francisco. Free. Located in the oldest standing building on the Presidio. Exhibits detail history of San Francisco since 1776. Hours: 10:00 A.M.–4:00 P.M., Tuesday through Sunday. 561–4115.

Fort Point National Historic Site. South tower of Golden Gate Bridge. Free. Restored by the National Park Service; interpretative tours daily, 10:00 A.M. –5:00 P.M. 556–1693.

Others: Wells Fargo History Room. 420 Montgomery St. Free. Monday–Friday, 10:00 A.M.–3:00 P.M. 396–2619. **Society of California Pioneers' Hall.** 456 McAllister St. Free. Monday–Friday, 10:00 A.M.–4:00 P.M. Closed July. Displays early Western historical documents. 861–5278. **Bank of California.** 400 California St. Free. *Money of the American West* exhibit. Open Monday–Friday, 10:30 A.M.–2:30 P.M.; 765–0400. **World of Oil.** Chevron U.S.A. Inc., 1st and Market, 555 Market. Free. Monday through Friday, 9:00 A.M.–4:00 P.M. 894–4895. **Cable Car Museum.** Reopened at 1201 Mason after extensive renovation. Daily, 10:00 A.M.–6:00 P.M. Free. Three original cars, plus 57 scale models. 474–1887.

S.F. Crafts and Folk Art Museum. 626 Balboa. New and popular. Wednesday–Friday, noon–5:00 P.M.; Saturday and Sunday, 1:00–4:00 P.M. 668–0406.

 FILMS. Such Northern California directors as George Lucas and Phil Kaufman are part of the Hollywood mainstream, but many more experimental filmmakers work in the area. Their films are often shown at the *Cinematheque,* located in the Art Institute at 800 Chestnut Street and *Video Free America,* 442 Shotwell St. The resource for avant-garde films is the Film Arts Foundation, 552–8760. Either of the daily papers will carry complete listings of films by location, as well as descriptive advertising of new movies.

In April, the city hosts the *San Francisco International Film Festival,* two weeks of approximately 75 films from all nations, many never before seen in America. The *Castro Theater* (Castro at Market) the *Ghirardelli Cinema* (Beach St. at Hyde) house the screenings. In addition, there are retrospectives and tributes to famous film artists, many of whom attend in person. Some free programs. Tickets and information, 221–9055.

The *Strand* (Market between 7th and 8th Sts.) is the busiest revival-repertory theater, with double and triple bills changing daily. The *Castro* is the grandest remaining movie palace, a registered city landmark built in 1922. It offers revival series and first-run foreign films, with Wurlitzer pipe organ interludes and the city's best hot buttered popcorn. The major first-run movie theaters are listed in the local papers.

 MUSIC. San Francisco is often called the "cultural capital of the West," for it supports many musical organizations, most of which play traditional classical music from Bach to Puccini. Avant-garde and contemporary music, with the exception of the Contemporary Music Players, is confined to colleges: Stanford University in the South Bay, University of California and Mills College in the East Bay. The major musical organizations in the city are listed below, but please check the pink "Datebook" section of the *Sunday Examiner and Chronicle* for the most current information. Tickets to many events are available at Sherman Clay, Post at Kearny (329–4400); Macy's on Union Square; Downtown Center, 325 Mason St. (775–2021); Ticketron (495–4088); and BASS outlets (735–3849).

San Francisco Opera (War Memorial Opera House, Civic Center) has two seasons—the 13-week international season which begins in mid-September, and the summer international season in June. This is the largest opera company west of New York and is considered to be of world class; stars such as Pavarotti, Domingo, and Marilyn Horne appear regularly. The 1984 Summer Festival programs, for example, included *Aida, Don Pasquale, Siegfried* and *Die Fledermaus.* The 1985 summer season is expected to include Wagner's entire *Ring* cycle of *Das Rheingold, Die Walkure, Siegfried* and *Gotterdammerung.* Tickets are extremely difficult to get in the fall; easier in the summer. Keep checking the box office on the day of performance, and often one can buy a ticket just before curtain time on the Opera House steps. Tickets and information, 431–1210. In addition, the opera sponsors an April showcase of rarely heard works in the adjacent Herbst Theater.

San Francisco Symphony (Davies Hall, Civic Center) plays an extended season from September through May. Like the Opera, the Symphony is a world-class group. Music director Herbert Blomstedt replaces Edo de Waart in the fall of 1985 and shares his baton with international guest conductors. Isaac Stern, Alicia de Larrocha, Maurizio Pollini are frequent guests. Many programs will include the magnificent new 7,373-pipe, $1.2 million Ruffati organ. The Symphony also sponsors a Great Performances Series of soloists and visiting orchestras, a new music series in the winter, Mozart series in February, Beethoven festival in June–July. It also presents modestly priced pops concerts in July and August in the Civic Auditorium, Civic Center. Tickets are scarce; follow the same procedure as at the Opera. Tickets and information, 431–5400.

Contemporary Music Players (Museum of Modern Art, Civic Center) perform 20th-century chamber music for mixed instrumental and vocal forces. Ten programs are offered fall through spring. Tickets and information, 751–5300.

Lamplighters (Presentation Theater, 2350 Turk Blvd.) is the nation's oldest Gilbert and Sullivan repertory troupe; local singers and full orchestra. Tickets and information, 752–7755.

Midsummer Mozart (Herbst Theatre, Civic Center) is an annual July festival conducted by San Jose Symphony director, George Cleve, with guest artists. Tickets and information, 775–2805.

Old First Church (Van Ness and Sacramento) offers a series of chamber music concerts throughout the year on Friday evenings and Sunday afternoons. Information, 474–1608.

Pocket Opera (Herbst Theater, Civic Center) gives two seasons (January–March and July–August); ten performances each of rare and unusual operatic repertory, staged in concert form. All works except Handel given in English. Tickets and information, 392–4400.

Stern Grove (19th and Sloat Blvd.) offers a series of outdoor summer Sunday-afternoon musical programs, including opera, jazz, ballet, and symphony concerts. Picnicking is encouraged. Free. Information, 398–6551.

In addition to the above, there are a number of concerts (free or small donation), recitals and other chamber music at *Grace Cathedral* (Nob Hill), *St. Mary's Cathedral* (Gough and Geary), the *H. M. de Young Museum* (Golden Gate Park), and the *Palace of the Legion of Honor* (Lincoln Park). All year long, weather permitting, there are free band concerts in Golden Gate Park (at the bandshell opposite the de Young Museum) on Sunday and holiday afternoons.

DANCE. *San Francisco Ballet* (War Memorial Opera House, Civic Center) offers two seasons: an annual run of Tchaikovsky's full-length *The Nutcracker* in November and December (a lavish, opulent production), and a repertory season from January through May, at which they première three or four new works, often by company choreographers. In addition, they present full-length ballets such as *Beauty and the Beast, Cinderella, Romeo and Juliet,* and *The Tempest.* Tickets and information, 621–3838.

There are innumerable modern and experimental dance groups in the city. The most prestigious of them are the *Margaret Jenkins Dance Co.,* which works in abstract movement, often with "sound scores" instead of music; *Oberlin Dance Collective,* the most purely entertaining of the local modern dance companies; *San Francisco Moving Co.* a modern ballet group oriented to storytelling and emotion. All three, along with many smaller contemporary dance groups, perform at the New Performance Gallery, 3153 17th; 863–9830. The city's other troupes range from the *Jazz Dance Company,* 456–8053, to the *Dionysian Duncan Dancers,* 282–9559, who continue Isadora's style.

98   SAN FRANCISCO

Dance Between the Lines is an innovative cabaret show about dancers (Music Hall Theater, Larkin at Geary, 776-8996). The source for all local performance information is the *Bay Area Dance Coalition,* 673-8172.

 STAGE. The *American Conservatory Theater* (ACT) is the largest resident theater company in the country, presenting a lengthy repertory season (at the *Geary Theater,* 415 Geary St.) of approximately eight plays from October through May. Repertory includes Shakespeare, Restoration comedy, Chekhov, Ibsen, French farce, Coward, modern American and European playwrights such as Hellman, Stoppard, and Shepard. Tickets and information, 673-6440.

Shorenstein-Nederlander is a theatrical booking group that keeps three theaters occupied with touring Broadway drama and musicals. The *Curran,* 445 Geary St.; 673-4400, is used for legitimate drama and intimate musicals; the *Orpheum,* 1192 Market St.; 474-3800, and *Golden Gate,* 1 Taylor St.; 775-8800, are used for big musicals. *Theater on the Square* (450 Post St., 433-9500,) and *Marines Memorial Theater* (Sutter at Mason, 441-7444) offer such smaller touring shows as *Torch Song Trilogy* and *Sister Mary Ignatius.*

Similar to New York City's TKTS service, the STBS booth on Stockton Street at Union Square, between Post and Geary, offers half-price tickets to many plays on the day of performance. Open Tuesday through Saturday, noon–7:30 P.M. It also handles full-price tickets for many neighborhood theaters. Information, 433-7827.

A number of smaller, experimental theater groups produce the best of avant-garde European and American drama. The most important of these are *Actor's Ark Theater,* Bldg. F, Fort Mason; *Asian American Theater Co.,* 4344 California St.; *Eureka Theater,* 2730 16th St.; *Julian Theater,* 953 De Haro St.; *Magic Theater,* Bldg. D, Fort Mason; and *One-Act Theater,* Showcase, 430 Mason St. The touring *San Francisco Mime Troupe,* 285-1717, is known for colorful political and social satire. The *Pickle Family Circus,* 826-0747, brings small-scale but professional entertainment to city parks and playgrounds in May and June.

"Performance art," with roots in art, music and dance, is the latest trend at *Project Artaud,* 450 Florida St.; *Soon 3,* 2678 California St.; *New Langton Arts,* 1246 Folsom St., and the theater named for its address, *544 Natoma.* Performing in a wide variety of settings and best contacted by telephone are *Gulf of the Farralones,* 431-1365; *Nightfire Theater,* 383-2900; and *Antenna Theater,* 332-4862.

 ART GALLERIES. Exploring San Francisco's exciting, stimulating art scene may range from a leisurely afternoon stroll along Sutter St. to a full week of cruising the city in the various areas offering art of all kinds. Most galleries are in the area between Kearny and Mason (east and west) and Bush and Post (north and south). The following selected galleries are specialists:

Art Glass: *Contemporary Artisans,* 530 Bush St. Collector-quality art glass by both American and European artists. New shows monthly of distinctive ceramics, textiles, and basketry, as well. *Compositions,* The Cannery, 2801 Leavenworth, features a distinctive selection of tradition and contemporary hand-blown art glass by more than 40 of America's most talented glass artists.

Alaskan and Canadian Eskimo Arts and Crafts. *Images of the North,* 1782 Union. Offers museum-quality Eskimo soapstone and ivory carving as well as fine-quality West Coast arts and crafts. The *Inuit Gallery,* in Tiburon, specializes in Canadian Eskimo prints and sculptures. By appointment; call 346–3232 or 435–5601.

California. Early California; plus Western American names like Russell and Remington shine at the *Hunter Gallery,* 278 Post, on the mezzanine. *Maxwell Gallery,* 551 Sutter, for over forty years a stellar institution in the art world, devotes a lower gallery to nineteenth- and early twentieth-century paintings and sculpture. A browser's delight. Original graphics, sculpture, and mixed-media works by 17th-century to contemporary artists are featured at the *Walton-Gilbert Gallery,* 590 Sutter, with a special exhibition of Navaho artist, R.C. Gorman.

Ethnic. *West of the Moon,* 3464 Sacramento, specializes in American Indian art and collectible antique quilts. *Kundus,* 1782 Union, is a grand bazaar of Indian and Nepalese treasures. *James Willis,* 109 Geary at Grant Ave., offers beginning collectors and connoisseurs outstanding African, Oceanic, and Indonesian tribal art and textiles.

European and Modern Masters. *Foster Goldstrom,* 257 Grant Ave., between Sutter and Post Sts. Distinctive collection of modern masters. *Hanson Galleries* at the Anchorage, 2800 Leavenworth, between Beach and Jefferson, highlights graphic arts with such celebrated artists as Miro, Chagall, Calder, Dali, and Picasso. *Pasquale Iannetti,* 575 Sutter St., near Powell, acclaims both old and new masters from the sixteenth to twentieth centuries.

Latino and Mexican. *George Belcher,* 500 Sutter St., features paintings, drawings, and sculpture and prints by Mérida, Orozco, Rivera, Tamayo, and Zuñiga. Shown by appointment only; 981–3178. *Moss Gallery,* 310 Sutter St. near Grant.

Photography. *Focus Gallery,* 2146 Union St., opened in 1966 and is noted for its outstanding one-man and group shows, from worldwide contributors. *Lowinsky Gallery,* 228 Grant, spotlights vintage photogravures by the greats, including San Francisco's own wonder, the late Imogen Cunningham. *Thackrey and Robertson,* 2266 Union St., suggests "Old Photographs for New Collectors."

This is but the tip of the iceberg. We suggest checking *Datebook,* the pink section in the Sunday San Francisco *Chronicle/Examiner,* for current exhibition information. Also *San Francisco* Magazine, and the free *San Francisco Gallery Guide,* available at most galleries.

SHOPPING. No need to travel to New York, Paris, London, or Rome seeking the best of shopping each of these world-class cities are acclaimed for. Tiffany's, Yves Saint-Laurent, Wedgwood, and Gucci showplaces offer their top creations in a city of under 700,000 residents.

But the smart shopper will travel around the city, seeking out the special neighborhoods and areas with their individual and selective offerings.

Union Square is perhaps the logical first encounter. And for the first-time visitors, often a shocker. The flower-bedded grassy mall attracts almost every type of person to be found in an urban community: the good and the bad. Any sunny noon will display a sampling of the city's elderly, gays, junkies, a religious guru and attentive disciples, and attractive office workers enjoying nutritious brown-bag delights, mimes and musicians.

Overseeing all are the well-known major department stores ringing the square. *I. Magnin,* sporting a new 1981 facelift, and neighbor *Macy's.* Both are extremely popular with the international guests who come with impressive shopping lists. A newcomer to the square is *Saks Fifth Avenue,* and its contemporary façade. And *Neiman-Marcus* ("Nee-mees"), with its restored landmark glass rotunda.

Specialty shops appeal to big-time spenders. *Bullock & Jones* is a luxe preppy establishment, spotlighting the acclaimed Burberry raingear.

Radiating off the square are dozens of exclusive shops, galleries, and haircutting salons, spread along Maiden La., Sutter, and Post Sts. One of the delights in this area are the charming and colorful corner flower stalls. And each spring Maiden Lane celebrates with a Daffodil Festival and street fair.

The most European and often expensive boutiques, galleries, and trendy shops are to be found in the carefully restored Victorians and carriage houses on Union St., from about Van Ness to Fillmore St. In the city's early days this area was known as "Cow Hollow," a pastoral dairy center. Some of the best coffee houses, brunch favorites, and lively bars are located in this neighborhood.

Polk St. is a colorful, relatively short thoroughfare running parallel to Van Ness Ave. The gay community sparked the renaissance in this district. Interesting boutiques and bookstores share space with some inexpensive and excellent ethnic eateries.

Certainly *Ghirardelli Square,* the photogenic former chocolate factory, affords hours of shopping exposure. Round-the-world collectibles in fashions, furniture, art, and handicrafts are available at affordable prices.

Just east of Fisherman's Wharf, *Pier 39* may be the ultimate in offering one-stop shopping, eating, and entertainment for the whole family.

While strolling around Fisherman's Wharf, examine the *Cost Plus* maze. Three of its warehouses bulge with thousands of imports to dress up yourself and your home at bargain prices. Shop the art and antiques section for treasures, often for a trivial cost.

Wander through *The Anchorage,* a contemporary courtyard complex bursting with everything from California handcrafted gifts and electronic games to the best selection of stuffed bears in the West.

At the foot of Columbus is *The Cannery,* formerly a plant for the Del Monte Fruit Company. This pre-earthquake brick landmark houses over fifty shops specializing in fashions and food, gifts, and games.

Though shopping is a fun and exciting pastime for most of us, a bit of caution follows. Beware the much-touted handmade arts and crafts items hawked along the Wharf and on the fringes of Union Square. The bulk of these "originals" are over-priced and often mass-produced. Frequently, it is the showmanship of the "artist-seller" that dazzles the buyer.

Quite a different atmosphere pervades posh *Jackson Square.* Known in the 1800s as the notorious Barbary Coast, the handsome rose brick buildings today house the shops and showrooms of some of the city's top decorators and wholesalers. Most of these establishments are off-limits to the general public. Some permit browsers.

Nearby, *Chinatown* features picturesque Grant Ave. bazaars aglitter with both trash and treasures from Hong Kong, Taiwan, and China. The best buys are craft items, especially straw baskets, embroidered table linens, festive silk-embroidered jackets, scroll paintings, and many varieties of tea. If you are interested in fine antiques or jade in any form, shop very carefully, and be sure to deal with well-established firms; many of these dealers are located in other areas of the city.

Japantown is our other Asian shopping specialty area. The five-acre Nippon Mall is about a mile west of Union Square. Besides tasty and inexpensive Japanese food, it is a showcase of the best of Japanese products. Cameras, calculators, cultured pearls, toys, trinkets, paintings, and porcelains are on display in abundance.

Throughout San Francisco are neighborhood favorites. Some of these we hope the visitor will discover as he walks this special city. North Beach has unusual bookstores as well as acclaimed Italian delicatessens. Local salami is a tasty remembrance to tote home. The Richmond district is the town's new Chinatown, and is a large residential section with ethnic shops and restaurants.

Following is more detailed information on individual stores and shops, plus bargain-hunting tips and a few guidelines on where to find exceptional and exotic items from antiques to wines.

SPECIAL SHOPPING NOTES

Sales are year-round, so if shopping for special items, allow time to shop the daily newspapers first. Store hours vary. Major department and retail stores usually open 9:30–10:00 A.M. and close at 6:00 P.M. Some downtown stores are open a few evenings and on Sunday. Phone for current policy. Boutiques and smaller shops/galleries often open later in the mornings and stay open into early evenings. This is true especially along Union St. and the Wharf.

Major credit cards are used (MasterCard, VISA, Carte Blanche, American Express, and Diners Club, though it is not accepted everywhere). Personal checks, with proper I.D., may or may not be accepted. This is also true of traveler's checks. Too many stolen traveler's checks have been appearing in the city in recent months. Before shopping, cash as much as required for a day's shopping at nearest bank. However, leave the bulk of your funds in a hotel safe-deposit box, available free (usually) at large hotels.

There are more good shops in San Francisco, and in more categories, than we could fit in a reasonable space in this book. Therefore the shops we list here are a selection of interesting and reputable establishments.

WOMEN'S SHOPPING

Be prepared to be bewitched, bewildered, and broke by the fabulous and funky fashions locally available.

Tastes differ; so do budgets. However, quality should be one's hallmark. Learn to look for fine workmanship, "pure" materials (real silk, 100 percent virgin wool, genuine leather). Avoid the popular "status" syndrome. Today, top fashion names—Dior, Pierre Cardin, Gloria Vanderbilt—adorn accessories of medium grade produced by licensees, often mass-produced in the Orient with higher price tags than if the same merchandise would be sold unlabeled.

I. Magnin and *Macy's* carry the original creations of noted designers such as the couture jackets and blazers of Giorgio Armani and Yves St. Laurent ($600 and more). Sportswear by Calvin Klein, Anne Klein, and Ralph Lauren each have their followers. Macy's glows with stunning knits by Missoni and Sonia Rykiel, affordable and becoming to a select few; plus Givenchy, Blass, Halston wearables. Handbags come in many shapes and sizes, and lots of them, with unfamiliar labels or none at all, are of good leather or fabrics.

For the cognoscenti, the status handbags are present too. Judith Lieber's evening fantasies; Fendi, Celine and Louis Vuitton initial-laden originals ($160 on up).

In the world of shoes, select timeless Ferragamo styling or trendy Maud Frizons. Macy's allows Charles Jourdan a separate boutique with snazzy shoe and boot fashions.

For more realistic designs and price tags, *Frank More* and *Kushins,* both on Union Square, are highly recommended. Frank More is known for his elegantly colored snakeskin and printed shoe and handbag combinations.

Fashion-following matrons flock to *Saks Fifth Avenue* for their Adolfo gowns and St. John's knits. More conservative and inflation-aware Grey Panthers love *Livingston's,* a locally owned favorite.

Post St. knockouts include *Celine* of Paris, *Gump's* for especially beautiful Thai and Japanese silk fashions, *Elizabeth Arden's* sports and late-day panache, and *Jaeger* for British-bred chic. *Eddie Bauer* carries slick safari and trekking togs. Stop in *Sidney Mobell,* the city's most imaginative jeweler. Perhaps the Cartier tank watch is out, budget-wise, as well as most of the diamond-decorated baubles. How about a sterling cable-car charm for a neck wire or bracelet? Anyway, don't miss viewing the half-million-dollar gold, platinum, and diamond backgammon set. Unless one of our three million visitors has carried it away! Long-time jeweler *Shreve's* carries fine jewelry, crystal, china and silver mementos, with an excellent repair shop for watches and pearl and semi-precious stone necklaces that are in need of restringing. *Gucci's* has tiny tote bags as well as the familiar Double-G buckle, around $50 and up. For the executive, *Mark Cross* suggests their solid-color suede briefcase, $450!

One of the most spectacular examples of contemporary architecture is the new *Galleria* at Crocker Genter, between Kearny and Montgomery, Post and Sutter. This Skidmore, Owings and Merrill block-long retail shopping complex is topped by a paned-glass arch and features a classic, Roman numeral clock at one end.

The blocks from Kearny to Mason on Sutter contain some of the most elegant shops to be found anywhere. It is also the center for some of the city's most important art galleries. Originally in Berkeley, the *White Duck* has exclusive designs in fine cottons, silks, and wool. Truly, art to be worn. Near-neighbors, and local high-style talents, are *Jeanne Marc*, whose colorful creations are also available at *I. Magnin* and *Saks Fifth Avenue*, and the romantic, lace-lavished lovelies of *Jessica McClintock*.

If you have the money, look for flashy Fendi foxes and minks that ranch at *I. Magnin*. *Roberts* on Post St. is famed for his red fox, lynx, and coyote one-of-a-kind fur pieces, though natives usually trot them out only for the Opera opening and summer-cool evening concerts.

For the total look in ultrasuede for him or her, look for the *Leather Hamlet*, on O'Farrell, rear of Macy's. Also suede specialists.

The Emporium-Capwell's department store on Market St. and *Joseph Magnin* on Stockton St. have moderate- to high-price fashions for all ages.

Stroll Union St. to see many tiny boutiques with original fashions. The *San Francisco Working Woman*, at 2250, offers the corporate image and *Elizabeth's*, 2758 Octavia, shows stunning originals.

MEN'S CLOTHING

The San Francisco male is a creature of many moods and modes. Weekdays, especially in the Financial District and expense account luncheon bastions, dress is usually conservative, quite à la *Brooks* or *Briggs* for upper-echelon achievers, and more moderately priced, off-the-rack safe suits from *Hastings* and *Grodins* for the up-and-away computer and brokerage-house recruits. However, on weekends in town or country, T-shirts, Levi's, or jogging outfits are almost universal.

A visit to trendy *Wilkes Bashford* at 336 Sutter can be a treat or torture. Extremely avant-garde sports, day, and evening wear are styled for a slender silhouette and a hefty wallet. Fabrics and tailoring are deluxe: pure wools, cottons, and silks. Colors are muted or rainbow-inspired. It takes courage, cash, and dash to adopt this look. Mr. Bashford's special look is also available for the gals.

Macy's on Union Square does very well by the male animal. Look for sportswear, suits and accessories from American and European designers. Their Calvin Klein shop stocks not only the designer's complete jean collection, but most of his other trend-setting male fashions.

Conservative-types head for *Brooks Brothers,* at 201 Post; *Jay Briggs,* 61 Post or *Cable Car Clothiers* at 150 Post. All offer traditional blazers, flannels, button-down shirts, shetlands, and loafers. They usually stock hard-to-find cotton hose, PJ's, and underwear.

Dunhill's at 290 Post has handsome, imported sports jackets and sweaters. Big-league prices.

Emporium-Capwell at Market and Powell stocks moderate-to-expensive men's wear. *Hasting's,* at the St. Francis Hotel and numerous other Bay Area locations, features suits by Hart, Schaffner & Marx, Dior and Cardin. Check the telephone directory for locations of *The Gap,* a jeans headquarters for the whole family.

CHILDREN'S CLOTHES

Macy's, Saks, and *I. Magnin* have extensive departments for the younger set. At *Dottie Doolittle,* 3680 Sacramento, there is an excellent selection of clothing for young girls (sizes 4–14) and girls and boys infants' and toddlers' togs.

TOYS

For over a century, *F.A.O. Schwarz* has been the hallmark for quality play-things from around the world. The two-story shop at 180 Post St. is a wonder world of Madame Alexander collector dolls, the latest in video games, and a menagerie of marvelous stuffed wildlife. *Jeffrey's,* at 445 Sutter and Ghirardelli Sq., has supplied both the usual and unusual toys, games, and hobby supplies for over three generations. It specializes in miniature cars for the collector and its extensive stock of hobby kits includes planes, ships, and vehicles from every era. *The Hobby Company* at 5150 Geary Blvd., near 16th Ave., can supply all one's hobby and crafts needs. Open seven days. *Mailways-Trains Are Us,* 200 Folsom, corner Main St., is mecca for all age railroad buffs. Check out the authentic H.O. scale models of the new S.F. Muni streetcar system, great gift or souvenir, and they actually run. Local kite shops include *Kite & Gift Inc.* at 333 Jefferson, by the Cannery on Fisherman's Wharf, and in Oakland at Jack London Village, and *Kites-Kites-Kites,* with a large selection of kites from around the world. Pier 39 has *Kitemakers of San Francisco,* which also offers an AKA discount. *Chinatown Kites,* 717 Grant, has a nice selection of inexpen-sive Mylar kites, including a 45-foot dragon style for $6. Take San Francisco home on a string; prices range from $6 to $80. Pier 39 is also the home of *Puppets on the Pier,* which features very charming stuffed-animal hand puppets from Furry Folk, who produce their wares in Emeryville, across the Bay near Oak-land.

JEWELRY

A *Tiffany* boutique at 252 Grant offers a sampling of the rare gems and jewelry, china, silver, and crystal that established their international reputation.

Both *Granat Bros.,* at Grant and Geary, and *Shreve and Co.,* at Post and Grant, are outstanding jewelry and gift stores.

Sidney Mobell, 141 Post and the Fairmont Hotel, is noted for his lavish diamond-studded original designs. *The Wedding Ring Shop,* 50 Post, specializes in traditional and modern engagement and wedding rings.

For gem-quality colored stones or diamonds, visit *Azevedo,* 210 Post, 3rd floor. They also do appraisals. Other fine jewelers are: *Fox's,* at the St. Francis Hotel; *Laykin,* at I. Magnin; *Boring & Co.,* 140 Geary, fresh-water pearl originals; *Wing's,* 190 Post, treasures of the East, especially pearls and jade; *Yokoo,* 210 Post, pearls of any luster, including golden; and *Robert E. Johnson,* for estate jewelry and rare coins, at 353 Geary.

LOVELY LUXURIES

Since 1861, *Gump's* has combed the continents to bring the rarest and most unusual gifts to their clientele. Be it a rare Late Ming Dynasty white nephrite bowl ($25,000), to a mini flowering cherry tree ($20), there indeed is something for everyone. Crystal lovers have always flocked to their superb Baccarat Room and the very new Crystal Lalique collection. It is also noted for its collection of old (ko) Imari, eighteenth- and nineteenth-century porcelains. Small pieces begin at $100 to a mid-eighteenth-century hibachi at $3,500. Modestly priced Japanese Seto porcelains, classic blue-and-white Thai porcelains, and Capiz Shell gifts from the Philippines are popular wedding and anniversary selections.

For several years, both handmade and machine-made Oriental rugs have found eager buyers. *Macy's* has perhaps the largest selection of both wool and silk rugs from China, Turkey, Pakistan, as well as Belgium reproductions of classic Chinese and Persian patterns. Two other Bay Area department stores, *Breuner's* and *Emporium-Capwell's,* have noteworthy departments.

One of the most charming Union Square stops is at *Wedgwood's* crystal and china cupboard, adjacent to *Dunhill's.* All-time favorites are here; however, a 5-piece place setting of their "Runnymede" pattern checks out at $165. Very affordable is the oven-to-tableware line or their fine earthenware, Queen's Ware, first appearing in the eighteenth century.

Victoria's Secret, 395 Sutter and 2245 Union, is a fantasy of luxe silk and satin lingerie. What every girl wants from Santa!

Sue Fisher King, 3075 Sacramento, is the Rolls of hand-embroidered crocheted and appliqued linens from China and Portugal—for bed, bath, or table. *Scheuer Linens,* opposite Hyatt Union Square, has hard-to-find Madeira hand-embroidered hankies, very much in vogue again.

The Enchanted Crystal, 1771 Union, is a 7-day wonder of dazzling lead-crystal figures and decorative pieces, handmade European silk flowers, and an eclectic collection of antique and modern jewelry.

At Ghirardelli Square or downtown, 59 Grant Ave., shop *Takahashi* with tasteful selections in table linens, kitchen items, contemporary glass and dinnerware, and Japanese decorative objects.

Hopefully, the reader was able to visit some wineries in Northern California and, after touring, sample a selection of their production. Or if not sampled at the site, then while dining at one of the nearly 3,000 restaurants at the ready. One might consider hauling a case back home. A wiser course would be to contact the *California Wine Merchant* at 3237 Pierce regarding cost and selection on out-of-town shipments. Or hand-carry by air, snuggled in soiled clothing, a sample of California's best. Perhaps a Domaine Chandon sparkling Napa Valley Brut or Blanc de Blancs for that next special occasion. (See the section on the *Wine Country* later in the book.)

LEATHER AND LUGGAGE

No doubt the visitor will need additional luggage to carry off the numerous goodies acquired in San Francisco. *Macy's* and *Emporium-Capwell* have selections of major brands. *I. Magnin* and *Saks* are noted for their Louis Vuitton and French collections. *Malm's*, at 222 Grant Ave., has been a local name for fine luggage since 1868. In addition to a wide selection of Vuitton classics, they feature Lark, Hartmann, Halliburton, Skyway, and many more. Handsome selection of traveling accessories and gifts and personal leather goods. At 3 Embarcadero Center, *Edwards* is a showplace of fashion luggage, attachés, and portfolios. Try *Harband's* at 517 Mission St.; closed Saturday, this firm offers a 20 percent discount on all merchandise. However, we suggest checking out the department stores, which often have sales of their various discontinued models.

ANTIQUES

Excellent buys of antiques are frequently made at auctions, but they are almost always made by persons who know beforehand the approximate values of the articles on which they bid. In addition, they examine them to ascertain their condition. Always visit the establishment before the sale. Note the articles of interest and establish the top limit of bid offer.

Butterfield's, 1244 Sutter St., has frequent sales of antiques. At *Butterfield's*, 660 3rd St., every Monday free appraisal clinics are offered. Bring in the item or a photo of it. The auctions at 660 feature a wide range of collectibles, 90 percent of which are sold for under $100.

Many people prefer established dealers. Following are some of the best locally.

French and English Furniture: *Arbes & Co.,* 701 Sansome; *Beaver Bros.,* 1637 Market; *Dillingham & Company,* 3485 Sacramento; *Dolphin,* 408 Jackson; *John Doughty,* 619 Sansome; *Hardy,* 855 Montgomery; and *Youll's Antiques,* 1651 Polk.

Antique Silver: *Argentum,* 1750 Union. *Meyer & Nutt,* 2284 Union, specialists in old American, English, Irish and Russian sterling and plate.

Orientalia: *Ashkenazie & Co.,* Fairmont Hotel, carvings; *Fabulous Things,* 1974 Union St.; *King Fook Goldsmith of Hong Kong, Inc.,* 838 Grant Ave., jade and gold jewelry; *Kuromatsu,* 722 Bay St.; *Peking Arts & Crafts,* 535 Sutter St., antique jade, porcelain, cloisonne, and contemporary Peking enamel and cloisonne; *Shige*, 1730 Geary St., kimonos, lacquerware, porcelain, scrolls; *Shiota*, 3131 Fillmore St., Japanese prints and porcelain; *Tom Wing & Sons*, 190 Post St., Ming to Ch'ing porcelain, jade, bronze; *Shibata's*, 3028 Fillmore St., *City of Shanghai*, 519 Grant Ave.

Collector Rugs: *Soraya*, 1025 Battery at The Icehouse; *Baktiari*, 2843 Clay Street; *Quality Rugs of the Orient*, 559 Sutter, and *Indigo*, 2340 Polk St. at Union, for antique tribal rugs.

American Antiques: *Keith*, 2455 Polk, *P. G. Pugsley & Son*, 4900 California; and *Pilgrim-Roy*, 372 Hayes St. *The Woodchuck*, 2215 Clement, specializes in turn-of-the-century oak furniture.

Clocks: *Robert R. Johnson*, 353 Geary; and *Walker's*, 1741 Polk.

Clothing: *Painted Lady*, 1838 Divisadero, turn-of-the-century, Twenties, Thirties, and Forties wearable art; *Grand Illusions*, 1604 Union; and *Matinee*, 1124 Polk.

BARGAIN SHOPPING

Be sure to check the telephone directory and call for addresses and hours of the businesses below. All shops mentioned are in the city and can be reached via public transport. Remember that all the major department stores have constant sales and special-purchases stock. Also, question method of payment, in advance: cash, check, credit cards (which are acceptable).

Women's Apparel. *Bon Marche*, 721 Market; *Company Store*, 1903 Fillmore; *Clothes Encounter*, 217 Kearny; *Factory Store*, 501 Bryant St., *Fran's*, 1539 Fillmore; *Spare Changes*, 695 3rd St., at Townsend; and *My Favorite Clothing and Shoe Store*, 33 Drumm St., across from Hyatt Regency.

Men's Clothing. *Clothing Clearance Center*, 695 Bryant, corner 5th St., and *Executive Clothes*, 520 Washington.

Children's Clothing. *Jamboree*, 5630 Geary. Sizes from infants through 14 in boys and girls clothing.

Art Supplies. *Flax's Warehouse*, 1699 Market.

China, Crystal. *S. Christian of Copenhagen*, 225 Post St. Hand-blown glassware by Rosenthal, seconds and irregulars about 60 percent below retail. A visit to Sausalito is a must for all visitors, so check out *Heath Ceramics*, 400 Gate 5 Rd. This award-winning designer offers slightly flawed dinnerware and heat-tempered cookware for 40 percent below retail.

FINE FOODS AND SELECT WINES

Everyone tastes sourdough bread while in the Bay Area. Treat yourself to a look at California's oldest French bakery, *Boudin's*, at 156 Jefferson, at the Wharf. Be sure to pick up some before departing. And add some savory North Beach salami. *Molinari*, at 373 Columbus, tops our list, with *Gloria*, at 635 Vallejo, a close second.

Connoisseur Wine Imports, 462 Bryant, two blocks from Moscone Center, celebrates the best of California and European wines.

Shop *Oakville Grocery,* 1555 Pacific, for imaginative pâtés and nine different country hams.

Out on California, in Laurel Village, is *Fantasia,* home of fabulous European desserts and pastries. Sample their coffeecake or croissants with coffee and pick up their mail-order brochure.

Visit *The Flying Crab,* North Terminal, San Francisco International Airport. Gourmet items include stuffed prawns and mushrooms and smoked salmon, and a variety of local fish, including salmon, sand dabs, rex sole, and snapper. Open seven days a week.

Downtown, *Macy's Cellar* is chock full of goodies from everywhere. In addition, there is a fine selection of wines and spirits.

Have you tasted California caviar? Locally, known as American Golden Caviar, it retails for $4.00 an ounce at *Jurgensen's.* Considerably more affordable than Iranian or Russian caviar selling for well over $200 a pound.

Check *I. Magnin* for the "Cartier" of chocolates, Moreau; try a maxi-bar (about $3). Chocolates at $38 a pound! A slightly less expensive product is Godiva, also at I. Magnin. The gold boxes are impressive and make a proper thank-you touch. Familiar to New Yorkers, and at sensible prices, are the cookies and chocolates bearing the Barton label at Grant and Geary. Popular in price, and with many locals, are See's Candies, all over the area. This editor finds them highly overrated.

For Italian roast espresso, French and Turkish styles, shop the *Capricorn Coffee Center* at 353 10th St. In North Beach, *Graffeo Coffee Roasting Company* sells retail as well as wholesale to leading restaurants. *Cost Plus* on the Wharf has a wide selection of coffees, bulk teas, herbs and spices.

Sample Monterey Jack Cheese. In the Richmond district, the *Sixth Avenue Cheese Shop* has a nibble on over 200 imported and domestic cheeses. They ship anywhere and have attractive party packages and picnic baskets. *The Cheshire Cheese* at 2213 Fillmore arrays cheeses, truffles, smoked salmon, and other delights in an appealing way.

BOOKS

The following downtown bookstores are recommended for very good to excellent stocks of books in general, and especially about San Francisco. Civic Center Area: *Civic Center Books,* 360 Golden Gate Ave. Embarcadero Center Area: *Foley Books,* 119 Sacramento St. (all NEW books at 20 percent discount); *B. Dalton,* 2 Embarcadero Center. Ghirardelli Square: *Ghirardelli Book Store,* 900 North Point. Polk Street Area: *Paperback Traffic,* 1501 Polk St. Union Square/Market and Powell Area: *Books, Inc.,* 140 Powell St.; *B. Dalton,* 200 Kearny St.; *Bonanza Inn Book Shop,* 650 Market St.; *Stacey's Bookstore,* 581 Market St.; *Albatross,* 166 Eddy; *Bookmania,* 160 California, a block from Embarcadero Center, is the West's biggest discount bookstore.

In North Beach, *City Lights Books,* at 261 Columbus, owned by Lawrence Ferlinghetti, is a bonanza of Beatnik books and still a gathering place for off-beat writers. Casual seating encourages browsing and reading. Open till midnight every day.

For mystery buffs, a trek out to tiny *Murder, Inc.*, at 746 Diamond, is a must. Mostly paperbacks, though one may uncover a rare first edition. Restricted hours: Friday and Saturday, noon till 6:00 P.M.

For French, German and Spanish books and periodicals, try the maps, guides, *European Book Company,* 925 Larkin. Japantown's *Kinokuniya* distributes Japanese books, tapes, magazines, and records.

Charlotte Newbegin's Tillman Place Bookshop, off Grant, between Post and Sutter, specializes in children's books, as does *Land of the Counterpane,* 3452 Sacramento.

To gourmet cooks and travel fans, Jean Bullock's select *Travel Books/Gourmet Guides,* 1767 Stockton in North Beach, is a winner.

Rare-book connoisseurs seek out *John Howell* at 434 Post St. Another specialist is the *Argonaut* at 786 Sutter; marvelous maps, prints, and autographs as well as rare books.

George Butler Company, 633 Battery, carries nautical books—as well as other nautical supplies such as sextants and fittings.

RECORDS

A vast array of records and tapes are available all over the Bay Area. Rock, soul, jazz, country, classical, pop, comedy as well as imported and rare and out-of-print records. Just a few retailers are listed. Check the telephone Yellow Pages for a more extensive listing and specific information. *Tower Records,* at Columbus and Bay, is one of the city's giants; open until midnight. *Record Factory,* 2075 Market and 1444 Polk, discounts tapes and records and has music books and accessories as well. *Let It Be Records,* 2434 Judah, stars Beatles memorabilia as well as rock items from 1950 to 1980. *Foreign Affair,* 2453 Fillmore, displays French, German, Italian, and Brazilian records. For collectors' items (opera, nostalgia, personality) visit *The Record House,* 389 Geary.

VERY SPECIAL SHOPS

Pier 39's *Rainbow Shop* is just that: special, with ceramic gifts, stationery, sculpture, jewelry, posters, and even suspenders! Bear freaks seek out Pier 39's *Ted E. Bear,* for new, tomorrow-rare bears like Misha of 1980 Moscow Olympic fame (be sure he's wearing his Olympic belt) to Steiff's 1980 reproduction of the 1903 original, only 11,000 created. Another marvel at Pier 39 is the year-round Christmas party at *S. Claus.* Many of the unusual ornaments are made by local craftsmen. Our favorite is the charming bread-dough cable car. *The Museum Shop,* 3119 Fillmore, off Union St., has a fantastic variety of artifacts and handicrafts from the four corners of the globe. Originally displayed and very hard to resist. At *Quilts Ltd.,* 1846 Union, custom quilts can be ordered or a huge selection of antique, traditional or contemporary designed quilts are ready to go. At 1800 Union, *Van Ginkel & Moor,* present over 10,000 items of nautical treasures, from authentic ships' wheels and lamps to handsome etchings and cable car bells. Special boxes for transporting Japanese bonsai (miniature trees) are provided by the *Bonsai Shop,* 712 Sutter, near the Canterbury Hotel. Over one hundred varieties of this traditional art form are offered, and instruction in care, etc., given by expertly trained staff. *Orvis,* on Maiden La. off Union Sq., carries a full line of top-quality sporting goods.

 TEATIME. Relax after shopping and sightseeing at the elegant, art-filled *Compass Rose,* St. Francis Hotel, Union Sq., 397–7000. 2:30–4:30 P.M. daily, except Sunday. For traditional scones, crumpets, savories and trifle, visit the *Bread and Honey Tea Room,* King George Hotel, 334 Mason St. 781–5050. 4:00 to 7:00 P.M. daily. Close to Union Sq. and the Geary St. theater district. *The Café on Mason* 542 Mason, is a tiny jewel for teatime reflections. Open Tuesday–Saturday, noon–4:30 P.M. Close to Union Sq. *Abigail's,* 246 McAllister, is a breakfast/tearoom in a small hotel. 861–9728. Close to Civic Center, Opera House and Davies Symphony Hall. Scones, crumpets, jams and jellies, and an interesting selection of teas. English-style luncheon also served. Open daily till 4:00 P.M.; weekends till 6:00 P.M. *The Cirque,* Fairmont Hotel, Nob Hill; 772–5000. English afternoon tea is served Monday through Saturday from 4:30 P.M. to 6:30 P.M. in this recently restored Art Deco rendevous.

 DINING OUT. If asked to describe a meal uniquely San Franciscan, most purists would probably concur on fresh, cracked Dungeness crab served cold with crusty sourdough bread, tender baby artichokes or avocados dressed with lemon juice, Monterey jack cheese, and vine-ripened melons or other fruit, all washed down, of course, with a fine California wine. These are foods indigenous to the area, but this meal would not reflect the city's diverse ethnic heritage. The early Mexican settlers, the influx of Europeans during the Gold Rush era, the Italian fishermen, the Chinese imported to build the railroads, and the twentieth-century immigrations of Japanese, Latin Americans, and Southeast Asians have left their mark on the city's eating habits. Perhaps a more typical example of "San Francisco Cuisine" would be an appetizer created by the Peruvian-born owner of a Richmond District restaurant (Alejandro's): Monterey jack cheese and minced Mexican jalapeño peppers stuffed into a thin Japanese pastry skin (gyosha), deep fried and served with lemon-mayonnaise. An ethnic mongrel, but absolutely delicious.

In no American city outside of New York can such a variety of restaurants be found in such a concentrated area as in San Francisco. New York also outranks San Francisco in the number of big-name chefs and, in general, the standards and quality of the top French and Italian restaurants. But San Francisco has a definitive culinary edge over New York and other Northeastern and Midwestern cities: the year-round availability of fresh local produce. Many of the better restaurants go to market daily at dawn to select the best of yesterday's crop: fruits and vegetables with flavors and nutrients that will decrease markedly each day away from their harvest. The same is true of the seafood from local

waters; if you're lucky that morning's catch will appear on your plate at noon
with the inimitable flavor of just-out-of-the-sea fish. The abundance and diversity
of fresh ingredients in the San Francisco Bay Area, along with the multiplicity
of ethnic groups, have in recent years resulted in the style of cooking known as
California cuisine.

Price Classifications and Abbreviations. The price classifications of the following restaurants, from inexpensive to deluxe, are based on the cost of an average
three-course dinner for one person **for food alone;** beverages, tax, and tip would
be extra. *Inexpensive* means less than $10.00; *Moderate,* $10.00 to $20.00; *Ex-
pensive,* $20.00 to $30.00; and *Deluxe,* over $30.00.

Abbreviations for credit cards are: AE, American Express; CB, Carte
Blanche; DC, Diners Club; MC, MasterCard; V, VISA. Most restaurants that
do not accept credit cards will cash traveler's checks; many will honor personal
checks if you have a major credit card.

Abbreviations for meal codes are: B, breakfast; L, lunch; D, dinner. As
restaurant hours and days of closing often change, you should call first to
confirm the hours open.

Remember, what we offer is only a *selection* of okay places, to give you a
range. See also "Wine Tasting in the Bay Area," later in this book.

VERY SAN FRANCISCAN

A certain breed of San Francisco restaurant does not fit easily into any ethnic
category because the food is often as cosmopolitan as the city itself, reflecting
local favorites and prejudices. But these places share a sense of history and an
ambience that is uniquely San Franciscan. It is also difficult to stamp these
dining places with a price tag. *Most can be expensive* if you don't keep an eye
on the right-hand margin, but in most the budget-wary diner can emerge with
his bank account intact, if he chooses with caution.

Bardelli's. 243 O'Farrell, Downtown; 982–0243. Founded in 1906 as
Charles' Oyster House, this turn-of-the-century showplace boasts high, vaulted
ceilings, massive marble columns, and stained glass. The menu mixes French,
Italian, and American fare with local specialties such as chicken Jerusalem
(sauced with mushrooms and baby artichokes) and superb fresh seafood. Popular for lunch and pre-theater dining. L, D, Monday–Friday. AE, MC, V.

Garden Court. Sheraton-Palace Hotel, Market and New Montgomery, Financial District; 392–8600. A high-domed ceiling of glass, monumental columns
of Italian marble, and gigantic crystal chandeliers make this one of the world's
most magnificent dining rooms. Sunday brunch at the Palace is a time-honored
tradition. The dazzling array of foods spread out on three enormous buffet
tables, plus the huge punchbowls of complimentary Bloody Marys and Screw-
drivers, makes the price seem quite reasonable. A buffet dinner is offered on
Sundays as well. L, Monday–Friday; brunch, D, Sunday. Major credit cards.

Jack's. 615 Sacramento, Financial District; 986–9854. Little has changed in
over 100 years in this bankers' and brokers' favorite. Regulars opt for the simple
fare—steaks, chops, seafood, and stews. The dining room has an old-fashioned,

no-nonsense aura; there are private rooms upstairs for top-secret meetings. L, D, Monday–Saturday; D, Sunday. No credit cards.

John's Grill. 63 Ellis, Downtown; 986–0069. A no-frills bar and grill that's been around since 1908 and was Dashiell Hammett's hangout when he wrote *The Maltese Falcon.* Good seafood. John's burned down in 1983, but was rebuilt just as before. L, D, Monday–Saturday. AE, MC, V.

STEAK HOUSES

San Francisco is not a meat-and-potatoes town, and top-grade aged beef is difficult to find in restaurants. In addition to the steak houses listed below, you will find good steaks at most of the top Italian, French or Continental spots. These serve excellent steaks, though often sauced and disguised by French names such as entrecôte (New York steak) or medallions (filet mignon). If you're a beef purist, you can always request the steak without the sauce. You'll also find steak in varying degrees of quality at most American restaurants that serve dinner.

Expensive

Alfred's. 886 Broadway, North Beach; 781–7058. Some of the best steaks in the city are served here with Italian accompaniments, such as a huge antipasto tray, in elegant surroundings reminiscent of Old San Francisco. L, D, Monday–Friday; D, Saturday–Sunday. Friday–Saturday. Major credit cards.

Harris', 2100 Van Ness, Midtown; 673–1888. Mrs. Jack Harris, who put together the award-winning restaurant at the famed Harris Ranch in Coalinga, has now opened her own place—appropriately in the old quarters of Grison's, but extensively remodeled with wood-paneled walls and a giant Barnaby Conrad mural of the Harris Ranch. Beef, of course, is king here with 21-day aged steaks and prime rib, accompanied with Texas red potatoes; though other meats and an array of appetizers are offered as well. L, D, daily. AE, MC, V.

SEAFOOD

In a city as renowned for its fish and shellfish as San Francisco, one would expect to find a first-rate seafood house in every block. This, unfortunately, is not the case. For decades the historic downtown grills, Sam's and Tadich, vied with each other almost exclusively for the trade of the local piscophiles. But in recent years a number of good dining places that specialize in fish have opened in outlying areas. Also, you usually can be assured of finding fresh seafood at the better Chinese, French, and Italian restaurants. Natives habitually shy away from Fisherman's Wharf, where much of the fish is frozen and the restaurants cater primarily to tourists. For a guide to the seasonal availability of various types of fish and seafood in San Francisco, see the Food section near the front of this book.

Moderate

Castagnola's. 286 Jefferson at Jones, Fisherman's Wharf; 776–5015. One of the more civilized of the Wharf's touristy restaurants and reliable if you navigate through the sea of fancy concoctions and stick with the fresh fish, simply broiled or sautéed. L, D, daily. Major credit cards.

Hayes Street Grill. 324 Hayes St., Civic Center Area; 863–5545. The freshest of fish is simply grilled here and served with a choice of several sauces and homemade fries. Desserts are exceptional. Close to the Performing Arts Center. L, D, Monday–Friday; D, Saturday. Wine and beer only. MC, V.

Ronayne's. 1799 Lombard, Marina; 922–5060. This pretty Irish pub offers fish in a variety of styles: grilled, broiled, sautéed, deep-fried, or dressed up with fancy sauces. Fresh vegetables; great desserts. D, daily. AE, MC, V.

Sam's Grill. 374 Bush, Financial District; 421–0594. Sam's and Tadich (following) are two of the city's oldest restaurants, and so popular for lunch that you must arrive before 11:30 for even a chance of a table. The atmosphere is starkly old-fashioned—some of the booths are enclosed and curtained—and the menu offers an extensive variety of dishes. But those in the know come here for the fresh local seafood and the shellfish flown in from the East Coast, and the excellent wines. L, D, Monday–Friday. MC, V.

Scott's Seafood Grill and Bar. 2400 Lombard, Marina; 563–8988. Embarcadero Three; 981–0622. As at most of the city's better seafood houses, you'll have to wait for a table. The day's catches, posted on a chalkboard, come either grilled or sautéed. Cioppino is another house specialty. L, D, daily at Lombard. L, D, Monday–Saturday; D, Sunday at Embarcadero. Major credit cards.

Swan Oyster Depot. 1517 Polk, Midtown; 673–1101. Eating facilities in this fish market are limited to one counter with only a dozen stools, but lovers of shellfish come from all over town for the Eastern oysters in the shell and giant seafood cocktails. L, Monday–Saturday. Wine and beer only. No credit cards.

Tadich Grill. 240 California St., Financial District; 391–2373. Owners and locations have changed over the 125-plus-year lifetime of this local institution, but the nineteenth-century atmosphere remains, as do the kitchen's high standards. Seating at counter and in private booths. L, D, Monday–Saturday. No credit cards.

The Waterfront. Pier 7, Embarcadero; 391–2696. The dramatic, multi-level, glass-walled dining room guarantees a Bay view from every table. The food doesn't always match the fabulous view, but the fresh fish and pasta are usually above average. L, D, Monday–Friday; Brunch, D, Saturday–Sunday. Major credit cards.

AMERICAN/CALIFORNIA

One doesn't think of San Francisco as a citadel of American cooking, but the list of good restaurants serving U.S. fare is surprisingly long. Its numbers have been boosted in recent years by a growing interest in regional food, especially from the south and southwest. Then there is the current phenomena of "New American" or "New California" cuisine, which relies primarily on fresh seasonal ingredients prepared in a creatively eclectic manner, drawing on a plethora of international cooking techniques.

Deluxe

Campton Place. 340 Stockton, Downtown; 781–5555. This luxurious hotel dining room has been the talk of the town since it opened with the noted chef Bradley Ogden at the helm and a sparkling menu reflecting the new American cuisine. All the foods are indigenous to or produced in America, but even the likes of blue corn cakes and apple pie are infused with Ogden's creativity. B, L, D, daily. Sunday brunch. Major credit cards.

Moderate

Cafe American. 317 Columbus, North Beach; 981–8266. The looks of a proper cafe (starchy white cloths and a big open kitchen) blend with the aura of a North Beach coffeehouse. The cooking, however is the new California style with an emphasis on mesquite-grilled seafood, and pizza from a brick oven. Pastries are wonderful and served from early morning until midnight in the cafe section. B, L, D, daily. Wine and beer only. MC, V.

Cafe Royale. 2080 Van Ness Avenue, Midtown; 441–1300. Creative cooking in the style of the new California cuisine in an Art Deco setting right out of a 1930s Hollywood movie. Seafood, mesquite-grilled meats and fish with unusual accompaniments are the specialties. A boisterous bar serves seafood appetizers —oysters, marinated calamari, golden caviar and the like—and a pianist plunks out nostalgic show tunes. D (open late), daily. AE, MC, V.

Courtyard. 2436 Clement, Richmond District; 387–7616. The menu is dubbed California cuisine, but the selection is more international, making use of local ingredients. Contemporary décor with skylights. Covenient to Golden Gate Park, Legion of Honor, and the beach. L, D, Monday–Friday; D, Brunch, Saturday–Sunday. Major credit cards.

The Elite Cafe. 2049 Fillmore, Pacific Heights; 346–8668. New Orleans Creole cooking and marvelous seafood—some of it flown in from the Gulf—is the draw in this very popular cafe that looks like it belongs on Bourbon Street. Homesick southerners should head right here for blackened redfish, gumbo or grits and grillades. Sazerac and gulf oysters help while you wait for a table—and you will. D, daily. Sunday brunch. No credit cards.

Golden Eagle. Embarcadero Four; 982–8831. Truly creative cooking, with everything made from scratch—even the ice cream. A la carte entrees range from corned beef with cabbage to the chef's inventions like prawns with horseradish and orange marmalade. L, D, Monday–Saturday. Major credit cards.

MacArthur Park. 607 Front St., Embarcadero Area; 398–5700. Restaurant mogul Jerry Magnin transformed an old warehouse into a contemporary gardenlike setting, but for years couldn't find a menu that succeeded. Now the kitchen is dedicated to ribs, links, and chicken, smoked and barbecued over mesquite charcoal—and it works. L, D, Monday–Friday; D, Saturday–Sunday. AE, MC, V.

Mama's. 1701 Stockton, North Beach; 362–6421. Macy's basement, Stockton and O'Farrell, Downtown; 391–3790. 1177 California, Nob Hill; 928–1004. Mama started serving exquisite salads, sandwiches, and omelettes in a tiny cafeteria-style café facing Washington Square in North Beach. She then went downtown for a similar operation in Macy's Cellar. Finally she opened a fancier branch on Nob Hill, with table service and Italian-accented dinners. The original North Beach locale is still the favorite of most San Franciscans. North Beach: B, L, D, daily; no credit cards; bring your own wine or beer. Downtown: B, L, D, daily; AE. Nob Hill: B, L, D (open late) daily; AE, MC, V.

Perry's. 1944 Union St., Cow Hollow; 922–9022. The West Coast equivalent of P. J. Clarke's in Manhattan. This popular watering hole and meeting place for the buttoned-down singles set also serves good, honest saloon food—hamburgers, London broil, corned-beef hash and the like, plus hearty breakfasts. B, L, D (open late), daily. AE, MC, V.

Ruby's. 500 Brannan, Moscone Center Area; 495–0457. Part of Ruby's charm is discovering a gracious mirrored interior behind an industrial facade. Its other charms are an imaginative menu and truly caring service accompanied by light piano music. L, D, Monday–Friday; brunch, D, Saturday, Sunday. Wine and beer only. No CB.

Zuni Cafe Grill. 1658 Market, Civic Center Area; 552–2522. In only a few years Zuni's has metamorphized from a comfortable coffeehouse to a first-rate restaurant with an experimental kitchen that ranks high among the practitioners of California cuisine. Only a rack full of magazines and newspapers is a reminder of the cafe's early days. L, Monday–Friday. D, daily. Weekend brunch. Wine and beer only. No credit cards.

Inexpensive

Bill's Place. 2301 and 2315 Clement, Richmond District; 221–5262. Famous for hamburgers named after its celebrity clientele. Outdoors seating in orchid-filled patios. L, D, daily. Wine and beer only. No credit cards.

Doidge's. 2217 Union, Cow Hollow; 921–2149. This new haven for breakfast/brunch lovers offers seemingly infinite variations on French toast, omelettes, and poached eggs. B, daily; D, Thursday–Sunday. No alcohol. MC, V.

Eagle Café. Pier 39; 433–3689. Nostalgia buffs will love this old-time waterfront cafeteria-saloon that was literally moved board by board across the street to Pier 39. They'll also love the yesteryear's prices for gigantic portions of plain honest cooking. Great view. B, L, daily. No credit cards.

Hog Heaven. 770 Stanyan, across from Golden Gate Park,; 668–2038. Mild Memphis-style barbecue, served with cornbread, slaw, and beans, in an attractive contemporary setting. L, D, daily. MC, V.

Sear's Fine Food. 439 Powell, Downtown; 986–1160. Breakfast at Sears' has been a San Francisco institution for some fifty years, with both locals and tourists lined up for tiny Swedish pancakes or fluffy French toast. B, L, Wednesday–Sunday. No alcohol. No cards. If the line at Sears' is too long for you, try **Pam Pam** at Geary and Mason Sts.

Zim's. Eleven locations throughout the city. The most reliable of the city's fast-food chains. Hamburgers, sandwiches, salads, quick dinners, and breakfast

24 hours daily. Special children's menus. Full bar or wine and beer in some locations. Credit cards in some locations.

CHINESE

For nearly a century Chinese restaurants in San Francisco were mostly confined to Chinatown. And the cooking was largely an Americanized version of peasant dishes brought here in the 1860s by the Cantonese laborers who built the railroads. In 1961 Cecilia Chiang, an elegant lady from Peking, changed all this when she opened The Mandarin, then a tiny restaurant on Polk St., and introduced San Franciscans to the full spectrum of Chinese cooking. Mandarin is not a regional style, but encompasses the finest dishes from all areas of China as they were prepared for the imperial households in Peking. Included in the Mandarin repertoire is Cantonese cooking, not the bland dishes with thick sauces found in most American kitchens, but light, subtly seasoned fare relying for flavor on the fresh produce and seafood that is abundant in the area around Canton. Seafood is also important in the cuisine of coastal Shanghai, but the dishes are more complex and intricately seasoned. In the Northern, inland regions of China around Peking, meat and flour replace fish and rice as the dietary staples. Beef and lamb, dumplings and pancakes characterize the Northern fare. The spiciest foods of China come from tropical Szechwan, where the searingly hot fagara pepper is used liberally, and its neighboring province Hunan, where smoked foods are very popular.

Today most of China's diverse cuisines are represented in many San Francisco restaurants, which are dispersed throughout the city with a concentration in the Richmond District. Chinatown cooking tends to become more Americanized, as it caters to the tourists while the locals go elsewhere.

Expensive to Moderate

The Mandarin. Ghirardelli Square; 673–8812. Madame Cecilia Chiang now holds court in a magnificent setting fit for imperial fare, decorated with paintings and embroideries from her family's palatial homes in Peking and Shanghai. This is one of the world's great restaurants, and its finest offerings, such as Mandarin duck, beggar's chicken cooked in clay, and the Mongolian firepot, must be ordered a day in advance. Bay view. L, D, daily. Major credit cards.

Moderate to Inexpensive

China Garden. 2110 Clement, Richmond District; 668–9599. The furnishings are of the Formica-and-vinyl genre, but the Peking-style cooking is a dining adventure, with many very unusual dishes, along with exceptional renditions of more familiar ones. L, D, Wednesday–Monday. Beer and wine only. MC, V.

Hunan. 924 Sansome, North Beach; 956–7727. 853 Kearny, Chinatown; 788–2234. Henry Chung's first café on Kearny had only six tables, but his Hunanese cooking merited six stars from critics nationwide. Henry's art flourishes in his new restaurant on Sansome, equally plain but with 250 seats to accommodate the crowds. Smoked dishes are a specialty, and Henry guarantees no MSG, L, D, Monday–Saturday. Sansome: full bar; major credit cards. Kearny: wine and beer only; no credit cards.

Ocean. 726 Clement, Richmond District; 221–3351. The current Cantonese darling of Chinese food fans who patiently wait in line at this plain café for the delicate, lightly sauced and dazzling dishes. L, D, daily. Wine and beer only. MC, V.

Sun Hung Heung. 744 Washington, Chinatown; 982–2319. This old-timer turns out classic Cantonese dishes with a consistency of quality not often found in Chinatown these days, though the service is somewhat indifferent. L, D (open late), Wednesday–Monday. MC, V.

Ton Kiang. 683 Broadway, North Beach; 421–2015. 5827 Geary Blvd., Richmond District; 387–8273. The Hakka cuisine of China, rarely found in this country, relies on a natural style of cooking. It has been attracting crowds to this unpretentious storefront café on Broadway and its newer slightly larger branch on Geary. L, D (open late), daily. Wine and beer only. MC, V.

Tung Fong. 808 Pacific, Chinatown; 362–7115. Dim sum—little morsels of seafood, meat, and vegetables, wrapped in dough—are the staple of this tea house. An endless procession is passed on trays; help yourself to what appeals. You will be charged by the number of empty plates left on your table. Tung Fong is one of the smallest, oldest, and best of the city's many dim sum parlors. L, Thursday–Tuesday. No alcohol. No credit cards.

Yank Sing. 671 Broadway, North Beach; 781–1111. 53 Stevenson, Financial District; 495–4510. 427 Battery, Embarcadero Area; 362–1640. This tea house has grown by leaps and branches along with the popularity of dim sum (see *Tung Fong*) in San Francisco. The original Broadway locale is small and plain; the Stevenson branch is of a dramatic contemporary design; the latest emporium on Battery seats over 300. Wine and beer only. Broadway: L, daily; D, Friday, Saturday; no credit cards. Stevenson: L, Monday–Friday; MC, V. Battery: L, daily; no CB.

CONTINENTAL/INTERNATIONAL

This catch-all category designates restaurants that combine more than one ethnic cuisine in their menus.

Deluxe

Alexis. 1001 California at Mason, Nob Hill; 885–6400. (Russian-French) Byzantine mosaic murals and Russian icons bespeak a Czarist splendor, as do the Franco-Russian menu and, most of all, the prices. The service also is noticeably undemocratic if you're not known here. The lamb dishes are among the best choices. D, Monday–Saturday. Major credit cards.

Blue Fox. 659 Merchant, Financial District; 981–1177. (Italian-French) Once a one-room café, later a speakeasy, the Blue Fox has grown into one of the city's most opulent restaurants. The spacious bar and three dining rooms are lavishly appointed with velvet chairs, gilt mirrors, and crystal chandeliers. Some question whether the food is worth the price but it is one of the few luxury establishments where strangers are treated as graciously as the regular clientele. D, Monday–Saturday. Major credit cards.

Fournou's Ovens. Stanford Court Hotel, 905 California at Powell, Nob Hill; 989–1910. (American-French-Italian) Lunch, with an eclectic array of choices from sandwiches to roast duckling, is served in the flower-bedecked greenhouses that flank the hotel. Dinner is a formal affair in the multi-level dining tiers that focus on the giant open-hearth ovens where many specialties—notably the rack of lamb—are roasted. By sunlight or candlelight, these are two of the city's loveliest dining areas. Service is attentive to detail, caring, and knowledgeable. L, Monday–Friday; D, daily. Major credit cards.

Expensive

Trader Vic's. 20 Cosmo Place, Downtown; 776–2232. This is the headquarters of Vic's empire. You'll find the usual tikis, the vast array of Cantonese and Polynesian dishes, and the exotic drinks. Concentrate instead on simpler fare like fresh seafood and Indonesian rack of lamb. The Captain's Cabin is where the local celebs hang out, but you're not likely to get a seat there unless you're known. L, D, Monday–Friday; D, Saturday–Sunday. (Open late.) Major credit cards.

EUROPEAN

Whereas French and Italian cooking has dominated San Francisco's culinary tradition, the cuisines of other European countries have had very little influence on the city's eating habits. Nevertheless, today a number of excellent restaurants specialize in the authentic cooking of a single European country or region.

Moderate

Gelco's. 1450 Lombard, Marina; 928–1054. (Yugoslavian) Don't be deceived by the motel locale. Inside, several tiny, dimly lit dining rooms provide romantic surroundings for four-course dinners that start with a lavish antipasto tray and end with a luscious dessert. The rack of lamb is, by far, the best bet. D, Monday–Saturday. Major credit cards.

Old Swiss House. Pier 39; 434–0432. (Swiss) A stand-out among the many restaurants in the waterfront's newest shopping-dining complex. The food here is not as Swiss as the atmosphere—Alpine-costumed waitresses, high-backed wooden chairs, flower-bedecked windows with bay views, But in the predominately French menu lurk a few unusual Swiss specialties. L, D, daily. Major credit cards.

Paprikás Fono. Ghirardelli Square; 441–1223. (Hungarian) Colorful Hungarian pottery, artifacts, and furnishings, along with a profusion of flowering plants and a Bay view beguile the eye while an extensive array of Hungarian country dishes intrigues the palate. Don't miss the palacsintas (crêpes) or the deep-fried langos bread. L, D. daily; open late weekends. AE, MC, V.

Moderate to Inexpensive

Archil's. 3011 Steiner, Cow Hollow; 921–2141. (Russian) Just off Union St., this homey little restaurant offers four-course Russian dinners. Entrées vary from the expected, like beef Stroganoff, to the unusual, with everythings prepared on the premises. D, Tuesday–Saturday. Wine and beer only. MC, V.

Luzerne. 1431 Noriega, Sunset District; 664–2353. (Swiss) A husband-and-wife team run this exceedingly popular little neighborhood café. Fondues and four-course French-Swiss dinners at budget prices draw the crowds. D, Wednesday–Sunday. Wine and beer only. No credit cards.

Schroeder's. 240 Front, Financial District; 421–4778. (German) Since 1893, this bastion of old-style German cooking has featured homemade sauerkraut, sausages, sauerbraten, and head cheese. Big and informal, the muraled and paneled dining room with its bare wooden tables looks like a German beer hall. L, D, Monday–Friday. AE.

Inexpensive

Des Alpes. 732 Broadway, North Beach; 788–9900. (Basque) The wood-paneled dining room with checkered oilcloth on the tables is a cozy site for the budget-priced five-course dinners, which include—in the Basque tradition—two meat courses. Guaranteed to keep the trenchermen happy—and discriminating diners, too. D, Tuesday–Sunday. MC, V.

Vlasta's. 2420 Lombard, Marina; 931–7533. (Czech) Vlasta prepares the hearty, three-course dinners as she would cook for her own family, who happen to serve them with justifiable pride in surroundings quite elegant for the modest prices. The duckling with dumplings is everyone's favorite. Or maybe it's the strudel. D, Tuesday–Sunday. Major credit cards.

FRENCH

As the fortunes made from Nevada's Comstock Lode were spent with extravagance in San Francisco during the late 1800s, French food was much in vogue with the Bonanza Kings. An account of a banquet for Senator William Sharon at The Palace Hotel in 1876 describes eleven intricately sauced French dishes served with nine wines from Burgundy and Bordeaux. Then, during the first half of this century, there was a hiatus in the growth and quality of Gallic restaurants. The 1960s and 70s, however, were marked by a revival of interest in French haute cuisine, as well as provincial fare, and in the 1980s many of the classic restaurants have even moved in the direction of *nouvelle cuisine*.

Deluxe

La Bourgogne. 330 Mason, Downtown; 362–7352. After its opening in 1961 this restaurant was widely acclaimed as the city's number one temple of classic French cuisine. A few years back a move to new quarters more than doubled its size and now many critics have questioned if the food is still worth the astronomical prices. D, Monday–Saturday. Major credit cards.

Cafe Mozart. 708 Bush, Downtown: 391–8480. Candlelight, roses and classical music make this intimate cafe a most romantic spot. The four-course fixed-price dinners offer many choices prepared by a creative Parisian chef in the style of *nouvelle cuisine*. The presentations themselves are works of art. D, Monday–Saturday. AE, MC, V.

Ernie's. 847 Montgomery, North Beach; 397–5969. (Italian-French) Like the Blue Fox, Ernie's developed from a humble trattoria into a mahogany-paneled, velvet-draped extravaganza reminiscent of a Barbary-Coast bordello. A young chef, Jacky Roberts, has changed Ernie's long-standing Continental fare to an almost all-French menu that combines *nouvelle cuisine* with his own version of classic dishes. D, daily. Major credit cards.

L'Etoile. 1075 California St., Nob Hill; 771–1529. One of the city's most formal and elegantly appointed dining rooms now offers an a la carte *nouvelle cuisine* menu with probably the most expensive prices in town. Be sure to stop by the bar to hear Peter Mintun at the piano. D, Monday–Saturday. Major credit cards.

Le Club. 1250 Jones, Nob Hill; 771–5400. Once a private club, this intimate hideaway lives up to its name, from the matches engraved with your name to the personalized service. Trust the staff's recommendations and you'll dine well here. D (open late), Monday–Saturday. Major credit cards.

Masa's. Vintage Court Hotel, 648 Bush, Downtown; 989–7154. Japanese-born, French-trained Masataka Kobayashi was the darling of New York's food world while chef at Le Plaisir. Now he has his own place and San Franciscans are willing to wait weeks for a table. The dining room is pretty, filled with flowers and bright accessories, but the true beauty lies in what is *on* the plate. Masa combines his classic training with the Japanese eye for artful presentation. If you want a seat here, however, you must reserve three weeks in advance. D, Tuesday–Saturday. AE, MC, V.

Pierre. Meridien Hotel, 15 Third Street, Moscone Center Area; 974–6400. A serene atmosphere with tables spaced far apart, attentive but unobtrusive service, and a menu that encompasses both innovative and conservative cooking, make this an excellent choice for important lunch dates during conventions at Moscone. L, D, daily. Major credit cards.

Rene Verdon's Le Trianon. 242 O'Farrell, Downtown; 982–9353. When the former White House chef of the John F. Kennedys took over this restaurant in the 1970s, the curious were attracted by his celebrity, but returned for his innovations on a classic and ambitious menu. Verdon is often named as one of the city's top chefs. D, Monday–Saturday. Major credit cards.

Expensive

Chez Michel. 804 North Point St., North Point (north of North Beach); 771–6077. A brilliant patchwork canopy contrasts with the simplicity of ash paneling and polished wood tables in this chic restaurant. Veal and seafood are especially recommended. D (open late), Tuesday–Sunday. MC, V.

Le Castel. 3235 Sacramento, Presidio Heights; 921–7115. Several restaurants have occupied this former Victorian residence with its slightly Moorish interior, and now it is one of the most delightful dining places in the city. Creativity abounds in the menu which includes both classics and the chef's concoctions. Service is thoughtfully attentive. D, Monday–Saturday. Major credit cards.

Fleur de Lys. 777 Sutter, Downtown; 673–7779. The romantic dining room has mirrored walls and a dramatic paisley-draped ceiling. The menu combines classic French cooking with dishes based upon the concepts of *nouvelle cuisine*. D, Tuesday–Sunday. Major credit cards.

Moderate

Castle Grand Brasserie. 1600 Folsom, Civic Center Area; 626–2723. Its proximity to the Performing Arts Center accounts for the popularity of this bistro, as do the nightly specials on the chalkboard menu. L, Monday–Friday; D, daily. Major credit cards.

500 Sutter. 500 Sutter, Downtown; 362–3346. A big, bustling café in front hides a quiet, decorous restaurant. Both share a common kitchen that was set up by the great French chef, Roger Vergé. The restaurant's *nouvelle cuisine* is expensive, but the café food comes at café prices. L, D, Monday–Saturday. Major credit cards.

Lafayette. 290 Pacific, Jackson Square; 986–3366. This once formal restaurant has been reincarnated in a new location as a light-splashed bistro with a young French chef whose cooking borders on California cuisine. Tables are jam-packed and noisy, but it's fun and the food is great. Same prices prevail at lunch and dinnertime, when a piano player adds to the din. L, D, Monday–Friday. D, Saturday. AE, MC, V.

Le Central. 453 Bush, Financial District; 391–2233. This boisterous bistro is noisy and crowded, and there's nothing subtle about the cooking either. Delicious garlicky pâtés, leeks vinaigrette, cassoulet, and grilled blood sausage with crisp French fries keep the crowds coming. L, D, Monday–Friday; D, Saturday. No CB.

Le Cyrano. 4143 Geary, Richmond District; 387–1090. In this popular neighborhood restaurant tables are close enough for a chat with your neighbor —who will probably agree that the four-course dinners here, with a choice of over fifteen entrées, are one of the best values around. D, Monday–Saturday. No credit cards.

L'Escargot. 1809 Union, Cow Hollow; 567–0222. Exceptionally good three-course dinners at very affordable prices are found in this intimate, candelit café. The rack of lamb and the snails are among the best in town. D, daily. Wine and beer only. MC, V.

Lipizzaner. 2223 Union, Cow Hollow; 921–3424. The owner-chef is Viennese as are some of his dishes—unbelievingly light wiener schnitzel and pastries such as sachertorte. Most of the cooking in this small cafe, however, is the chef's own style, which is more French than Viennese. The artful presentations alone are worth the price of admission. It's no wonder that his place has been playing to a full house since opening. D, Tuesday–Saturday. Wine and beer only. MC, V.

Zola's. 1722 Sacramento, Midtown; 775–3311. This charming new cafe features a seasonally changing menu based upon regional French cooking, with its own touches. Cassoulet, seafood stews, homemade sausages and pastries are among the specialties. D, Monday–Saturday. Wine only. AE, MC, V.

GREEK AND MIDDLE EASTERN

The foods of Greece and the Middle East have much in common, especially a preponderance of lamb and eggplant dishes. Cooks from the eastern Mediterranean countries also share a widespread fondness for *phyllo,* a paperlike pastry used in a myriad ways: wrapped into triangles around cheese, meats, or vegetables (known as tiropitas or boreks), layered into pies with vegetable and meat fillings, or encasing sweet custards or nuts for desserts. Another signature of these cuisines is pilaf or pilau: sautéed rice or other grains steeped with vegetables and/or nuts and meats.

Moderate

Bali's. 310 Pacific, Jackson Square; 982–5059. (Armenian) *Sedlo*—rack of lamb marinated in pomegranate juice—is the star here, and the menu offers a very limited selection of other entrées. Another star often found here is Rudolf Nureyev, who makes Bali's his headquarters when he's in town, as do many other ballet dancers. L, Monday–Friday; D, Wednesday–Saturday. Major credit cards.

Pasha. 1516 Broadway, Midtown; 885–4477. (Middle Eastern) The ornate, tented dining room and belly dancers can detract from the food. A pity, because the array of Middle-Eastern appetizers is one of the most dazzling shows in town. D, Tuesday–Sunday. Major credit cards.

Xenios. 2237 Polk, Midtown; 775–2800. (Greek) Brick and mirrored walls and tile floors don't keep the noise level down but do enhance the Aegean ambience. The extensive menu is like a culinary tour of the Greek islands. D, Wednesday–Monday. Major credit cards.

Moderate to Inexpensive

Caravansary. 310 Sutter, Downtown; 362–4640. (Middle Eastern–Mediterranean) This attractive dining room is hidden upstairs above one of the city's leading gourmet shops. Dinners, preceded by a platter of Middle Eastern appetizers, offer a wide range of entrées. Lunch features favorites like moussaka and creative sandwiches. L, D, Monday–Saturday. AE, MC, V. (There is a breach at 2263 Chestnut St., in the Marina District; 921–3466.)

Panos'. 4000 24th St., Noe Valley; 824–8000. (Greek-Mediterranean) This bright little neighborhood café provides a limited choice of classic Greek dishes and a fairly broad selection of seafoods sautéed with garlic, herbs, and vegetables. L, D, Monday–Friday; Brunch, D, Saturday–Sunday. Wine and beer only. MC, V.

S. Asimakopoulos Cafe. 288 Connecticut, Potrero Hill; 552–8789. Excellent Greek food at reasonable prices keeps the crowds waiting for seats at the counter or bare-topped tables in this storefront cafe. The menu is large and varied. Convenient to Showplace Center. L, D, Monday–Friday, D, Saturday. Wine and beer only. MC, V.

ITALIAN

The style of Italian food in San Francisco spans the "boot" from the mild cooking of northern Italy, where butter, cream, and subtle seasonings prevail, to the spicy cuisine of the south, redolent with garlic and olive oil. Then there is the style indigenous to San Francisco, known as North Beach Italian—dishes like cioppino (a fisherman's stew) and Joe's special (a mélange of eggs, spinach, and ground beef attributed to several restaurateurs named Joe). Pasta is usually freshly made at the better restaurants, and even if they don't make their own, restaurants have access to fresh noodles from several excellent pasta factories. Tortellini (delicate little noodle crescents stuffed with ground meat) is a specialty of this area.

Expensive

Donatello. Pacific Plaza Hotel, Post and Mason Sts.; 441–7182. (Northern Italian) Intimate, quiet dining amidst silk-paneled walls and paintings and tapestries by Eric Chapman. Superb, low-keyed service; plan to spend 3 to 4 hours at the table. Delicious pastas. Select fish or veal entrées. L, D daily.

Julius Castle. 302 Greenwich, Telegraph Hill; 362–3042. Recently renovated by new owners, this turreted old building clings to the cliffs of Telegraph Hill and commands sweeping views of the bay. Try the unusual agnoletti pasta, seafood, and veal. L, D, Monday–Friday; D, Saturday–Sunday. Major credit cards.

La Pergola. 2060 Chestnut, Marina; 563–4500. An overhead grape arbor is festooned with Chianti bottles and Italian hams, while thousands of wine bottles line the walls of this intimate restaurant. But it is the northern cooking of Tuscan chef Angelo Piccini that draws the crowds. D, daily. Wine and beer only. MC, V.

Modesto Lanzone's. Ghirardelli Square; 771–2880. The best tables are in the loggia room, with its wicker furnishings and beautiful views of the Bay. An extensive menu of 40 selections includes many unusual pastas, plus veal, chicken, beef, lamb and seafood. L, D, Tuesday–Friday; D, Saturday–Sunday. Open late. Major credit cards.

Modesto Lanzone's: Opera Plaza. 601 Van Ness, Civic Center; 928–0400. This new branch has many dishes found at the Ghirardelli restaurant, but is developing its own style with traditional Italian dishes rarely found in this country. Modesto's large collection of contemporary painting and sculpture is on a par with shows at the San Francisco Museum of Modern Art, which is just down the street. L, D, Monday–Friday; D, Saturday. Major credit cards.

Ristorante da Luciano. 2018 Lombard, Marina; 922–1900. Luciano Maggiora, formerly co-owner of La Pergola, presents the the cooking of northern Italy, from simply sautéed veal to intricate concoctions such as chicken baked in clay. Surroundings are somewhat stark, but the service is first-rate. D, Tuesday–Saturday. Wine and beer only. AE, MC, V.

Expensive to Moderate

North Beach Restaurant. 1512 Stockton, North Beach; 392–1587. The copious size of this restaurant and its menu can cause problems in food and service when it is crowded, which is most of the time. But often enough meals here are excellent. Don't miss the antipasto tray. L, D, daily. Major credit cards.

Moderate

Basta Pasta. 1268 Grant Avenue, North Beach; 434–2248. Pasta is made on the premises, and the restaurant's own boat furnishes the "catch of the day." Freshness and informality are the bywords here. There's usually a wait for dinner, when no reservations are accepted. L, D (open late), daily. Wine and beer only. Major credit cards.

Buca Giovanni. 800 Greenwich, North Beach; 776–7766. Giovanni Leoni, long-time chef at Vanessi's, has now opened his own place as a showcase for the dishes of his birthplace: the Serchio Valley in Tuscany. Pastas, made on the premises, are a specialty. D, Monday–Saturday. Wine and beer only. MC, V.

Café Riggio. 4112 Geary, Richmond District; 221–2114. The décor here is contemporary and chic, as is the food—mostly regional Italian dishes adapted for the restaurant's sophisticated clientele. The no-reservations policy translates into long waits on weekends. D, daily. MC, V.

Caffè Sport and Trattoria. 574 Green, North Beach; 981–1251. Owner Tony La Tona is both an artist and chef, covering every inch of walls, ceiling, and furniture with carvings, paintings or collages. Gigantic portions of Sicilian pasta and seafood assure perennial crowds. Funky atmosphere, not-too-fast service. L, D (open very late), Tuesday–Saturday. Wine and beer only. No credit cards.

Ciao. 230 Jackson, Jackson Square; 982–9500. The décor of this trattoria—all white splashed with brass and chrome—is high tech, but the menu features old-fashioned pasta, all made freshly. L, Monday–Saturday; D, daily. AE, MC, V.

La Traviata. 2854 Mission, Mission District; 282–0500. BART stops four blocks from this storefront restaurant, a mecca for opera buffs who like the recorded arias and creative Italian cooking. A large selection of entrées accompanied with pasta and sautéed vegetables. Wine and beer only. D, Tuesday–Sunday. MC, V.

Little City Antipasti Bar. 673 Union, North Beach; 434–2900. Reminiscent of the tapa bars in Spain, Little City offers a variety of snacks from a number of cuisines; go with a group and share. In the evenings pasta and grilled entrees are offered as well. It's very popular and no one seems to mind the noise level from the bar that fills about a third of the space. L, D, Monday–Saturday. AE, MC, V.

Little Italy. 4109 24th Street, Noe Valley; 821–1515. Homesick New Yorkers head here for Sicilian specialties seldom found outside of Manhattan's Little Italy. It's garlicky peasant-style cooking is best enjoyed sharing à la carte dishes family style, in the usually crowded and noisy dining room of this restored Victorian. D, daily. Wine and beer only. MC, V.

Ristorante Parma. 3314 Steiner, Marina; 567–0500. A warm, wonderfully honest trattoria with excellent food at modest prices. The antipasto tray, with a dozen unusual items, is one of the best in town, and the pasta and veal are exceptional. Don't miss the spinach gnocchi, served only on weekends. D, Tuesday–Sunday. Wine only. MC, V.

Washington Square Bar and Grill. 1707 Powell, North Beach; 982–8123. You're apt to rub elbows with the city's top columnists and writers in this no-frills saloon—which seems lately to presume beyond its class. The food is basic North-Beach Italian. Cioppino, Joe's Special, several versions of calamari, pasta, and fresh seafood share honors with basic bar fare such as hamburgers and steaks. Pianist at night. L, D (open late), daily; Sunday Brunch. AE, MC, V.

Moderate to Inexpensive

Capp's Corner. 1600 Powell, North Beach; 989–2589. Owner Joe Capp, always with cap on head and cigar in mouth, greets and seats customers at the long noisy bar and keeps an eye on the narrow Formica tables where diners, elbow to elbow, feast on bountiful six-course, family-style dinners. For the budget-minded or calorie-counters, a shorter dinner includes only soup, salad, and pasta. L, D, Monday–Friday; D, Saturday–Sunday. MC, V.

Tommaso's. 1042 Kearny, North Beach; 398–9696. Long known as Lupo's, this quaint Neapolitan trattoria supposedly introduced pizza to San Francisco. The nineteen varieties from oak-burning ovens are hard to resist, but don't overlook the equally broad selection of pasta or the excellent veal. No reservations—and no bar—means long lines on weekends. D, Wednesday–Sunday. Wine and beer only. MC, V.

JAPANESE

Japanese cooking had little impact on the cuisine of San Francisco until the middle of this century. In the last few decades, however, the number of Japanese restaurants has increased enormously every year. The food of Japan is very healthful, with the emphasis on obtaining the freshest ingredients, an abundance of vegetables, and foods low in cholesterol and high in protein, such as fish, chicken, and tofu (soybean curd). To understand a Japanese menu, you should be familiar with the various basic types of cooking: *yaki,* marinated and grilled foods; *tempura,* fish and vegetables deep-fried in a light batter; *udon* and *soba,* noddle dishes; *domburi,* meats and vegetables served over rice; *ramen,* foods served in broth; *nabemono,* meals cooked in one pot, often at table. *Teppan* is a new Westernized style of Japanese cooking where seafood, meats, and vegetables are cooked on an electric grill built into the dining tables—usually with much dramatic fanfare from the chef. *Sushi* bars are also becoming extremely popular in San Francisco; they offer a selection of *sushi*—vinegared rice combined with an array of vegetables and/or (usually) raw fish—and *sashimi* (raw fish served with dipping sauces). In some Japanese restaurants you will be asked to remove your shoes and put on slippers—a time-honored tradition. Western seating refers to conventional tables and chairs; *tatami* seating is on mats at low tables.

Expensive

Yamato. 717 California at Grant, Chinatown; 397–3456. The city's oldest Japanese restaurant is by far its most beautiful, with inlaid woods, painted panels, a meditation garden, and a pool. There is tatami seating in private shoji-screened rooms; also Western seating and a teppan room. Come for the atmosphere; the menu is somewhat limited and more adventurous dining is found at some of the smaller places. L, D, Tuesday–Friday; D, Saturday–Sunday. Major credit cards.

Moderate

Cho Cho. 1020 Kearny, North Beach; 397–3066. Both counter and table seating in a dimly lit dining room with service by kimono-clad waitresses. Good tempura and sukiyaki prepared at table. Western seating. L, D, Monday–Friday; D, Saturday. Major credit cards.

Kinokawa, 347 Grant, Downtown 956–6085. Sushi fanciers argue forever about the finer points of this or that bar, but most agree that the best act in town and the freshest fish is found at Kinokawa's counter. Sushi bar, Monday–Saturday. Major credit cards.

Inexpensive

Kichihei. 2084 Chestnut at Steiner, Marina; 929–1670. There is both Western and tatami seating in the small dining room that looks into a pretty garden. A good selection of nabe, teriyaki, and tempura, plus many unusual dishes. For a sampling, order the multi-course *omakase ryori* dinner. D, Thursday–Tuesday. Wine and beer only. Major credit cards.

Sanppo. 1702 Post St. at Buchanan, Japantown; 346–3486. This small place has an enormous selection of most every type of Japanese food; yakis, nabe dishes, donburi, udon and soba, and exquisite tempura, plus interesting side dishes. Western seating only. L, D, Tuesday–Saturday; D, Sunday. Wine and beer only. No credit cards.

MEXICAN/LATIN AMERICAN

Considering San Francisco's Mexican heritage and its large Latin American population, there are remarkably few good restaurants specializing in these cuisines. The Mission District contains a swarm of little Mexican and Latin cafés, but in most of them the food at worst is greasy and gummy and at best the cooking is wildly inconsistent. The following choices have demonstrated a high level of consistency over the years.

Moderate

Alejandro's. 1840 Clement, Richmond District; 668–1184. (Peruvian-Spanish-Mexican) Many rate this tops in the city for Latin food. The Mexican "combinations" are as good as any in town, but overshadowed by the marvelous Peruvian and Spanish dishes and by Alejandro's innovations. The dining room is attractive—whitewashed walls and Peruvian artifacts—but noisy. D, daily (open late). Major credit cards.

Cadillac Bar. 1 Holland Court, Moscone Center Area; 543–8226. Patterned after a landmark bar and grill in Laredo, Texas, this barnlike newcomer is noisy and crowded, but outstanding fresh seafood with slightly piquant sauces and typical Mexican fare make the din bearable. L, D, Monday–Friday; D, Saturday. Major credit cards.

Inexpensive

El Sombrero. 5800 Geary, Richmond District; 221–2382. (Mexican) Easily the city's most popular Mexican spot, with long lines to prove it. The menu is standard Cal-Mex—enchiladas, tostadas, tacos, and burritos, with rice, beans, and salad—but everything is meticulously fresh. Even the tortillas are made on the premises. L, D, Tuesday–Saturday. No credit cards.

MOROCCAN

San Francisco's Moroccan restaurants share a similarity of décor, menu, and ritual. Diners are seated on pillows or hassocks at low, round tables and treated to the ancient hand-washing ceremony, with scented water poured from a large brass pitcher; important, because you must eat with your fingers in the North African tradition. Then, course after course, the feast proceeds: a spicy, lentil-based soup drunk from the bowl; platters of vegetables scooped up with Arabic bread; and *bastilla,* slivers of chicken, hard-boiled eggs, and almonds layered with honey and cinnamon in paper-thin pastry dusted with sugar. You may choose from over a dozen entrées, most of which are chicken or lamb stewed with various combinations of fruits and vegetables. The finale is sweet Moroccan pastries washed down with mint tea. The following restaurants offer consistently good banquets at quite moderate prices, considering the abundance of food.

El Mansour. 3123 Clement, Richmond District; 751–2312. D, daily. Wine and beer only. Belly dancers, Sunday–Thursday. AE, MC, V.

Mamounia. 4411 Balboa near 45th Ave., Richmond District; 752–6566. D, Tuesday–Saturday. Wine and beer only. MC, V.

SOUTHEAST ASIAN AND INDIAN

In recent years San Franciscans have seen a tremendous influx in restaurants specializing in the foods of Indonesia, India, Thailand, and Vietnam. The cuisines of these countries share many similarities, but one characteristic in particular: the cooking is always spicy and often *very* hot.

Moderate

Gaylord. 900 North Point (Ghirardelli Square); 771–8822. Embarcadero One; 397–7775. (Indian) The mildly spiced food of northern India is featured here, along with meats and breads cooked over coals in the tandoor oven, and a wide range of vegetarian dishes. The dining rooms at both branches are elegantly furnished with Indian paintings and gleaming silver service. Ghirardelli also offers Bay views and an elaborate buffet lunch on Sundays, with Indian music and dancers. L, D, daily at Ghirardelli. L, D, Monday–Saturday at Embarcadero. Major credit cards.

Khan Toke. 5937 Geary, Richmond District; 668–6654. (Thai) The lovely dining room with garden view is furnished with low tables and cushions. The six-course dinners, with two entrées from an extensive choice, provide a delicious introduction to Thai cooking (the seasoning will be mild, unless you request it hot). Classical Thai dancing on Sundays. D, daily. Wine and beer only. AE, MC, V.

North India, 3131 Webster, Cow Hollow; 931–1556. Small and cozy, this new restaurant has a more limited menu than Gaylord and hotter seasoning. Both tandoori dishes and curries are served, plus a range of breads and appetizers, and everything here is cooked to order. D, daily. Wine and beer only. MC, V.

Sari's. 2459 Lombard, Marina; 567–8715. (Indonesian) This serene little place is noted for its *rijsttafel* (rice table), a wide array of dishes accompanied with rice, which permits a thorough sampling of the restaurant's fare. D, Tuesday–Sunday. Wine and beer only. DC, MC, V.

Moderate to Inexpensive

Garden House (Vietnamese), 133 Clement, Richmond District; 221–3655. This charming little place is a standout among the city's many Vietnamese cafes. The menu is extensive—65 dishes—plus interesting and unusual nightly specials and desserts. D, daily. Wine and beer only. AE, MC, V.

VEGETARIAN/NATURAL FOODS

Vegetarians should also consider Gaylord's (see *Southeast Asian* restaurants), which offers a wide variety of meatless dishes from the Indian Hindu cuisine.

Moderate

Greens at Fort Mason. Building A, Fort Mason, North Point (Marina); 771–6222. Few new restaurants in recent years have caused such a sensation as this beautiful dining room (with Bay views), owned and operated by the Tassajara Zen Center of Carmel Valley. The meatless cooking is spectacularly creative and the bread promises Nirvana. L, Tuesday–Saturday; D, Friday–Saturday. Wine only. MC, V.

CALIFORNIA CULINARY ACADEMY

One of the city's most unusual dining experiences is lunch or dinner at the *California Culinary Academy* (CCA) at 215 Fremont Street in the South-of-Market-Street area. In addition to training professional chefs, the school serves its lessons *dujour* in an attractive dining room, where the public has a clear view of the white-hatted men and women students in the glass-walled kitchen.

What may well be the nation's most sophisticated cooking school opened in 1977 in the former international headquarters of Del Monte Food Products.

CCA's sixteen-month course runs the gamut from basic soup stocks to "advanced French pastries." Tuition is high—over $7,000 for the course—yet CCA graduates yearly 180 cooks trained in the art of classic Continental cuisine. In addition, there is instruction in the selection of wines, both Californian and French.

Many CCA graduates plan to apprentice at a two- or three-star restaurant in France and eventually run small restaurants in various areas of the U.S.

Reservations for either lunch or dinner are essential, usually at least a week in advance. Phone 543-2764 for reservations and serving hours.

BREAKFAST/BRUNCH

The following restaurants, described above, are recommended for breakfast and/or weekend brunch. *Very San Franciscan:* Garden Court. *American:* Campton Place, Courtyard, Elite Cafe, Mama's, Perry's, Doidge's, Eagle Café, Ruby's, Sears' Fine Food, Zuni Cafe. *Greek/Middle Eastern:* Panos'. *Italian:* Washington Square Bar and Grill. *Seafood:* The Waterfront. *Southeast Asian/Indian:* Gaylord. *Cafés* (see below): Buena Vista.

CAFÉS. People-watching is the favorite indoor-outdoor sport of most café-goers; newspaper reading perhaps ranks second. In the following cafés you can also find food to enjoy with your paper and/or the passing show. The latter is the big attraction at *Enrico's Sidewalk Café* (504 Broadway) in North Beach. It's a draw whether the best performance is found at the outdoor tables, where lots of local celebrities hang out, or on the sidewalk where passersby range from neighboring night-club strippers to dark-suited businessmen on their way to Vanessi's. North Beach also boasts a number of typical Italian coffee houses, where you can fantasize that the poet at the next table might be Allen Ginsberg. Two of the most popular are *Caffè Roma* (414 Columbus) and *Caffè Puccini* (411 Columbus). Both serve a wide range of coffee drinks—espresso, cappuccino—and wonderful Italian pastries and sandwiches.

The boisterous bar of the *Buena Vista Café* (2765 Hyde) provides one of the best people-watching shows in town, plus a view of the bay. Best known for its Irish coffee, the BV also serves good, honest food—hefty breakfasts, and sandwiches throughout the day. Up the street in Ghirardelli Square, the show at *Portofino Caffè* is the panoramic view of the bay from the outdoor deck. Sandwiches plus a great selection of chocolate and coffee drinks are the fare here. And art buffs can assuage their hunger at two of the most pleasant cafés in town, located in the *San Francisco Museum of Modern Art* (Van Ness and McAllister) and the *de Young Museum* in Golden Gate Park.

NIGHT LIFE. As a combination of seaport and Gold Rush commercial center San Francisco from its beginnings in 1849 has been known as a hard-drinking, fun-loving night-life center. In recent years, as tourism has become San Francisco's principal industry and many tens of thousands of workers have populated the new high-rise office buildings by day, some of the city's distinctive saloon and cabaret atmosphere has faded away.

Certainly the North Beach area still has the most interesting of bars and clubs, and they are all within easy (and pleasant) walking distance of one another. The "downtown" section, those blocks surrounding Union Square (and including many hotels), has lost much of its World War II-era night life, but here and there are interesting watering holes, some with music. In the Embarcadero Center area (where the high-rises cluster near the waterfront) most of the bars and modern restaurants are jammed at noon and early evening, but thin out by 9:00 P.M. The Fisherman's Wharf–Cannery–Ghirardelli Square strip along the north waterfront is, these days, pretty much overrun by tourists, and the saloon life crowded and undistinguished.

With a large gay community, and one that spends money on entertainment, night life, and booze, San Francisco has whole areas whose lifestyle is notably different from that of the rest of the city. The Castro Street area, for instance, has an East Coast flavor, with many bars and clubs (and restaurants) flourishing into the wee small hours.

In the Mission District most clubs are Spanish-speaking, and in a number of neighborhoods (such as Clement St. in the Richmond District) the flavor is more like an isolated smaller city than a segment of San Francisco.

THE MUSIC CLUBS

San Francisco's saloons and clubs offer a remarkable variety of regular musical presentations. Some are world-famous for certain types of music (jazz, punk rock, etc.), while others mix all manner of styles into their bookings. Except for a very few spots there are no credit cards accepted; the exceptions are the clubs with either a box-office or a full restaurant operation. Regardless, it is always worthwhile to phone ahead to the larger clubs to confirm the night's entertainment and check on showtimes. Door charges at the bigger establishments run from $3.00 to $4.00 to perhaps $12.00 (if a major star is playing at, say, the Great American Music Hall or Wolfgang's).

Bajone's. 1062 Valencia St.; 282–2522. Has modern jazz every night of the week and San Francisco's best jam session on Sunday. A mellow club liked by musicians and fans alike.

Baybrick Inn. 1190 Folsom, 431–8334. A women's music club and bar featuring outstanding local (and occasionally national) talent. A fine new club.

Brick House, 1028 Geary St.; 928–9636. Features folk, blues, comedy, some jazz, and comfortable surroundings. Fairly close to downtown, inexpensive.

Camelot. 3231 Fillmore; 567–4004. A popular bar featuring local jazz of various styles every night of the week. Lively, crowded, busy location.

Chi Chi, 440 Broadway; 392–6213. For years this was a theater-club but now features new-wave, punk, rock and some jazz. A nice room, but the noise level is often overwhelming.

Earthquake McGoon's. Pier 39; 986–1433. Former home of the Turk Murphy Traditional Jazz Band, known worldwide for its New Orleans jazz and ragtime stylings. The club is large, with adequate dance space and San Francisco memorabilia on the walls. Continuous music, with ragtime piano or banjo relieving the band every half hour. Kids okay.

Ghirardelli Square Wine Cellar. 900 North Point; 776–5021. Has folk music of various sorts seven nights a week in a cozy tavernlike atmosphere. Excellent supper-snacks, too.

Kimball's. 300 Grove St.; 861–5555. A jazz room within a restaurant-bar operation. Music most nights by both local and traveling groups. Monday night Jazz Society jams. Good food and drinks; often crowded and chaotic.

The Last Day Saloon. 406 Clement; 387–6343. A two-floored neighborhood restaurant-saloon that presents country, blues, rock, and folk acts, and serves also as a watering hole for the surrounding area. Excellent booking of first-rate local acts (different every night) with a lively crowd, some dancing.

Mabuhay Gardens. 433 Broadway; 956–3315. The oldest punk-rock saloon in town. A Filipino family restaurant until 11:00 P.M., the Mab becomes one of the nation's best known punk emporiums a few minutes later. The sidewalk scene outside the Mab is worth a glance.

Major Pond's. 2801 California St.; 567–5010. May have Dixieland jazz, blues-rock, country music, and boogie-woogie on four successive nights. Very popular (something of a "singles" place), the room is usually crowded; excellent bar, dancing if there's room.

Pasand Lounge, 1875 Union St., 922–4498. Features excellent local jazz combos, a relaxed atmosphere and good bar.

Paul's Saloon. 3251 Scott St.; 922–2456. Has been featuring bluegrass groups nightly for years. A friendly saloon and often crowded. Try Mondays for a lively jam session. Good drinks, no cover charge.

Pier 23. Embarcadero and Pier 23; 362–5125. Epitomizes what most folks think of as a "Dixieland saloon": A waterfront dive, and proud of it, The Pier has noisy old jazz from Wednesday to Sunday and a noisy, boozy crowd to match. There's a café, and good drinks at the bar. Dancing if you want to push aside chairs, tables, and bodies.

Plough & Stars. 116 Clement; 751–1122. Features Irish music, Irish dancing, and Irish drinking. Traveling Irish troupes often drop in. Singing and good times nightly—and, of course, a first-rate bar.

Spatz, 353 Jefferson, 771–3330. A favorite jazz jam site for mainstream stylists (swing, trad, bop, etc.) and a peculiarly laid out bar and restaurant. In the midst of Fishermen's Wharf.

The Stone. 412 Broadway; 391–8282. Part of a triumvirate—Keystone Palo Alto and Keystone Berkeley are the partners in the conglomerate. Featured at all three clubs is an amalgam of rock, reggae, blues, occasional jazz, and whatever. The Stone is a big refurbished older show-club; a young crowd, often chaotic

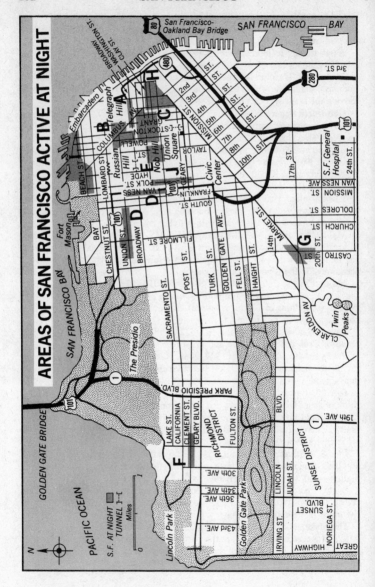

AREAS OF SAN FRANCISCO ACTIVE AT NIGHT

presentations, adequate bar, some dancing—if the act on stage is dynamite, the Stone is a great place to hear it.

Washington Square Bar & Grill. 1707 Powell (North Beach); 982–8123. A chic, trendy bar and restaurant with plenty of old elbow-benders at the bar. The nightly piano music makes it a superb place to have a drink and listen to keyboard legends. The music format hasn't changed in years—veteran Fats Waller–Jelly Roll Morton specialist Burt Bales plays early in the week, Norma (Jack's sister) Teagarden is there too, as is stride-pianist Mike Lipskin, usually on Sunday. Go late for piano and booze.

THE MUSIC "HALLS" AND A CLASSIC SUPPER CLUB

The only difference here with the "Music Clubs" category is that these establishments tend to book better-known acts (often on national tour) and set a specific nightly schedule. Also, they *may* take credit cards, especially if tickets are bought in advance through such a computerized operation as BASS or Ticketron. Although specific reservations cannot be made, tickets usually will be held at the door or box office for these venues; thus, you at least get in.

Wolfgang's. 901 Columbus; 441–4333. In July 1983, impresario Bill Graham closed his Old Waldorf nightclub operation, moved it into the former site of the

---

A Broadway. Seedy; sex clubs. Vanessi's, Enrico's Café, and Finocchio's for its revue are OK. Area could be dangerous after midnight.

B North Beach. Lots of cafés, restaurants, bars, and music clubs. An extremely popular area for both locals and visitors, but not much street life.

C Chinatown. Many restaurants. Nighttime strolling and shopping. Especially crowded weekends.

D Union St./Fillmore/Van Ness. Great bars, cafés, restaurants. Boutiques and upscale shops. First-run movie houses on Union and Van Ness. Union is popular for strolling and *is* San Francisco's singles street. Avoid Fillmore south of Sutter (Western Addition).

E Nob Hill. Deluxe hotel bars and restaurants, sky rooms. Area is fashionable and expensive; very little strolling.

F Clement St. Reasonably priced ethnic restaurants and bars, some clubs. A polyglot neighborhood.

G Castro. The heart of the City's gay community. Lots of bars and restaurants. Intense street action.

H Financial District. A number of bars and restaurants; a few clubs. Relatively quiet (to very quiet) street scene, but the spots are active weekdays right after work into early evening.

I Northern Waterfront. Pier 39, Fisherman's Wharf, and surrounding areas have numerous bars and restaurants. Strolling is popular, especially in summer and on weekends, along Beach and Jefferson Sts. and the end of the Embarcadero.

J Polk St. From Geary to Clay, lots of bars, night clubs, some restaurants. A heavy concentration of gay places between Post and Pine. Late evening could be dangerous.

Mission St. area northeast of the Castro (not coded on map) is a largely Hispanic area active at night.

Franklin St. area behind Civic Center (not coded). New clubs sprouting up around Performing Arts Center.

Boarding House club, and renamed it. Wolfgang's has a touch of an old-fashioned, fan-shaped supper club, with a large stage, perfect sight lines, a small balcony, and excellent sound and lights. Big-name rock groups, some rhythm-and-blues, jazz, Latin, folk, etc. Bookings are usually one- or two-night affairs, and sellouts are common. Door charges may run over $10 for a big act; drink minimums enforced; a well run club.

The Great American Music Hall. 850 O'Farrell; 885–0750. The most impressive music room in the city, perhaps the nation. Gilded ceiling, plush carpeting, a European balcony, and the best sound system in town. The GAMH is carefully managed to bring in only performers who can do well. Thus locals and traveling groups, big-name singers (Sarah Vaughan, Carmen McRae), big bands (Basie, Herman), and all the great ones mix with fine local favorites of all kinds of pop music persuasion. First-rate bar, gracious service, impressive short-order food: a San Francisco best-buy for jazz, folk, country, comedy, etc.

The Venetian Room, Fairmont Hotel. Mason & California (Nob Hill); 772–5000. One of the few supperclubs left in the nation, the Venetian Room continues to present very big names on a two-week booking policy, starting usually on Tuesday nights. Tony Bennett, Joel Grey, Anthony Newley, Pointer Sisters, Ella Fitzgerald, Sammy Davis, Jr., other greats have played the room many times. Two shows: one about 9:45 P.M., the other shortly after midnight. The dinner show, with all complications, will cost about $60.00 per person; the midnight show, carefully handled (and, perhaps, taking a tour bus) can cost you only $10.00 or so per person. The room and service are marvelous; the food mediocre; the shows usually quite fine—and you're close to big stars. Dancing.

CABARET STYLE

"Cabarets" in San Francisco are constantly opening and closing; offered is entertainment (usually singers), drinks and sometimes food.

132 Bush. 362–4484. A multi-floored drinking and eating establishment with a small cabaret room on the top. Cozy atmosphere for twilight performances.

1177 Club. 1177 California St.; 776–2101. A small saloon featuring cabaret shows and light jazz acts. Charming and intimate; good drinks. Some fine little shows have begun at the 1177, which is next door to Mama's in the Gramercy Towers.

Fanny's. 4230 18th St.; 621–5570. Very well run, serves good food and drinks, and has entertainment every night. All the city's cabaret stars play or have played Fanny's. A good place to drop in if you're in the Castro district.

Mame's, Bay & Mason Sts.; 986–4553. Opened recently on the site of the legendary Veneto Restaurant. A large "Gondola Room" has cabaret entertainment nightly. Attractive, convenient, good drinks and imaginative bookings.

The Plush Room. 940 Sutter St.; 885–6800. Presents cabaret singers, light jazz groups, little musicals, and showcase productions almost every night. A comfortable, small room with particularly excellent service and lighting.

Purple Onion. 140 Columbus Ave.; 781–0835. The small basement club where the Kingston Trio, Phyllis Diller, the Smothers Brothers and many others started. Two shows a night (usually packed with tour-bus customers); good local talent. The Onion doesn't cater to the general community any more and is ignored by most natives.

DRINKS AND PIANISTS

The best resident saloon pianist in San Francisco is Peter Mintun, a fixture at **L'Etoile's Lounge** in the Huntington Hotel on Nob Hill; 771–1529. The drinks are good but expensive, the crowd large and noisy, and Mintun weaves through everything from old pops and show tunes to definitive readings of Fats Waller and Zez Confrey keyboard classics.

At the **Stanford Court Hotel,** 905 California St.; 989–1910, the Fournou's Ovens restaurant bar has background piano, good drinks, and a view of two cable-car lines; the **Hyatt Regency Hotel,** Market and California Sts.; 788–1234, has good—but expensive—drinks in its atrium lobby and fine small-combo jazz playing many evenings a week.

The **Starlite Roof** of the Sir Francis Drake Hotel, Powell and Sutter; 392–7755, has a good view and drinks to go along with various musical activities—sometimes there is even a musical revue in the room, and there is always dancing; hors d'oeuvres early in the evening.

The **Redwood Room** in the Clift Hotel, Geary and Taylor Sts.; 775–4700, is an elegant spot, nicely located as a place to meet friends. There is piano music and good drinks; famed restaurant alongside. The **Compass Rose** in the Hotel St. Francis on Union Square; 397–7000, is a new name for a favorite old meeting place for San Franciscans. Drinks, piano sounds, and lots of Orientalia. Also offering drinks and piano music in the Union Square area are: The **Curtain Call,** 456 Geary; the **Geary Cellar,** 413 Geary (both tied in to the Geary and Curran Theater crowd), and **Lefty O'Doul's,** a hofbrau-style saloon which is noisy, often has a good pianist, and is dripping with baseball nostalgia—it's at 333 Geary; kids okay.

The **New Bell Saloon,** 1203 Polk St.; 775–6905, for some time has presented a combined piano-cabaret entertainer named David Kelsey; he's very good on his own and even better with the Pure Trash Dixieland band on Sundays. Good drinks, crowded, mostly gay.

Casablanca. 2323 Polk; 441–2244. Has a slicked-up Moroccan décor, Continental food, and a splendid lounge for drinking and listening to such fine jazz pianists as Merrill Hoover, the resident keyboardist when he's not on tour. Open for food, drink, and music well after midnight.

Curtain Call, 456 Geary; 474–5918. A noisy, theater-oriented piano bar, whose walls are covered with 8x10 glossies (most autographed) of performers who have worked the Geary or Curran theaters across the street. Delis on either side of the club, too.

Gold Dust, 247 Powell; 397–1695. A noisy, busy "Barbary Coast" style saloon that features piano jazz in the ragtime and New Orleans styles.

THE THEATER CLUBS

Since all San Francisco legitimate theaters have full bars as part of their operation, the "theater club" term can be used to cover the smaller musicals and theatricals which often as not are playing in clubs and often serve drinks during the performances. Always phone ahead for these venues; their bookings are sporadic, to say the least.

The Alcazar Theater. 650 Geary; 775–7100. Rather consistently booked, usually with musicals. Wine, beer, soft drinks, and a nice lounge.

Club Fugazi. 678 Green St.; 421–4222. Not really a club at all, but the home of San Francisco's longest-running and wildly successful musical revue, *Beach Blanket Babylon.* Once an Italian social club's hall, Fugazi was often used (prior to BBB) for jazz and folk concerts, musical revues, and poetry readings. Drinks are available, but it's not a "club."

Finocchio's. 506 Broadway; 982–9388. Has been presenting hour-long revues with female impersonators for so long most people forget it was once just an upstairs nightclub. Primarily a tourist attraction now; the natives have long since gone elsewhere.

The Open Theater. 441 Clement St.; 386–3086. Sometimes a musical theater, sometimes a comedy room, sometimes presenting jazz and blues. Whatever is on stage, however, the bar continues to function—food, too. Small, congenial, fun.

On-Broadway Theater. 435 Broadway; 398–0800. Presents musicals (often jazz-oriented) most of the time. It was here that Jon Hendricks' "Evolution of the Blues" debuted. Full bar, some service during shows. On weekends after the stage performances the On Broadway becomes a punk-rock venue, presenting acts booked by the Fab Mab, which is downstairs.

The Warfield Theater. 982 Market St.; 775–7722. Part of impresario Bill Graham's empire presenting in concert form many of the rock, pop, and blues acts which are "too big" for Graham's Old Waldorf night club. A full bar operates on the mezzanine.

BOOZE AND BELLY LAUGHS

Comedy in clubs goes back a long way in San Francisco; in recent times it hit its peak, perhaps, when Mort Sahl, Lenny Bruce, Jonathan Winters, and Woody Allen played the hungry i and frequently hung around town, sitting in at other clubs.

These rooms now are devoted almost entirely to comedy; many other clubs frequently book comedy acts (such as the Punch Line, Great American Music Hall, Old Waldorf, and Boarding House):

Cobb's. 2069 Chestnut; 563–9658. Round-the-clock comedy with major local talent on weekends and auditions at other times. One of the city's big-four comedy rooms—with Holy City Zoo, Other Cafe and Punch Line. A wonderful neighborhood, too.

The Holy City Zoo. 408 Clement (Richmond); 752–2846. Began the current comedy rage years ago. Robin Williams and other successful comics broke in here, and frequently drop by when they're in town. There is always something going on here—give a call first and find out what new shows they're presenting. Beer and wine only.

The Other Café. 100 Carl St.; 681–0748. Presents full-bills of comics almost every night, including some of the bigger TV comedy names. A smallish room nicely suited to its current use. Beer, wine, and food.

The Punch Line. 444 Battery St.; 474–3801. Booked by the week, the Punch Line headlines major comics, with a couple of lesser lights opening up each show. A perfect room for comics with full bar, good sound, and a comfortable feeling.

Valencia Rose. 766 Valencia; 552–1445. A popular gay hangout, which features gay comedy regularly but also presents folk, jazz, musical revues, rock, etc. An interesting scene—and the comedy can get pretty ripe.

SOME OF THE BEST BARS

Everyone has favorite bars, especially in a hard-drinking town like San Francisco. Atmosphere, view, congeniality, special drinks, location—all contribute. Here are a couple of dozen of San Francisco's best.

The Albatross. 155 Columbus; 434–3344. A spiffed-up bit of authentic San Francisco history. Sometimes crowded (there's a restaurant adjoining), this is a fascinating place with a good bar.

Buena Vista. 2765 Hyde St. at the Northern Waterfront; 474–5044. Not a "best bar," but it is probably the best-known San Francisco bar and restaurant, because it is supposedly where Irish coffee was introduced into the United States—and that is what people, mostly tourists, go there to drink, till 2:00 A.M. There *is* a nice view of the waterfront, if you can maneuver to be in the layer of people on that side of the bar. Good breakfasts, too.

Carnelian Room. 555 California; 433–7500. At the top of the Bank of America Building—highest in the city. Something of an executive's bar, with elegant furnishings, about the best view of the Bay Area, and good, reasonably priced drinks.

Caspian. 517 Clement; 387–0603. A neighborhood bar that is more a "cocktail lounge"; well appointed, good drinks, and a table with fruit, crackers, cheeses, and (usually) caviar.

Chelsea Place. 641 Bush St.; 989–2524. One of the better dart-bars, with a number of boards and lots of dart-tossing. A common interest among the patrons makes for a cozy, friendly atmosphere.

Cookie's Star Buffet. 708 Kearny St.; 362–5167. Maybe more interesting to locals than to visitors, this is just an old-time, raunchy bar in a good location tended by Cookie Picetti, a North Beach character for many a year. (Until the late 1960s the San Francisco Hall of Justice stood close to Cookie's—thus his much-displayed contacts with the San Francisco Police Department.)

Day's. 24 Ellis; 421–2894. Slightly down-at-the-heels, Day's is a leftover from somewhat better Ellis and Market Street eras. Drinks are strong and inexpensive, there are darts, pool, backgammon, and indications that Day's has been "home" to many a downtowner over the years.

Eagle Café. Pier 39; 433–3689. For decades the Eagle was an Embarcadero legend—redevelopment tore the original down but, surprisingly, the "new" Eagle has settled into the old tradition and even looks like the original. Breakfast and lunch are served, kids are okay, the view is great, the drinks better.

Edinburgh Castle. 950 Geary; 885–4074. All kinds of beers, ales, hard booze, darts, fish and chips—plus an old-time jukebox and bagpipes on the weekends. Naturally, this sort of pub draws a crowd that, in itself, is part of the action. Lots of tables (it's a big place), so you can have some privacy if you want.

Gino and Carlo. 548 Green St.; 421–0896. Taken for granted by many North Beach habitues as the most solid of mainstream Italian bars. Powerful drinks, a pool table, noisy across-the-room conversations, constant phone messages—if you want atmosphere, this is it. But there is a bit of the "closed-club" feeling.

Happy Valley Bar. Sheraton Palace Hotel, Market and New Montgomery; ·392–8600. Buried inside the vaultlike Palace, the Happy Valley is a little gem. Old San Francisco surroundings with swing-era records, good drinks, and intimate tables.

Henri's Room at the Top. Hilton Hotel tower, O'Farrell and Mason; 771–1400. Has lots of windows, snacks during the cocktail hour, and leisurely service which gives you time to enjoy the views.

Hoffman's. 619 Market St.; 421–1467. More an old-fashioned businessman's meat-and-potatoes restaurant than it is a bar—but, still, it's a solid place to have a couple of belts, too. Comfortably crowded with hard-headed banking types at lunch; a bit of Old San Francisco, when men-only midday dinner establishments were the rule (see *Sam's Grill* and *Tadich's* in the *Dining Out* section for similar atmosphere).

S. Holmes, Esq., 480 Sutter; 398–8900. A big favorite with the Baker Street crowd of Sherlock Holmes addicts. The surroundings are as authentic as possible, with all manner of Holmes memorabilia about. Many intimate tables and booths; in the Holiday Inn, Union Square.

House of Shields. 39 New Montgomery St.; 392–7732. Another old-time south-of-Market saloon (across from the Palace Hotel) that has resisted modernization. If you're bar-hopping late in the day, a drink at House of Shields, then a walk across the street to the Palace, a look into the Garden Court, perhaps a glance at the Maxfield Parrish painting in the Palace's Pied Piper Bar, then a sip at the Happy Valley Bar *(q.v.)*, will give you a pretty heavy dose of what pre-World-War-I San Francisco was all about.

Jerry and Johnny. 81 3rd St.; 362–7028. A south-of-the-"slot" (Market St.) saloon of the old school. Old, and aware of it; a bit seedy and loaded with old newspaper memorabilia (three major San Francisco papers were once within a block or so), J&J has lusty drinks, a fascinating clientele, some curious sandwiches, and is about all that's left of the once-famous San Francisco newspapermen's bars.

John's Grill. 63 Ellis; 986–DASH—the "Dash" is for Dashiell Hammett. A good-enough bar near the Tenderloin that figures in *The Maltese Falcon* and others of Hammett's that involve Sam Spade. Loaded with Hammett memorabilia.

Li Po. 916 Grant Ave.; 982–0072. A sort of in-bar (or in-joke) among Caucasian barhounds around Chinatown and North Beach. It's amazing how many diehard San Franciscans think of Li Po as their own private discovery. First-rate drinks, an unbelievable mishmash of décor, some strange jukebox discs, and a cozy atmosphere.

Main Stem. 2 Turk; 776–3330. Originally a beer, sausage, and sandwich saloon (or brauhaus), and really hasn't changed much since the World War I days. Cluttered with pictures not only of old San Francisco but also of old America in its simpler days. Inelegant neighborhood—to say the least—but a good midday food-and-drink spot; inexpensive and memorable.

New Pisa. 550 Green St.; 362–4726. May be what you get into when you're looking for Gino and Carlo *(q.v.)*, since they're neighbors. This is a Bay Area sports fan's delight, especially if you remember Stanford's Bobby Grayson, or the Seals' Joe DiMaggio, or Cal's 1938 Rose Bowl team. Less hectic than Gino and Carlo, and somewhat larger, New Pisa seems best in late afternoon when there is room, idle conversation, and little interest in what's happening outside the doors.

Peer Inn. Pier 33 (Embarcadero at the end of Bay St.); 788–1411, is about the best of the waterfront saloons that have escaped tourist-trappings. There is a restaurant in the structure, and enough room so that waterfront shipping activity can be observed while drinking.

Penny Farthing Pub. 679 Sutter; 771–5155. Close to many downtown hotels, yet it has a distinctly British village-pub feeling; the food seems also to reflect an authentic British-pub touch.

San Marcos (or "Café" San Marcos). 2367 Market St.; 861–4186. A mod restaurant-bar with considerable space, good drinks, unusual views, and a mostly gay clientele. A good spot to use as a base for checking out the Castro St. area's shops, clubs, and saloons.

Schroeder's. 240 Front St.; 421–4778. San Francisco's best German restaurant with a century-old reputation. There is a wonderful bar, adjacent to the restaurant, which serves fine brew (of course) and well-made hard stuff. If you can't make the restaurant here, a drink at the bar will give you a nice feeling for the establishment.

Templebar. 1 Tillman Pl; 362–6661. From the 1930s until, certainly, 35 years later, this was (along with now long-gone El Prado) *the* shopping-area bar. Husbands, wives, paramours, girl-and-boy friends, and all manner of professional folk used it as their elbow-bending downtown home. The bar is still there, the drinks are still fine, the snacks are plentiful at the end of the working day, and many still think of the Templebar as *their* San Francisco bar.

(Specs') Twelve Adler. 12 Adler Pl.; 421–4112. A wonderful old bar that's hard to find, which is to its advantage, and loaded with memorable San Francisco mementos. Get to the Broadway-Columbus intersection, walk south from the southeast corner and you'll pass Adler Pl.; if you're inattentive, you'll miss it. Too bad—a couple of drinks at Specs' (even the name is obscure) will expose you to an unusual slice of North Beach.

Tosca. 242 Columbus; 986–9651. Virtually next door to Twelve Adler (see above), and so give it a whirl, too. For decades Tosca was assumed to be the home of espresso and cappuccino. It was a North Beach ritual to leave an Italian restaurant (*any* of them) and go to Tosca for coffees, desserts, opera-on-records, and the probability of meeting old friends. The old generation has passed at Tosca now, but the joint's the same—including the perfectly awful pseudo-Italian wall murals.

Vesuvio. 255 Columbus; 362–3370. Across the street from both Tosca and Adler Pl. (see above) and if you can handle it, worth visiting (along with the Albatross) in a night's bar-tour. Far more a residence-bar, with tables full of animated conversation, loners reading by themselves, and notable disinterest with the North Beach commercial whirl out on the street, Vesuvio comes closest to the Beatnik bars of the 1950s—and Lawrence Ferlinghetti's City Lights Bookshop is across the alley.

SINGLES BARS

Perhaps better identified by the indelicate term "pickup bars," what is involved here are a few of the saloons which are especially popular at the end of the work day with (generally) young people. Many, of course, continue to be packed all night; and a number of the bars mentioned elsewhere in this section also have *their* "singles" action. Hors d'oeuvres, music, dancing, and hubbub are built-in aspects of these establishments.

Balboa Café. 3199 Fillmore; 922–4595. Very popular, in a crowded working-singles residential area.

Dartmouth Social Club. 3200 Fillmore; 922–8515. Across from the Balboa (see above) and somewhat newer, the DSC has all the requirements of the genre—an Ivy League/British tone, ferns, long bar, open space, plenty of bartenders.

"Embarcadero Center" (actually two saloons—The Upper Level, 956–8768; and The Holding Company, 986–0797). These are really hot bars these days, filled with office workers from Embarcadero Center 1 and 2. Upper Level, somewhat older, has excellent finger-food if you can get to it. Great places to try new pickup techniques.

Harrington's. 245 Front St.; 392–7595. An immensely popular saloon patronized by the singles crowd from nearby office towers as well as the older Irish drinkers. Lively, noisy, convivial; the unofficial headquarters of S.F.'s uninhibited St. Patrick's Day celebration.

Hart's California Street Restaurant and Bar. 230 California; 434–2525. As Harrington's reflects a certain officeworker tone, Hart's (farther up toward Montgomery St.) may have more junior executives. Plenty of hors d'oeuvres and singles, too.

Henry Africa's. 2260 Van Ness Ave.; 982–7044. Just as the Balboa, Dartmouth, and Pierce St. Annex *(q.v.)* are a triumvirate, so are Henry Africa's, Lord Jim's, and the Royal Oak: all are within easy walking distance, each has crystal-clear windows, mirrors, and bar accessories. Henry Africa's, the oldest of the three though now at a new location, sports considerable "authentic" H. Africa memorabilia and a model railroad train—also good food and drink.

The Iron Horse. 19 Maiden La. off Union Square; 362–8133. One of San Francisco's original singles saloons, it has especially good snacks, and a respected restaurant, too. With the emergence in the last decade of the Embarcadero Center business community, The Iron Horse has been geographically shifted aside—but is still a good bar for making friends.

Lord Jim's. 1500 Broadway; 928–3015. Situated at Henry Africa's original location, it is perhaps the most *observed* bar in the city; thousands of cars a day pass the Broadway and Polk intersection and Lord Jim's Tiffany lamps and (in early evening) hundreds of young drinkers and seekers.

MacArthur Park. 607 Front St.; 398–5700. Also part of the Embarcadero (i.e., new) business community, MacArthur Park is always jammed around 5:30 P.M. not only for the booze and socializing, but also because of a lavish hors d'oeuvres spread.

Paoli's. 565 Commercial St.; 781–7115. An older saloon with the best free food spread in town, it has good big drinks, music, and a usually fascinating bunch of people; a little "older," this crowd is also more sophisticated.

Perry's. 1944 Union; 922–9022. *The* "in" bar in San Francisco, it is, in essence, a "singles" or "pickup" bar all the time. Always crowded and often jammed, there is a long bar, lots of tables, decent food, and the feeling that many in the saloon are there either to observe the hopefully famous personages who are in attendance, or to be seen themselves. Button-down shirts fit in here.

Pierce St. Annex. 3138 Fillmore; 567–1400. One of the Balboa-Dartmouth triumvirate, but with the youngest clientele by far, this is one of a number of similarly named saloons around the country. Lots of action, especially later in the evening; rock-dancing, too.

Royal Exchange. 301 Sacramento St.; 956–1710. A combination of English pub and American fern-bar; nicely located between the old and new business areas and usually filled with a blend of singles from each.

LET'S DANCE—WITH DRINKS AROUND

A combination of California state laws (through the Alcoholic Beverage Control law, "ABC" to all) and San Francisco city statutes results in multiple complications for clubs, restaurants, cabarets, and bars that might want to encourage dancing on the premises. The result, of course, is that those establishments which publicize their nightly dancing are very few compared to those saloons and clubs that actually *do* have dancing. The same sort of foolishness also allows teenagers into places of entertainment which serve liquor *if* food is available. Thus you'll find many saloons advertising "food available," although it may mean a microwave oven and a collection of frozen sandwiches and dishes listed on a dittoed "menu." Thus, the Fairmont Hotel or Earthquake McGoon's have no age restriction on admission (although their music may not at all appeal to teenagers) yet, say, The Stone or the Old Waldorf, both of whom present music highly appealing to teenagers, have to somehow contrive a "kitchen" in order to let under-21s into their joints.

If you're interested in dancing, then check through the other listings included (many indicate dancing) and note these, too:

Alexis. 1001 California St. at Mason; 771–1001. The cocktail-lounge at Alexis, which is like a Moroccan fantasy, also doubles as a mini-disco. An elegant, expensive room, but a good way to end an evening at the top of Nob Hill; Alexis Restaurant is very fashionable, with prices to match.

Cesar's Latin Palace. 3140 Mission; 826–8899. A huge warehouse-like ballroom, with bar, bandstand, almost acres of tables and dance floor, and a nightly procession of Latin bands coming and going. Parking is easy, the beat is strictly Latin, and if you're out for a salsa night this is a good start. There is an admission charge at the door, fairly expensive drinks; safe parking, and you're close to some late-night Latin-food emporiums in the Mission District.

Harrison St. Club. 715 Harrison; 495–8660. Typical of what's happened to virtually all of San Francisco's disco palaces—either they've bellied-up or they've ceased being "private" and have brought in new-wave (punk) bands some nights to spell the record-spinning and, it's hoped, to bring in some new, younger, customers. Harrison St. Club is a restaurant, dance floor, lavish spread —but you'll have to phone ahead to find out what's happening.

Earl's (at Bali's). 310 Pacific; 982–5059. A small, seemingly private mini-disco that has always been quite cordial when we've dropped in—although there's a feeling that maybe it's a private club. The location, five minutes from Broadway and Columbus, is superb—there's a good bar, and you might run into some famous people. Bali's as a restaurant and focal-point for high-end ballet folk is quite famous—you might even disco-dance with Rudy Nureyev; you also might not.

I-Beam. 1748 Haight St. at Cole; 668–6006. A huge, relatively well-appointed room with a disco setup and bar. Like many of the dance-to-records clubs, the I-Beam now often features new-wave (i.e., "punk") bands playing live or new-wave records rather than the old-styled "disco" records.

Lehr's Cabaret Disco. 726 Sutter (in the Canterbury Hotel); 673–1717. More like a tea-dance room than a disco, there is dancing room, mainstream disco music, bar, and lots of ferns. Convenient—near Union Square.

Maxwell's Plum, 900 North Point (in Ghirardelli Square); 441–4104. The disco aspect of this lavish spread is more, we think, to continue the tradition of other Maxwell Plum establishments—those built when discos were "in." But it's a lively room and bar—mostly tourists, but attractive ones. Bar and restaurant, of course.

Mumm's. 2215 Powell; 433–3414. Established in the height of the disco-craze, Mumm's was a membership-only disco and restaurant-bar. It "went public" later on, if dinner-reservations were made. A convenient Fisherman's Wharf location, and built for dancing with a fancy sound system. Better phone first—Mumm's may have gone into a new phase by the time you get to San Francisco.

Oz. At the top of the Hotel St. Francis Tower, 335 Powell; 397–7000. A great disco-dance room; it's hard to tell if it is still "private" or not, but give a call. The view is marvelous, the drinks fine (service good, too), and the ambience encourages a good long evening and many new friends.

Park Exchange. 600 Montgomery; 983–4800. In the shadow of the Transamerica Pyramid, favored by the Financial District set—disco, drinks, etc.

Roland's. 3309 Fillmore; 921–7774. An old-fashioned "cocktail lounge" that has been offering music for decades. There may be a big-band around, or a pianist, or a small combo; whatever, if there's room there is dancing—and good drinks, no door charge. Close to Lombard St.'s motel row.

The Stud. 1535 Folsom; 863–6623. A long-standing and representative example of the many S&M, leather & metal, male gay saloon-and-dance halls in San Francisco. Although straights are certainly admitted, generally it's a world quite unknown to outsiders—especially those outside the San Francisco gay community. There is lots of drinking, lots of picking-up, constant loud music and dancing, and considerable action outside—well into the early morning hours.

Trocadero Transfer. 520 Fourth St.; 495–0185. This is about all that's left of the once-flourishing commercial disco scene. Still very popular, the Trocadero has restrictions, memberships, regulations, etc., but it's *the* place if you're still working out *Saturday Night Fever.* Phone first—there are new "rules" every week; sometimes there are live disco-soul artists around.

OAKLAND

by
VERN HAWKINS

Vern Hawkins, an East Bay resident, is a freelance travel writer and contributor to national magazines and newspapers across the country. Since 1965 he has produced and written travel films for KTVU in Oakland and KCRA in Sacramento.

Oakland will probably never shake its image as "that other city across the bay." It's only 8½ miles across the Bay Bridge from San Francisco—a 75¢ toll one way, and no charge the other. The joke is still repeated, "It doesn't cost anything to go to Oakland." But now San Francisco has stopped laughing. While San Franciscans have argued over just what to do with their aging waterfront, Oakland has prospered by expanding her modern container-cargo facilities. Oakland, with 19 miles of port, is the fifth largest port in the world. The new port meant new jobs and a new look for Oakland.

The city (population 328,000) begins on the bay and winds up on rolling hills 1,900 feet up. It is ringed by regional parks. Along the way are charming old houses on winding streets. Like many old cities, it's a town made of neighborhoods and districts—each a little different from the other.

The climate is mild year-round: cool summers with some of San Francisco's fog that spills across the bay, but clear by noon.

A section of downtown is dotted with some lovely old Victorians in various states of battered elegance. Commercial "Vics" line both sides of Ninth St. between Broadway and Washington. In the 1870s, they were the bustling downtown center. The Delger Building on the northwest corner of Ninth and Broadway housed the city's first newspaper, the *Oakland News*. The southwest corner hosts the Wilcox Building, which was the town's first brick building. Now, only a few pawnshops occupy the graying relics of another era. They are protected by zoning controls and slated for restoration. For a closer look at some of Oakland's downtown neighborhoods there are free guided walking tours every Wednesday or Saturday at 1:00 P.M. Call Oakland Tours at (415) 273-3234 or 273-3831.

There are also areas of Oakland that visitors can afford to miss. The city is plagued with every problem common to urban "core" cities. Both unemployment and the crime rate are high in the area known as the "flatlands." For the sixth-largest city in the state, its downtown lacks a thriving center.

But that doesn't mean it's not worth exploring. Jack London Square, on the waterfront, is a mixture of lure and lore. A string of restaurants overlooking the harbor offer pleasant if not exceptional dining. And here is found the memorabilia of the author, including the sod-roofed Yukon cabin where Jack London spent the winter of 1897. It's now the First and Last Chance Saloon, located near the estuary where London pirated oysters in the late 1800s. The square is mainly a place for drinks and dining. Seagoing tankers parading by offer changing scenery. For shopping, Jack London Village is just next door. It's a weather-worn-looking two-level complex of 100 specialty shops and restaurants.

The area begins at the foot of Broadway, where the tiny port village of Oakland got its start. There is ample and inexpensive parking and frequent bus service to the area.

Not too far away is the brief but busy block called the Bret Harte Boardwalk, 500 Fifth St.—home of yet another author who wrote of the Gold Rush era. It's now a row of specialty shops and restaurants attractively renovated in Victorian buildings.

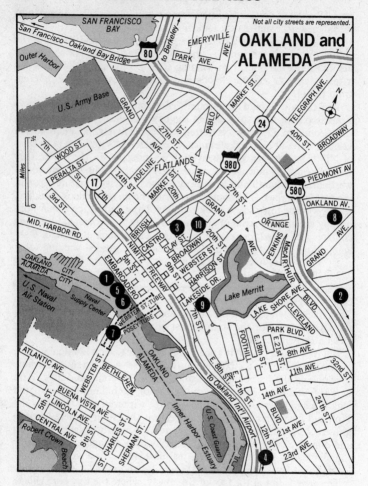

Points of Interest

1) Bret Harte Boardwalk
2) To Chabot Planetarium
3) City Hall/BART Station
4) To Oakland—Alameda County Coliseum
5) Jack London Square
6) Jack London Village
7) Mariner Square
8) Morcom Rose Garden
9) Oakland Museum
10) Paramount Theatre

At 20th and Broadway is the classic Art Deco showplace, the Paramount Theatre, opened in 1931. Its creator was architect Timothy Pfleuger, who also designed I. Magnin, the Castro Theatre, the Top of the Mark, and the Pacific Telephone Building—all located in San Francisco. The League of Historic American Theatres estimates that more than 50 major theater houses have been saved around the country and Oakland's Paramount is one of the best restorations. It's now a state historical landmark, restored in 1973, and a spark to area redevelopment. It is also the home of the Oakland Symphony.

Lake Merritt also offers music and some history. It has been there only since the 1870s. A former tidal marshland, it is now an attractive oasis in the midst of the city. Its 155 acres (the world's biggest saltwater body within a city proper) is ringed by more than three miles of paths, well worn by joggers, strollers, and naturalists. Its shoreline and islands are winter stopovers for migratory waterfowl. Pause for a lecture offered by park naturalists. Its lakeside park beckons bicyclists, picnickers, lawn bowlers, and for boaters there is everything from canoes to paddleboats for rent. While parents tune into an afternoon concert at the bandstand, the youngsters can see puppet shows at nearby Children's Fairyland or escape on its rides and enjoy its settings based on Mother Goose rhymes.

Nearby on the lakeshore stands the classic Camron-Stanford house, built in 1876. Guided tours are offered through the Italianate Victorian, restored to its 1880 vintage. It was a private home until 1907, then housed the Oakland Museum.

Today's Oakland Museum, also within walking distance of Lake Merritt, is a unique four-block work of art camouflaged by lush vegetation. Many visitors, standing beside it, have trouble finding it. The museum is a museum of California, covering the state's arts, natural sciences and history, featuring both permanent and changing exhibitions. More than a million visitors wander through its three levels each year. Foreign visitors, especially, make it a must as an overview during their California tour. Its art work depicts California when it was young. Its relics range from Spanish armor to an 1890 fire engine. The Natural Sciences Gallery wanders from the seacoast to the deserts and mountains, a journey that can require some nourishment. So, there's a fine restaurant featuring California wine—open Tuesday through Friday—and a snackbar to help you through the trip.

Oakland's Chinatown can't hold a fortune cookie to San Francisco's for size and variety, but its dozen blocks teem with intriguing markets, bakeries, and some good restaurants. Worthy of a look is Yang Sang Co., 411 Ninth, a Chinese herbal pharmacy.

Emeryville, a small community at the east end of the Bay Bridge, is known as "the artists' capital of the world" because it supposedly has more artists per capita than any other city.

From March to December a display of 8,000 rose bushes with 400 varieties in bloom is a unique delight at the Morcom Rose Garden, located on Jean St. off Grand Ave.

To set your sights higher, star gaze at the Chabot Planetarium, 4917 Mountain Blvd. Its 20-inch refractor telescope is the largest one open year-round for public outer space viewing.

While Oakland's airport handles only a tenth of San Francisco's number of flights, it's much easier to use and Bay Area visitors are finding Oakland is also easier on the pocketbook. Hotel space is limited, but often half the price of San Francisco's. And with BART, the Bay Area Rapid Transit—a 75-mile modern train system linking 15 communities with San Francisco—it's only ten minutes to San Francisco, under the Bay. A bike permit lets cyclists take their bikes on BART during noncommuter hours. BART trains run Monday–Saturday from 5:00 A.M. to midnight and start at 9:00 A.M. on Sunday.

PRACTICAL INFORMATION FOR OAKLAND

HOW TO GET THERE. Oakland lies just across the bay from San Francisco. **By car:** Use the Bay Bridge. **BART** (Bay Area Rapid Transit System) is headquartered in Oakland and serves 71 miles of routes in Alameda, Contra Costa, and San Francisco counties.

Bus service is provided by A/C Transit to all points in Oakland and surrounding communities, inclusive of service from the airport to the nearby BART Coliseum station. The city and the area are also serviced by Greyhound and Continental Trailways.

There is **limousine service** to Oakland Airport and between Oakland–San Francisco airports; see the Yellow Pages.

By train: Oakland is the major station for Amtrak's coastwide service from San Diego to Vancouver and from Oakland to Chicago. Free bus shuttle is provided into the San Francisco East Bay Terminal from Oakland.

By air: 18 airlines fly into Oakland Airport, located just 10 minutes from downtown and 20 minutes from the San Francisco financial district. It is the only area airport connected by shuttle bus to BART. Phone 444-4444 for flight information and reservations.

TELEPHONES. The area code for Oakland—as well as for Berkeley, Marin County, and San Francisco—is 415. From outside the area, directory information can be obtained toll-free by dialing (415) 555–1212. Dial (800) 555–1212, directory information for toll-free 800 numbers, to see if there is an 800 number for the business you want to reach.

HOTELS AND MOTELS. Hotel and motel rates are based on double occupancy. Categories determined by price are: *Deluxe*, $80.00 to $100.00 and, of course, over; *Expensive*, $70.00 to $79.00; *Moderate*, $60.00 to $69.00; and *Inexpensive*, anything under $60.00.

Claremont Resort Hotel. *Deluxe.* North Oakland, close to U.C. Berkeley; Ashby and Domingo Aves.; 843–3000. Victorian landmark for 50 years, newly renovated. Attractive grounds on 22 acres. Spectacular view of the entire Bay Area from the lounge and dining room. Pool, whirlpool, sauna. Ten lighted tennis courts. Free parking. Transportation to Oakland Airport.

OAKLAND AIRPORT AND COLISEUM AREA

Oakland Airport Hilton. *Expensive.* One Hegenberger Rd.; 635–5000. Spacious grounds, twin buildings back from a busy thoroughfare. Pool, restaurant, and lounge. Limousine service to Oakland Airport.

Oakland Hyatt. *Expensive.* 455 Hegenberger Rd.; 562–6100. Newly redecorated. Accommodations spread over landscaped grounds. Popular disco, attractive coffee shop and restaurant, lounge. Pool. Free Limo service to airport and BART. Near Coliseum.

Holiday Inn of Oakland. *Moderate.* 500 Hegenberger Rd.; 562–5311. Alongside freeway. Pool, restaurant, and lounge. Limousine service to airport and BART. Children under 12 free.

Oakland Airport TraveLodge. *Moderate.* 150 Hegenberger Rd.; 635–5300. Pool, sauna, therapy pool. Restaurant and lounge. Limousine service to airport.

JACK LONDON SQUARE AREA

Boatel Motor Lodge. *Moderate.* 88 Jack London Sq.; 836–3800. Quiet, offers best accommodations on the Square. Small rooms overlook the harbor. Pool. Docking available at hotel's landing.

DOWNTOWN AREA

Hyatt Regency. *Deluxe.* 1001 Broadway; 893–1234. New 21-story luxury hotel. Pool. Coffee shop, restaurant and lounge. A few steps from BART.

London Lodge. *Moderate.* 423 7th St.; 451–6316. Noisy downtown location. Basic rooms and facilities. Restaurant and lounge. Pool. Limousine service to the airport. 60 kitchenettes.

NEAR BAY BRIDGE

Holiday Inn—Bay Bridge. *Expensive.* 1800 Powell St.; 658–9300. Emeryville. A high rise—ask for rooms overlooking San Francisco and the Bay. Restaurant and lounge. Pool. Full-service hotel.

GETTING AROUND. Oakland via public transportation is easy; bus transfers are available at the stations and Oakland's new weekday shuttle bus circles downtown every ten minutes between 9:30 A.M. and 4:30 P.M. Regular fare is 25¢; for 50¢ you get an all-day pass allowing unlimited stops.

BART especially eases the parking and transportation problems of attending the Oakland-Alameda Coliseum. The Coliseum features a three-decker stadium, convertible for football or baseball, and seating for 52,000. There is also a 16,000-seat indoor arena and large connecting exhibition and meeting hall for trade shows and conventions.

To get to Alameda, take Route 17 at the Oakland end of the Bay Bridge and exit at the "Alameda Tube" sign; follow the signs along the parallel access road until you come to the Tube entrance turn-off, which is marked by a rather small sign. Along the access road, by the way, you'll see the turn (a right turn) marked for Jack London Square, which is on the Oakland side of the estuary.

TOURIST INFORMATION. Oakland Convention and Visitors' Bureau, 1330 Broadway, Oakland, CA 94612; 839–9000. BART Transit Information, 800 Madison St., Oakland, CA 94607; 788–2278. (Note: The Yellow Pages of the telephone directory has a BART route map.)

TOURS. May through August, the Port of Oakland conducts free tours of the port. They leave twice on Thursdays, at 10:00 A.M. and 12:00 noon from (and return to) the Harbor Tours dock in Jack London Square at the foot of Broadway. The tours last 90 minutes and travel the Oakland Estuary into San Francisco Bay, with a circuit of the main cargo terminals affording a close look at merchant ships berthed at container yards. Reservations are required for the tours individually or with groups. Call 839–7488.

CHILDREN'S ACTIVITIES. Lake Merritt, in addition to having boating facilities for all ages, is the location of *Children's Fairyland,* with puppet and clown shows—a mini-world of tiny fairytale scenes. The *Knowland State Park Zoo,* 98th Ave. and Mountain Blvd., has the usual furry friends plus children's rides and attractions. The *Oakland Museum's* natural science exhibits appeal especially to teens.

SPORTS. Oakland offers all types of spectator and participant sports—pro baseball (the Athletics), football (the Invaders), basketball (the Warriors) are all played at the Oakland Coliseum. Call 638–0500 or 638–4900 for Coliseum information. (At press time, the Raiders appear to be remaining in L.A., though there is the possibility they may return to Oakland.) Lake Merritt offers boating, swimming, fishing, bicycling, tennis, and jogging. There is water-skiing, sailing, and boating on the Oakland Estuary; indoor and lawn bowling and golf on municipal and private courses.

 MUSIC AND DANCE. The Paramount Theatre, 2025 Broadway, a sightseeing destination in its own right, is the home of the Oakland Symphony. Oakland is also the home of a contemporary dance company now coming into national prominence, Ronn Guidi's Oakland Ballet.

Oakland's 86-member Oakland Symphony performs October through May. Classical concerts are held at the Zellerbach Auditorium at UC Berkeley as well as at the Paramount (444–3531). Six Friday evening "Pops" programs are also held at the Paramount, which was named a National Historic Landmark in 1977. For information and tickets phone 465–6400, Monday through Friday, from noon to 6:00 P.M.; Saturdays from noon to 5:00 P.M. Tickets may be charged to Visa and MasterCard.

 LIBRARY. The Oakland Public Library, the main branch located at 125 14th St., has a small but comprehensive collection of Jack London memorabilia in a special room. Included are copies of his works in numerous foreign editions. Call 273–3134.

 MUSEUMS. *Mills College,* at the junction of Rtes. 580 and 13 in South Oakland, has an excellent museum with a varied art collection of more than 4,000 works. Five major groupings include: works on paper, sixteenth to twentieth century; nineteenth and twentieth century, American and European paintings. Textiles: international, but especially fine Japanese, Chinese, South and Central American works; ceramics: pre-Columbian, Chinese, Japanese, and American; and sculpture. Note the Chinese Fu-dogs (1368–1644) of the Ming Dynasty; they guard the entry. Museum hours are 10:00 A.M. to 4:00 P.M., Tuesdays through Sundays. Inquire regarding summer hours. Phone 430–2164. Admission free. Mills College Campus, 5000 MacArthur Blvd., Oakland.

Oakland Museum. Stepping up an in-town hillsite on the shores of Lake Merritt, the Oakland Museum is an urban gathering place for science, history, and the arts. The museum building drips with Babylon-like greenery, sparkles with reflecting pools and huge sheets of glass, and muffles city sounds with massive, vine-covered walls. Internationally praised for its unique concept and structure, the three-tiered terrace complex has four main levels, embracing seventeen court areas. Museum visitors may enter the garden levels from any gallery level. There are guided 45-minute tours to all the galleries. There's a well-stocked museum store and a buffet/restaurant that's open 10:00 A.M. to 3:00 P.M., Wednesday through Saturday and from noon until 4:00 P.M. Sunday. The restaurant overlooks the gardens and reflecting pool. There are also picnic areas in the gardens. Oakland Museum focuses on the regional concept and has acquired an outstanding collection of California works, while the Natural Sciences Gallery covers the terrain of Northern California. Because the building itself is world-famous, it's worth a visit. Hours are Wednesday through Saturday, 10 A.M. to 5:00 P.M., and Sundays, noon to 7:00 P.M. Free, with charges for special exhibits. Located at Oak and 10th Sts.; (415) 273–3401 or (415) 834–2413. For restaurant reservations: (415) 834–2329.

 DINING OUT. The price categories are based on dinner for one person, *not* including cocktails, wine, taxes, or tips. *Deluxe,* $25.00 and over; *Expensive,* $16.00 to $24.00; *Moderate,* $8.00 to $15.00; and *Inexpensive,* under $8.00.

Deluxe

A. J. Toppers. On the 21st floor of the Hyatt Regency; 893–1234. Dramatic views of San Francisco, Oakland and the Bay. Veal, pasta and fresh fish. Extensive wine list. Dinner only. All major credit cards.

Trader Vic's. 9 Anchor Dr., Emeryville (Powell St. exit off I-80, sits on a point allowing views of San Francisco Bay); 653–3400. Original Trader Vic's began in Oakland. Handsome décor, Polynesian motif. Exotic drinks and South Seas hors d'oeuvres. Host Freddy Fung will assist you to select from an extensive menu which includes several Chinese oven barbecue specialties. Stuffy about neckties. Reservations necessary. All major credit cards.

Expensive

Beau Rivage. 1042 Ballena, Alameda, just minutes from Oakland; 523–1660. Intimate dining, plus décor and fireplace. The chef is a former personal chef to the premier of France. Beef Wellington is excellent. Fresh fruit daiquiris. Reservations necessary. All major credit cards.

La Brasserie. 542 Grand Ave.; 893–6206. French Provincial, chef-owned. Cassoulet is the house specialty. Highly praised is veal à la Dijonnaise, filet au Roquefort. Lunch Wednesday–Friday, 11:30 A.M.–2:00 P.M. Dinner served Wednesday–Sunday, 5:30–10:00 P.M. Reservations recommended. All major credit cards.

Broadway Terrace Cafe. 5891 Broadway Terrace; 652–4442. Small, quiet dining room. Mesquite charcoal broiled fish, poultry, meat and superb "starters." Excellent service and wine list. Located in the Oakland hills; call for directions. Reservations necessary. No credit cards. Dinner Tuesday through Sun. Sunday brunch.

Duck's and Company. Oakland Hyatt, 455 Hegenberger Rd.; 562–6100. Rustic country atmosphere. Gourmet salad bar with grilled garlic bread. Seafood, steaks, pasta. Duck is the specialty. Dessert bar. Lunch Monday through Friday. Sunday brunch. Dinner, dancing and entertainment nightly. Major credit cards.

Mirabeau. Kaiser Center Roof Gardens, 344 20th St.; 834–6575. French-Continental. Quiet, with extremely elegant décor, overlooking a rooftop garden along Lake Merritt. A fair selection of California wines. Reservations recommended. All major credit cards. Validated parking.

Moderate

Bay Wolf. 3853 Piedmont Ave.; 655–6004. Converted Victorian home, relaxed atmosphere. Mediterranean-inspired dishes. Lunch and dinner; 7 days; large outdoor deck. Reservations necessary. V, MC.

Capri. 1103 Embarcadero; 839–4800. Attractive, split-level setting for a fine Italian menu, overlooking the estuary. House favorites include fettuccine Alfredo and linguine with crab, garlic, and mushrooms; also excellent veal offerings. Music in the lounge Thursday through Saturday nights. Reservations recommended. Major credit cards.

Caribbean. 567 5th St., Bret Harte Boardwalk; 444–6183. For something different both in décor and dining, this somewhat drafty, dimly lit Victorian house attractively fitted with colonial furnishings and tropical vegetation offers West Indian delicacies. The menu includes curried goat, herbed lamb shank, and spicy jumbo shrimp. Caribbean beer is available. Service can also be in the Caribbean pace, a little slow. Taped music of the islands. Small, so reservations recommended. No lounge. All major credit cards.

El Caballo. 67 Jack London Sq.; 835–9260. Large, attractive Mexican hacienda. Comfortable lounge with complimentary snacks. The usual Mexican dishes, including enchiladas and rellenos; some of the food slightly bland. Pleasant outside patio dining, weather permitting. Open seven days. Reservations accepted. Major credit cards.

The Grotto. 70 Jack London Sq.; 893–2244. An East Bay reliable since 1936. Extensive fresh seafood and traditional favorites. Situated on Jack London Square by the estuary, it offers pleasant views of sailboats and freighters gliding by. Attractive cedar interior, linens, and fast service. There is a large bar for waiting for those who have not made reservations. Major credit cards.

Gulf Coast Oyster Bar. 8th and Washington; 839–6950. Near Hyatt Regency. Local and imported shellfish in creole dishes, special salads and homemade pecan pie. Good beer and wine list. Lunch, dinner, Sunday brunch. Ample parking. Major credit cards.

Pacific Fresh. 2203 Mariner Sq. Loop, Alameda (take the Webster St. Tube under the water to the first exit); 521–6577. A fine fish restaurant and market. Oak and brass abound for an airy, spacious feeling. The Garden Room is less noisy than the larger main dining room. Fifty varieties of fish; calamari steak, swordfish, and thresher shark broiled over mesquite wood charcoal. A daily fresh fish and wine special. Good California wine list at reasonable prices. Very popular, reservations recommended. Major credit cards.

Regency Cafe. On the 2nd floor of the Hyatt Regency; 893–1234. Atrium setting featuring fresh fish and Latin style beef in a special salsa. Wine available by the glass. Breakfast, lunch, dinner. All major credit cards.

Silver Dragon. 835 Webster St. at 9th Ave.; 893–3748. In the heart of Oakland's Chinatown, this attractive three-level restaurant offers extensive Cantonese selections including Peking duck and stuffed crab claws (advance notice for preparation). Two full bars. Reservations recommended. V, MC.

Yoshi's. 6030 Claremont; 652–9200. Traditional Japanese cuisine and sushi counter. Reservations recommended. Major credit cards.

Inexpensive

Oakland Grill. 301 Franklin; 835–1176. Located in Oakland's produce mart; the vegetables are fresh daily. The restaurant's walls are open to the mart activity during the summer. Salads, steaks, good breakfasts (served anytime) and fresh coffee cakes. Opens at 6:00 A.M., Monday through Friday. Dinner 7 nights until 9:30 P.M.

 NIGHT LIFE. Eli's Mile High. 3629 Grove St., Oakland; 655–6661. The best blues club anywhere around the Bay Area. Run-down neighborhood (though generally safe), nondescript saloon furniture, decent and inexpensive drinks, and gut-level blues every night. Not exactly on the "night-life tour bus" route, but for blues enthusiasts the Mile High is it.

Red Sails. 2337 Blanding Ave., Alameda (an island south of Oakland along the Bay); 522–4536. This is one of many bars, restaurants, and cabarets that front on the estuary—a finger-like extension of the Bay known to practically no one—where you can drink, look at the boats coming and going, and enjoy the unusual view, to the west, of San Francisco.

The Round Up. 3553 Mt. Diablo Blvd., Lafayette (northeast of Oakland); 284–4817. A Western saloon that really *was* in the country when it opened in the 1930s. Now it is in the heart of suburbia, but still has country bands, dancing, drinks, and a rowdy atmosphere.

BERKELEY

by
VERN HAWKINS

Berkeley is more than just a college town. Its ideas and lifestyles have spread throughout the country. The city's politics have been called radical, and ordinances that are rarely even discussed in other cities have been adopted here. Berkeley is different.

It is only a 20-minute drive from the Bay Bridge and San Francisco. Situated between the Berkeley Hills and the Bay, there is a spectacular view of "The City" and the Golden Gate Bridge—often shrouded in fog. Its downtown is a blend of tradition and fad.

During the 1960s, Berkeley was infamous. It was at the University of California–Berkeley (U.C. Berkeley) where the first campus sit-in was held. Stores and banks near the campus that grew tired of replacing windows during the riots are still today fortified with steel and brick façades. But today, the atmosphere is as mellow as any ivy-clad university town in the Midwest.

It's a city of very distinct communities. The western flatlands stretching toward Oakland and the Bay house light industry and low-income families. The hillside community, near the university and bordering the 2,000-acre Tilden Park, is filled with affluent neighborhoods of rambling estates. Boutiques and bistros along College and Ashby Aves. give the city a European flavor.

A drive through the hillside neighborhoods offers a variety of architectural sightseeing. Homes range from informal shingled cottages to Spanish castles to versions of Swiss chalets and English Tudor estates. The chief landmark is the fairytale-styled Claremont Hotel, built in 1914. It is a sprawling, whitewashed spectacle, surrounded by 22 acres of lush grounds tucked into the South Berkeley Hills. It is on the Oakland-Berkeley city boundary, and for years both cities claimed it, with the argument still underway. Several million dollars were recently pumped into its restoration to bring it back to its former grandeur. Its restaurant and lounge, with their memorable views, are alone worth a visit.

But most visitors are drawn to the university and its attractions. At the foot of the hills sprawls the University of California—Berkeley, the oldest of the nine University of California campuses. It was chartered in 1868 and graduated its first class in 1873. Today, the university—a city in itself—has some 30,000 students and is one of the world's most renowned educational, scientific, and cultural institutions. More Nobel laureates dwell here per acre than anywhere else.

The cyclotron and the discovery of plutonium were both Berkeley firsts. The heart of the campus is Sproul Plaza. Near Bancroft Way and Telegraph Ave., the plaza is a perennial carnival with musicians, puppeteers, vendors, evangelists, and students from every land.

At noon, debates on every imaginable topic are found in just as many booths. Featured speakers take to the microphone on the steps of Sproul Hall. Visitors would think they are in London's Hyde Park.

The campus Student Union, below the Plaza, has the usual student eateries, including a creamery (closed weekends), lounges, and a well stocked bookstore, all open to the public.

In the main lobby of the Student Union building is the Visitors' Center (642–5215). Here, information and pamphlets are found as well as free student-led tours of the campus. The tour leaves the center at 1:00 P.M. weekdays and lasts one hour.

Just north of Sproul Plaza lies Sather Gate, the fabled main south entrance. From here one may stroll along broad tree-lined avenues and by white granite buildings capped with green-copper and red-tile roofs.

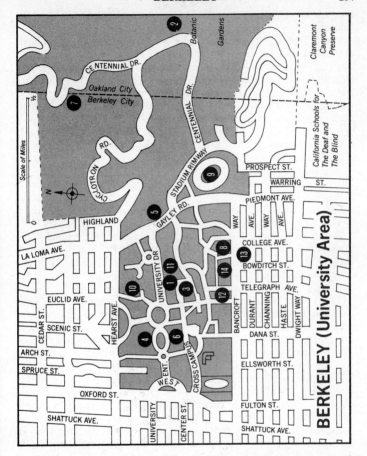

Points of Interest

1) Bancroft Library/Exhibits
2) Botanical Garden
3) Doe Library/Exhibits
4) Essig Museum of Entomology
5) Greek Theatre
6) Jepson Herbarium; Museum of Vertebrate Zoology; University Herbarium
7) Lawrence Hall of Science
8) Lowie Museum of Anthropology
9) Memorial Stadium
10) Museum of Geology; Museum of Paleontology; Seismographic Station
11) Sather Tower
12) Sproul Hall
13) University Art Museum
14) Worth Ryder Art Gallery

Large grassy knolls, streams, and pines offer space and serenity to the campus.

Sather Tower, the Campanile, is Berkeley's most photographed landmark. The graceful bell tower was built in 1914 and modeled after St. Mark's Campanile in Venice. The original twelve English bells grew to a carillon of forty-eight. Above the carillon is a separate bell, which has tolled the hours since 1899. The carillon is heard each weekday at 7:50 A.M., noon, and 6 P.M., except during finals. On Saturdays, the bells perform at noon and 6:00 P.M., and on Sundays at 4:00 P.M. The tower is open 10:00 A.M. to 4:30 P.M. daily except on university holidays. It costs only a dime to ride the elevator to the observation platform for an unforgettable view of the Bay.

You may not even feel the earthquake, but it will be recorded in the Earth Sciences Building. Here, the famed seismographic station is constantly at work. The seismograph is in the lobby and other instruments are on the 5th floor, Room 565. It's open 8:00 to 5:00 weekdays. Group tours of ten or more can be arranged by calling 642–3977.

But don't leave the building just yet, as the first and second floors house the Museum of Paleontology. Fossils and skeletons that date back to the dinosaur age, including a plesiosaur, reveal the evolution of man and animal through time. It's open weekdays 6:00 to 5:00, weekends 1:00 to 5:00 when the university is in session.

The Lowie Museum of Anthropology in Kroeher Hall has both changing and permanent exhibits that may include the archeology of ancient America, Polynesian, or Eskimo art. Artifacts are selected from the museum's research collection of a half million pieces. It's open 10:00 to 4:00 weekdays, noon to 4:00 weekends. There is a nominal admission fee.

U. C. Berkeley's most interesting piece of modern architecture is the University Art Museum, found just across the street from the main campus—2626 Bancroft Way. The fan-shaped building by Mario Ciampi looks like a huge concrete sculpture. Inside, spiral ramps and balconies surround open galleries. Light is provided by large floor-to-ceiling windows and skylights. Its permanent collection features canvases of Rubens and Cézanne, sculpture by Maillol and Paolozzi, as well as the abstract work of Mark Rothko, Helen Frankenthaler, and others. The museum also houses the world's largest collection of Hans Hofmann. There is a sculpture garden in back of the museum for hands-on climbing.

The Pacific Film Archive in the museum offers nightly films (642–1124).

In the lower level of the museum is the Swallow Restaurant, with good snacks at low prices. The museum is open 11:00 to 5:00 Wednesday through Sunday (642–0808). Admission is free except for special showings.

Another museum—not affiliated with U. C. Berkeley—is the Judah L. Magnes Memorial Museum at 2911 Russell St. Considered the Jewish museum of the West, it has the nation's largest collection of Jewish ceremonial objects. Museum officials have also restored six Jewish cemeteries in California's Gold Rush areas and conduct guided tours to them.

Not far from the main campus is the California Memorial Stadium, home of the Golden Bears. It seats 76,780 and was completed in 1923 in time for the annual Big Game with Stanford University, Berkeley's greatest rival since 1892.

Uphill from the stadium in Strawberry Canyon is the world's largest Botanical Garden, of some 80,000 plants. They are arranged geographically over 32 acres. The largest selection is, of course, native Californian. The garden is open daily 9:00 to 5:00 except for Christmas Day. Free tours are offered weekends at 2:30 P.M. (642–2343).

Perched in the Berkeley Hills on Centennial Drive, with a panoramic view of the campus and bay, is the Lawrence Hall of Science. The fortress-like hall is named for Ernest O. Lawrence, the university's first Nobel laureate and inventor of the cyclotron. The hall is a mecca for all ages.

Exhibits are offered in math, chemistry, physics, astronomy, and biology. There are telescopes, mineral displays, an optics tunnel, and a planetarium. In the wizard's lab are do-it-yourself experiments with light, optical illusions, and electricity. Visitors can play with tarantulas, rabbits, and other critters in the biology lab or play on computers. The Galaxy Sandwich Shop is open daily until 4:30 and the Discovery Corner sells unusual games and toys. The Hall is open daily from 1:00 P.M. to 4:30 P.M., Thursday until 9:00 P.M.

The Holt Planetarium is open daily except in December. Call 642–5132 for information regarding exhibits and workshops.

Much of the university and surrounding areas can be explored on foot. Distances are short. On campus there is no choice, as only cars with permits are allowed. Forget roller skates and skateboards; they are not permitted. But getting to and from the campus is easily done by bus.

The Humphrey go-BART connects with the 75-mile Bay Area Rapid Transit system (BART) and the bus is free during the week. It connects the main Berkeley BART station with various campus locales, the Botanical Garden, and Lawrence Hall of Science. Check the schedule and map at the campus visitors' center.

Napa may have its winery tours and testing but Berkeley offers a unique tour of the first and largest sake works in the United States. The

2,000-year-old Japanese rice wine came to the United States in the late forties, almost exclusively for Japanese-Americans. Its popularity here grew, and in 1978 the Numano Sake Company began what is now a half-million-gallon-a-year production plant that distributes sake to 43 states, Canada, and even Japan. The Numano Sake Company is at 708 Addison St. near Hwy. 80. Tasting hours are 10:00 A.M. to 8:00 P.M. daily. Tours on weekdays by appointment. Saturday and Sunday tours from 12:00 to 4:00 P.M. (540–8250).

For sheer color stroll along Telegraph Ave. near the campus. It's something of a street vendors' haven. Whatever can be handcrafted can be found here. There are also trendy boutique shops, ethnic restaurants, and some of the finest bookstores on the West Coast (some are on Bancroft Way, too). Dress, to say the least, is casual. And on any corner newsstands peddle publications you're not likely to find at home. Much of the mood of the sixties persists here: leaflet-littered streets, strolling students with canine companions, crowded walkways, noisy traffic—all parts of Berkeley's mystique.

At the Bay end of Berkeley is the new Marina and Yacht harbor complex. It's a perfect place at the end of the day to watch the sun sink beyond the Golden Gate Bridge through smoky-colored windows of comfortable lounges.

Here also are Berkeley's newest accommodations, among the quietest in the Bay Area and at prices much less than in San Francisco, yet only minutes away.

PRACTICAL INFORMATION FOR BERKELEY

HOW TO GET THERE. By car. To get to the University of California, take the San Francisco–Oakland Bay Bridge, U.S. 80, and keep left on 80 at the end of the bridge, then either turn right off 80 onto Ashby Ave., driving up to Telegraph Ave., then left on Telegraph and drive till you come right into the university—or turn right off 80 farther up, onto University Ave., and keep on University until you come to the university.

By public transportation. Call BART at 788–2278.

TELEPHONES. The area code for Berkeley—as well as for Oakland, Marin County, and San Francisco—is 415. From outside the area, directory information can be obtained toll-free by dialing (415) 555–1212. Dial (800) 555–1212, directory information for toll-free 800 numbers, to see if there is an 800 number for the business you want to reach.

HOTELS AND MOTELS. The price categories for double occupancy are: *Deluxe,* $80.00 and over; *Expensive,* $70.00 to $79.00; *Moderate,* $60.00 to $69.00, and *Inexpensive,* under $60.00.

Marriott Inn. *Deluxe.* 200 Marina Blvd., Berkeley Marina; 548–7920 or (800) 228–9290. Convenient yet secluded location along the bay. Views. Indoor heated pool. Whirlpool. Tennis. Sauna. Entertainment. Private boat dock, charter fishing and cruising, even sailing lessons.

Claremont Resort Hotel. See "Oakland Hotels."

Best Western Berkeley House Motor Hotel. *Moderate.* 920 University Ave.; 849–1121 or (800) 528–1234. Convenient location. Pool. Coffee Restaurant.

Best Western Golden Bear Motel. *Moderate.* 1620 San Pablo; 525-6770.

The Durant Hotel. *Moderate.* 2600 Durant; 845–8981. Close to campus. Restaurant and lounge.

BED-AND-BREAKFAST. Gramma's Bed and Breakfast Inn. *Deluxe.* 2740 Telegraph, near campus; 549–2145. An old mansion with antique rooms and modern bathrooms. Breakfast only. Sunday Brunch. V, MC. **The French Hotel.** *Deluxe.* 1538 Shattuck; 548–9930. Modern décor. 16 rooms and suites. Café. **East Brother Light Station,** 117 Park Place, Point Richmond, CA 94801; 233–2385, is a lighthouse converted into an inn, right on the Bay northwest of Berkeley.

INDUSTRIAL TOURS. In Berkeley, across the Bay from San Francisco, *Numano Sake* conducts tours of its facilities weekdays by appointment. The traditional revered drink of Japan, *sake,* is usually served warm and has been a major beverage for over a thousand years in Japan, Korea, and other Asian countries. Numano Dry California Sake is an extra-dry pure rice wine, made from a specially selected strain of California rice, called Tsuru Mai, and highly purified water from the Sierra Nevada mountains. Perfect on the rocks, or as a cocktail base. The rice drinks are brewed in the age-old tradition, without alcoholic additives or preservatives. The Koshu White Rice Wine is also light and dry, a bit like a chablis. Their tasting room is open daily from 12:00 P.M. to 6:00 P.M.,. For more information on sake and the plant tour, write to: Numano Sake Company, 708 Addison St., Berkeley, CA 94710; 540–8250.

FISHING. *Berkeley Marina Sport Center,* 225 University Ave. Berkeley Marina, CA; 849–2727 or 849–2728. 24-hour reservation service. *Chinook,* Captain Ernie Feigenberg; foot of University Avenue, Berkeley Marina, CA; 521–9275. *JAWS,* Captain Rick Powers; foot of University Avenue, Berkeley Marina, CA; 849–2727 or, after 6 P.M., 653–5463. *Hank Schramm's Sport Fishing Center,* 3310 Powell, Emeryville Marina, CA; 654–6040. An eleven-party boat fleet.

HISTORIC HOUSES. Several blocks from the Oakland Museum is the *Camron-Stanford House,* an Italianate Victorian on the shores of Lake Merritt at 1418 Lakeside Dr. Hours: Wednesday, 11:00 A.M.–4:00 P.M. Sunday, 1:00 P.M.–5:00 P.M. Docent tours. Phone: 836–1976. Another Victorian, owned by the city of Oakland, is the *Dunsmuir House,* 48-acre estate open Wednesdays and Sundays, April through September, during the hours of noon to 4:00 P.M. Tours: 1:00 P.M., 2:00 P.M., 3:00 P.M. Admission to both the house and garden: $3.00; admission to gardens: $1.00. Located at the north end of Covington St.; 562–7588.

In Martinez, the *John Muir House,* a National Historic Site, is operated by the National Park Service. Open daily: 8:30 A.M.–4:30 P.M. Home of the famous naturalist and writer. Free. Located at 4202 Alhambra Ave., at California Rte. 4. 228–8860.

MUSEUMS. *The Lawrence Hall of Science,* located in the hills above the Berkeley campus, on Centennial Dr., is another hands-on museum that features astronomy, computer games, planetarium, and science experiments for both children and adults. Hours are 10:00 A.M.–4:30 P.M. weekdays; to 5:00 P.M. Saturday, Sunday; to 9:00 P.M. Thursday, Thursday nights free. 642–5132.

The Lowie Museum of Anthropology is located directly across the street from the University of California Art Museum; it has an outstanding permanent collection. Open 10:00 A.M.–4:30 P.M.; closed Wednesday; from noon to 4:30 P.M., Saturday and Sunday; 642–3681. Admission charge.

The University Art Museum of University of California–Berkeley is a unique, multi-level concrete building, with galleries rimming a central open wall. Permanent collection includes Otto Dix, Karl Hofer, Alexei Jawlensky, and Paul Klee. The museum's Pacific Film Archive is a film center that offers approximately 800 film programs each year. Gallery hours are Wednesday through Sunday, 11:00 A.M.–5:00 P.M.; 642–0808. General admission is $3.00; $1.50 for senior citizens and UC students. For theater schedule, phone 642–1124; it's open daily. The Swallow Restaurant, which serves indoors and al fresco, is open Sun–Tues from 11:00 A.M. to 5:00 P.M.; to 8:00 P.M. Wednesday–Saturday. 2626 Bancroft Ave., Berkeley.

STAGE. *Berkeley Repertory Theater,* 2025 Addison St. at Shattuck, is second in importance to San Francisco's ACT among the Bay Area resident theaters. Repertory includes Shakespeare, Shaw, European playwrights, with more emphasis on such contemporary Americans as David Mamet and Christopher Durang. A season of approximately six plays runs September through May, with additional summer comedies. Tickets and information, 845–4700.

September. Performances are in John Hinkel Park, off Arlington Circle in the Berkeley hills. Tickets and information, 548–3422.

 DINING OUT. The price categories are for dinner for one person, *not* including cocktails or wine, taxes, or tip. *Deluxe,* $25.00 and up; *Expensive,* $16.00 to $24.00; *Moderate,* $8.00 to $15.00; and *Inexpensive,* under $8.00. The following restaurants are, of course, only a selection.

Deluxe

Chez Panisse. 1517 Shattuck Ave.; 548–5525. French in the nouvelle cuisine techniques, this restaurant consistently receives *the* top rating from restaurant critics and gourmets. Only the best and freshest California produce, fish, and meat are featured on a daily-changing *prix fixe* menu which is posted for the week each Saturday. (Every July 14 Chez Panisse has a garlic-day festival, with all garlic meals!) The wine list is nothing special but includes reasonably priced California wines, or bring your own for $10.00 bottle corkage. The first sitting is at 6:00–6:30 P.M.; the second is at 8:30–9:15 P.M. but often means a wait. Reservations are mandatory. Closed Sunday and Monday. No credit cards.

Narsai's. 385 Colusa Ave., North Berkeley; 527–7900. Located in a quiet neighborhood, this restaurant offers a pleasant bar and understated elegant dining room. The service is excellent; the wine list is the most extensive in the Bay Area. The chocolate decadence dessert is fantastic. Reservations recommended. All credit cards.

Santa Fe Bar and Grill. 1310 University Ave.; 841–4740. Former train depot converted into airy, continental dining room. Mesquite charcoal-grilled fresh fish, steaks, warm and cold salads, fresh pasta and excellent desserts. Pianist nightly. Dinner and lunch daily. Sunday brunch. Reservations recommended for dinner. Major credit cards.

Expensive

Pavilion Dining Room. *Claremont Hotel.* Ashby and Domino Aves.; 539–0904. An outstanding Sunday brunch set with a spectacular view of San Francisco and the entire Bay Area. The buffet is endless, followed by a choice of entrée and desserts. Reservations recommended. Major credit cards.

Moderate

Café at Chez Panisse. 1517 Shattuck Ave.; 548–5525. This is the upstairs of Chez Panisse, where light meals of soup, pizzas, salads, and a fresh fish selection are available at reasonable prices. A good offering of inexpensive wines. No reservations, and the wait can be long. Open 11:30 A.M. till midnight. No credit cards.

Fourth Street Grill. 1820 Fourth St. near I-80 and Spenger's Fish Grotto; 849–0526. The feeling of a small European café, a little cramped often with standing room only at the bar. Excellent Italian dishes, pastas made daily. Fettuccine in clam sauce and Louisiana hot sausages are menu regulars. Has a respectable wine list at reasonable prices. Homemade desserts; especially good are the lemon tarts. No reservations. V, MC.

Norman's. College and Alcatraz Aves.; 655–5291. Dimly lit, comfortable atmosphere with plush bar. Seafood, California cuisine, good treatment of fresh vegetables. Reservations recommended. All credit cards.

Omnivore. 3015 Shattuck Ave.; 848–4346. Home-grown restaurant in off-beat neighborhood. Reservations accepted. No credit cards.

Petrouchka. 2930 College Ave.; 848–7860. Vegetarian and Russian cuisine. Reservations accepted. V.

Spenger's Fish Grotto. 1919 Fourth St., near I-80; 845–7771. One of the Bay Area's largest seafood restaurants, offering everything from mixed seafood plates to fresh lobster. The most popular dishes are shrimp scatter and fish and chips. Service is fast, but the wait can be long and noisy around the enormous bar area. Reservations for six or more only. All credit cards.

Warszawa. 1730 Shattuck Ave.; 841–5539. Stylish brick setting, intimate atmosphere. The menu is entirely Polish; all selections are cooked to order by the chef-owner. Try the *pierogi.* Reservations recommended. All credit cards.

Yoshi's. 6030 Claremont Ave., on the Oakland/Berkeley line; 652–9200. Traditional Japanese motif except for the upstairs bar where there is a band and a video game, necessary because even with reservations a wait is usual. There are 21 dinners listed; among them crisp tempura, nicely seasoned sukiyaki, chicken or beef skewered yakitori. Attentive service. Reservations recommended. V, MC.

Inexpensive

Casa de Eva. 2826 Telegraph Ave.; 540–9092. Unusual and authentic Mexican dishes; good combination plates, tamales in homemade sauce, and fresh corn and flour tortillas. Small, pleasant dining areas with outstanding Mexican and Indian art. Good selection of Mexican beer. Reservations for six or more. No credit cards.

 NIGHT LIFE. Larry Blake's. 2367 Telegraph Ave., Berkeley; 848–0888. Has a downstairs bar with sawdust on the floor, jazz and blues (live) every night, a real Joe College feeling, and a cozy atmosphere although the loud music makes conversation difficult. Upstairs on the mezzanine over the restaurant there is a cocktail lounge, which is a convenient place to meet friends.

The Claremont Hotel. Ashby and Domingo, Berkeley; 843–3000. The big white tower structure you see when looking due east from San Francisco toward the Berkeley Hills. What is now called the **Terrace Lounge** (although it has had other names over the years) affords an unexcelled view of San Francisco; it's not as well appointed a barroom as it should be, but get there at sunset, have a drink, and you're not likely to forget the experience. You might also find the creaky old hotel and its grounds worth a stroll.

Dock Of The Bay. Berkeley Marina; 845–7656. One of a few saloons that are part of the Berkeley yacht harbor area at the foot of University Ave. Rather new, with views in all directions and a warm, wooden interior. Drinks are good, the music (whether live or taped) is varied, and there are famous hors d'oeuvres at twilight.

Erle's. 1403 Solano Ave., Albany; 524–9314. A small club that has developed a nice mix of jazz, blues, comedy and cabaret acts, which bring in a large young audience. Gets pretty crowded on weekends; rather high door charge. Set in the midst of Berkeley's Chinese restaurant row, a few minutes off I-80, about a block from the Berkeley line.

La Pena. 3105 Shattuck Ave., Berkeley; 849–2568. Features Central and South American food, drink, music, and politics. Crowded with Berkeley left-wingers, La Pena presents nightly fare of music, dancing, films, lectures in a comfortable neighborhood-saloon atmosphere. Inexpensive and interesting.

The Hotel Mac. Washington Ave., Point Richmond; 233–0576. Used to be the funkiest old saloon in the East Bay. It still has charm and good drinks, but all the authenic old Richmond memorabilia and accumulated junk have been replaced by chic, pseudo-authentic décor. A very popular lunch spot in the midst of a strange little community.

The Point. 2 West Richmond, Point Richmond; 233–4295. This *is* an authentic old saloon with plenty of barstools, tables, a rickety piano, and excellent New Orleans jazz on weekend nights. Conversations at the Point may involve carbon compounds (a huge Standard Oil plant is nearby) or old jazz records or various contemporary art forms; Point Richmond is a strange place.

MARVELOUS MARIN

by
JOAN McKINNEY

They call it "Marvelous Marin" (pronounced MaRINN) and, even allowing for some chauvinism on the part of its inhabitants, the county directly north of the famed Golden Gate Bridge has much to offer.

Just 20 minutes from downtown San Francisco brings you to a county that contains, within its 607 square miles, almost a microcosm of California terrain.

There are 115 miles of spectacular coastline, sheer cliffs fronting the Pacific Ocean, interspersed with golden beaches and wooded coves and, to the east, a gentler landscape facing the northern half of San Francisco Bay. Together they form a paradise for sailors, fishermen, skindivers, surfers, and even hardy swimmers—that water is cold!

Marin County, with one of the highest per-capita incomes in the country—and so in the world—is also renowned for being the place of origin of the "laid-back" Hot-Tub Culture, with a propensity for Porsches and new psychologies.

There are picture-pretty small towns in the south, rolling farmlands in the north, and to the west wide-open, windswept grasslands leading down to an ocean where breakers crash and sea lions roar.

There's even a mountain, Mount Tamalpais, named for the Indian maiden whose silhouette, it is said, forms its crest, visible for miles to north and south. Nestled beneath it there is a stand of redwoods in Muir Woods National Memorial that will whet your appetite for a trip north to the Redwood Empire.

Almost one-third of the county's land is set aside for parks: national, state, county, and city. That's a total of more than 100,000 acres of pure heaven for hikers, campers, birdwatchers, nature lovers, and camera buffs. And none of it more than an hour's drive from the Golden Gate Bridge.

The biggest—and youngest—of the parks is the Golden Gate National Recreation Area, stretching from both sides of the bridge north and west along the coastline, and the Point Reyes National Seashore, the northern third of which abuts GGNRA. Together they total 78,546 acres.

Marin also boasts what is reputed to be one of the world's six best climates. This means that it is mild in winter, with an average January temperature of 47 degrees, and mild and dry in summer, when average temperatures hover around 66—though hotter as you go north and away from the water. This is not to say that the climate is flawless. The county's coast gets more than its fair share of fog, both summer and winter. For trips to the GGNRA and Point Reyes, carry a windbreaker and be prepared to find that, some days, you can't even see the sea.

Marin's recorded history is among the oldest in California. It begins in 1579, when Sir Francis Drake, halfway through his historic voyage of circumnavigation, beached his ship, the *Golden Hind,* here for repairs. Scholars still argue over the exact spot of Drake's landing, some saying it was on the Bay side where San Quentin prison now stands. But the most favored spot is the wide, sandy beach that lies southeast of Point Reyes. It is known as Drake's Bay and is part of the National Seashore.

Here Drake and his crew met the friendly Miwok Indians, native to the area. Drake named it "Nova Albion" and claimed it for Queen Elizabeth, who knighted him, not for this feat, but for his piracy of Spanish merchantmen. No Britons returned to settle their new land—at least not for several centuries.

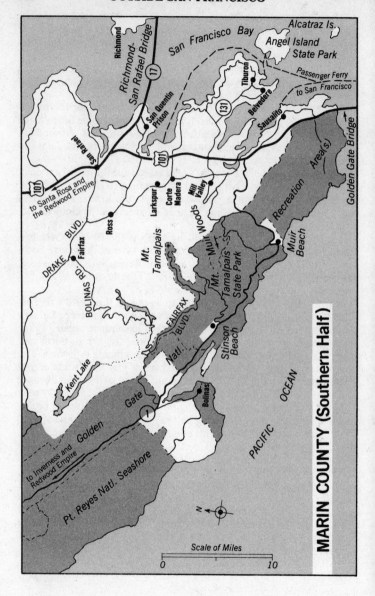

MARIN COUNTY (Southern Half)

In the interim, the Spaniards came north from Mexico, founding San Francisco in 1769. Six years later, the first ship known to enter San Francisco Bay anchored at a spot the Spaniards named *Salcelido* or "little willow," for the willow trees that stood there. Also a Miwok Indian home, it later became known as Sausalito and, with its houses perched on wooded hills and its houseboat colony of artists and non-conformists, it has become a major tourist attraction.

Much of Marin County in early days was in the hands of a few men who were given Spanish land grants. The whole Tiburon-Belvedere Peninsula was one, and the central corridor where now stand the "twin cities" of Corte Madera and Larkspur, another. As the land grants were divided, the southern part of Marin became a favored summer-home spot for San Franciscans, who traveled back and forth to the city by a railroad (which no longer runs), and ferries that carried their cars. Now Marin has ferries again, running from San Francisco to Sausalito, Tiburon, and Larkspur, but they are for people only. Visitors to Marin can take these ferries for a day of exploring the towns they service, leaving from a terminal at the foot of Market Street in San Francisco.

Sausalito

Sausalito is one of Marin County's main tourist attractions. If you have only a day to spend in Marin, chances are that's where you'll spend it—in the village that clings to the side of wooded hills above the Bay, sometimes called the Portofino of California.

Sail over to Sausalito on the ferry and tour the Village Fair, a four-story warehouse converted into a complex of international specialty shops. Have lunch over the water at the Spinnaker, or in any of the small restaurants crowding Bridgeway, the main street, to the south of the ferry terminal. For an evening's splurge, dine at Ondine, on the water, or Casa Madrona on the hill above. The wide deck at the Alta Mira, with its great view, is the favorite spot for Sunday brunch.

Whether you come to Sausalito by ferry, tour bus, Golden Gate Transit bus, or by car, once you are there you must walk to get the flavor of the town.

From the ferry slip or main parking lot which abuts it, walk west on the short street called El Portal. On your right is Plaza Vina del Mar, the small park site donated to Sausalito by the North Shore Railroad in 1904 and now named for Sausalito's sister city in Chile. The lamp-bearing elephants and the fountain came from the 1915 Panama-Pacific Exposition.

To the left is the old Sausalito Hotel, which has been refurbished with Victorian antiques; stop in to see the lobby.

Bridgeway, Sausalito's main drag, now stretches to left and right before you. It has recently been named a historic district by the Secretary of the Interior. The two-story buildings originally had shops below, living quarters above. Now the second stories also house gift shops, galleries, and the like.

Turn left, or south, on Bridgeway. Soon you will have the Bay on your left, specialty shops on the other side of the street. Beyond Scoma's and Ondine, restaurants built out over the water, look for the sea-lion sculpture on the rocks. Created by local artist Al Sybrian in 1958, it was recast in bronze in 1966. The Sausalito Foundation sells small copies to raise funds for historic preservations.

High on the hill to the right you'll see the massive foundations of what was to have been William Randolph Hearst's northern "castle." The project was never completed, and the foundations are now surmounted by a house designed by local architect Joseph Esherick.

Continue south until Bridgeway ends at Richardson St., then follow the boardwalk past the refurbished "Castle by the Sea," where Jack London is supposed to have written *The Sea Wolf.* At the other end of the boardwalk is the town's oldest restaurant building, opened as a German beer garden in 1893 and more recently occupied by ex-madam Sally Stanford's Valhalla Inn.

Return to Bridgeway via the boardwalk or Second St., and look for a tiny park, called Tiffany, and a flight of steps climbing the hill to your left. This is your only steep climb, and it's not a long one—stop for breath and admire the view over the Bay.

At the top, turn right on Josephine, which leads into Atwood Ave. At the meeting of Atwood, Bulkley, and Harrison is a resting place known as Poet's Bench, because lines by Sausalito poet Daniel O'Connell are carved into it.

On the east side of Bulkley, follow the footpath that curves down, past old brown shingled houses set amid trees, to Princess St. Bear left and upward again on Bulkley. On your left you'll pass a Queen Anne shingled Victorian called Laneside, appropriately set at the side of Excelsior Lane. Beyond it is the Spanish-style Alta Mira Hotel, with its big deck which is full to bursting for outdoor Sunday brunches but accessible other days of the week.

Take Excelsior to your right, past the First Presbyterian Church, designed in 1909 by Ernest Coxhead. The lane finally ends in a flight of steps which will take you back down to Bridgeway.

Half a block to your left is the four-story Village Fair again. A few doors farther north is The Quest, where you will find the work of local artists plus treasures from north of the border, where the gallery originated.

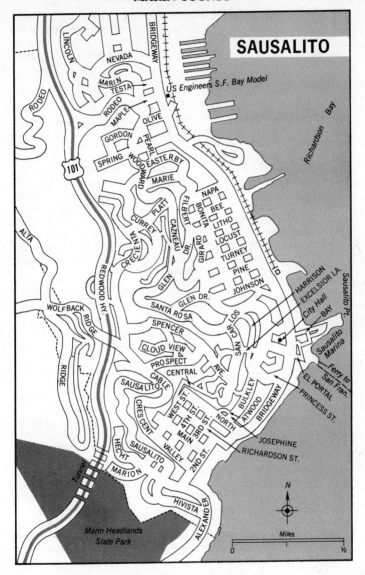

SAUSALITO

US Engineers S.F. Bay Model

Richardson Bay

LINCOLN

BRIDGEWAY

NEVADA

MARIN
TESTA

RODEO

RODEO

MAPLE

OLIVE

GORDON

PEARL

SPRING

WOODWARD

EASTER BY

MARIE

NAPA

BONITA

BEE

PLATT

FILBERT

LITHO

CURREY

CAZNEAU

GIRARD DR.

LOCUST

CRECIENTA

TURNEY

PINE

GLEN

JOHNSON

GLEN DR.

SANTA ROSA

HARRISON

EXCELSIOR LA.

City Hall

Sausalito Pt.

BAY

WOLFBACK

RIDGE

SPENCER

SAN CARLOS

Sausalito
Marina

CLOUD VIEW

PROSPECT

Ferry to
San Fran.

CABLE

CENTRAL

EL PORTAL

SAUSALITO

AVE.

BULKLEY

ATWOOD

BRIDGEWAY

PRINCESS ST.

REDWOOD HY.

CRESCENT

WEST ST.

4TH ST.

3RD ST.

NORTH

RIDGE

HECHT

SAUSALITO

MAIN

2ND ST.

JOSEPHINE

ALTA

VALLEY

RICHARDSON ST.

MARION

Tunnel

HIVISTA

ALEXANDER

Marin Headlands
State Park

N

Miles

0   ½

101

Directly across Bridgeway is the Sausalito Yacht Harbor, crowded with boats of all sizes and origins. After a spot of boat-watching, relax in Gabrielson Park, by the side of the Bay and right next to the No. 1 parking lot. It's a good spot for a picnic before heading for home.

Tiburon and Larkspur

An alternative is the ferry to Tiburon, its Main Street with clapboard-front stores a mélange of restaurants, from Tiburon Tommie's Polynesian-style place at one end to Carlos O'Brian's, fresh from Mexico, at the other. In between are Sabella's, The Dock, and Sam's Anchor Café, where everyone goes Sunday mornings to sit on the sunny old dock, drink gin fizzes, eat crab burgers and watch the yachts coming and going from the Corinthian Yacht Club next door.

Or sample the sleek modern ferries to Larkspur and tour Larkspur Landing, a brand-new complex clustered around a central patio. There are shops of all kinds, and restaurants, including Scoma's for seafood, Yet Wah for Chinese fare, and the Good Earth for vegetarians.

Shuttle buses from the ferry terminal will take you to quaint Larkspur, where you can lunch at the Blue Rock Inn, a former stagecoach stop, or the Lark Creek Inn, a restored Victorian home.

North on Route 1

Marin is well served by commuter buses and there is special service on weekends connecting with Point Reyes National Seashore and the Marin Headlands. But undoubtedly the best way to explore the county is by car.

There are two main highways running north and south through Marin. U.S. 101, or the Redwood Highway, runs up the central corridor, through San Rafael, the county seat, with its striking blue-and-tan Civic Center, designed by Frank Lloyd Wright, and California State Highway 1, which branches off 101 outside Mill Valley and hugs the coastline for much of its length.

That's the one to take to sample the best of Marin's scenic beauties.

Take Hwy. 1, which soon becomes a winding, uphill route, until the road to Mount Tamalpais branches off to the right. Follow that road, along Panoramic Hwy., up to the very top of the mountain. Park and walk around the path cut around the summit for a panoramic view of the whole Bay Area—on a clear day, that is. There are days when Mt. Tam is shrouded in mist and you're better off sticking to Hwy. 1 as it winds down to the coast, past Green Gulch Ranch, now owned by Zen Buddhists who grow produce there for their popular vegetarian restaurant, Greens, at Fort Mason in San Francisco.

This road isn't for people who can't stand heights or cliff edges, as it swoops down and around the hills to the ocean at Muir Beach.

Stop at The Pelican, a lovingly created facsimile of an old English inn, where you can quaff a pint of British ale and eat such Limey fare as bangers-and-mash and shepherd's pie for lunch. Or stay overnight in one of the six bedrooms, all furnished with antiques. Breakfast (English-style) comes with the price of the room.

You might even find yourself there on one of the monthly "Shakespeare at the Inn" free events.

The Pelican, named after Drake's ship, which was only later renamed the *Golden Hind,* is one of a chain of charming bed-and-breakfast establishments that have sprung up in West Marin over the past few years. They include the Olema Inn; the Holly Tree Inn near the Point Reyes National Seashore headquarters; 10 Inverness Way; and the Inverness Valley Inn in the village of Inverness.

North of Muir Beach, if the weather is good, the Muir Beach overlook is worth a stop for pictures and a look at the staggering view of the rocky coastline. Then the road is a cliffhanger again for a few miles down to Stinson Beach, where the 53-acre stretch of sand from which the village takes its name is a magnet for surfers and sunlovers.

There are one or two galleries, shops and places to eat, such as the Sand Dollar, before you head north, past Bolinas Lagoon to the left and the Audubon Canyon Ranch to the right. The 1,000-acre ranch, run by the Audubon Society, is a major nesting area for great blue herons and American egrets. It is open to the public from March 1 through July 4.

A little farther on an unmarked road to the left leads to Bolinas, one of Marin's oldest towns, once a thriving center for the lumber industry. Now it's a mixture of old-time residents who don't welcome strangers (hence no signpost) and artists and craftspeople who lend the village a slightly funky air.

Northward, the road runs inland along the eastern boundary of the Point Reyes National Seashore. This is the path of the San Andreas Fault, whose stirrings in 1906 caused the Great San Francisco Earthquake and Fire.

Stop for lunch at Jerry's Farmhouse in Olema, on the corner where Sir Francis Drake Blvd., which stretches from U.S. 101 to Point Reyes, meets Hwy. 1. Owned and operated by a Swiss family, the Bunces, it specializes in oysters from nearby Tomales Bay. The soups and barbecued chicken also are recommended.

The turnoff to the National Seashore headquarters is a few hundred yards beyond. There rangers will dispense information on the facilities, which include miles of trails, a youth hostel, camping areas, a Morgan-horse ranch, and a model Miwok Indian village.

You can drive down to Limantour Beach from here, or continue on through the village of Inverness to Point Reyes, nestled in trees along the shore of Tomales Bay, which slashes into the land from northwest to southeast. Founded in 1889 as a summer resort, Inverness has retained its Old World, country charm, but is by no means sleepy. In the summer there are weekly yacht races on the bay.

There are also a number of good places to eat, notably Manka's Inverness Lodge, where Czech cuisine is featured; and Talli's, which features trout, scallops and chicken.

The last miles to Point Reyes wind through wonderfully wild country, reminiscent of the moors of Scotland and passing through active cattle ranches.

You have your choice of beaches: McClure's or Tomales Bay State Park to the northwest; Drake's Beach, several miles farther west and off to the left; and, most magnificent of all, Point Reyes beach, which stretches north from the point for several miles. This is a walking beach, a picnicking beach when the weather is good, but not a swimming beach—two minutes in those breakers would finish the strongest swimmer.

For the energetic, where Sir Francis Drake Blvd. finally peters out there is another quarter-mile walk to the lighthouse—and 300 steps down and up again!

For those who prefer just to look at wildlife, there is a vista point where you can watch sea lions disport themselves on rocks hundreds of feet below. And in January and February, you can see the great gray whales making their annual migration to their mating waters in Baja California, far to the south.

Before you leave this "land that time forgot," take the turnoff to Johnson's Oyster Farm, if you're partial to that delicacy. Sold in quart and pint jars, they've just been shucked by Mrs. Johnson herself and still taste of the sea.

On the way back, go north through Point Reyes Station, which will remind you of a Western movie set, and turn off Hwy. 1 north of town, to the right. This road will take you past the Nicasio Reservoir and, if you stay on it for a couple of miles, to the Cheese Factory.

This is the home of Rouge et Noir French-style cheeses, and the owners have made a delightful picnic place out of it, with tables set in an orchard and around a big duck pond. You can buy cheese, sandwiches, bread, wine, and soft drinks and there are free tours hourly around the small factory.

Return to Hwy. 101 via Nicasio, a tiny spot in the road with a marvelous red schoolhouse and a little church that has been featured in many films. East of Nicasio the road forks. Either fork will bring you back to the freeway, one by Lucas Valley, the other via San Geronimo and Woodacre, Fairfax, and San Anselmo.

This is a long trip that can be done in a day if you get up early and don't linger anywhere for long. Much better to take a couple of days and stay at one of the B & Bs (bed-and-breakfasts).

For those who don't even have a day to spare, there are some good short trips, too.

Angel Island

For nonpareil views, cross Golden Gate Bridge, then double back under the highway as if returning to the city. Just before you hit the bridge again, there's a road climbing up to the right. Take it. You are now on the Marin Headlands and at every turn in the road there's a view that will catch your breath. All those fantastic photographs of San Francisco with the bridge in the foreground were taken from this road. Bring a camera.

Follow the road to the end, which is Point Bonita, where there is another view area. Then wind down to Rodeo Beach at Fort Cronkhite, a former Army base now part of the National Recreation Area. The beach has its share of sunlovers and agate hunters, and the soaring cliffs and ridges that surround it are awesome. There's a youth hostel here, too, in former Army bachelor officers' quarters.

Or take a boat from Fisherman's Wharf to Angel Island, across Raccoon Straits from the Tiburon Peninsula. Formerly a military garrison and a place where Asian immigrants were interned pending admission into the U.S., the island is wooded, full of deer, and small enough to walk around. A trolley runs around it on weekends. There is a food concession stand at Hospital Cove, where the boats dock, but it's better to take your own picnic basket.

There are seasonal events not to be missed in Marin, such as the Renaissance Pleasure Faire, operated by the Living History Centre on weekends from mid-August to mid-September in Black Point Forest by the Bay north of San Rafael. This re-creation of a country fair in Elizabethan England, with crafts, entertainment, and all manner of tasty foods, is so enjoyable that locals make a point of returning year after year.

There are also annual art fairs in Sausalito (Labor Day weekend) and Mill Valley (later in September) that showcase the work of local artists, and a county fair around July 4 at Marin Civic Center.

In addition to weekend offerings by a number of little theater groups, a major theatrical event of the year is the annual Mountain Play, given for two weekends in July in the huge, open-air amphitheater high up on Mt. Tam.

For those who like to fish, a number of party boats leave from Sausalito early in the morning to seek salmon and striped bass in the Bay or outside the Golden Gate.

And, for the flea market aficionado, Marin has one of the biggest and best, operating Saturdays and Sundays at Marin City, right off Hwy. 101 at the northern entrance to Sausalito.

PRACTICAL INFORMATION FOR MARIN COUNTY

HOW TO GET THERE. Golden Gate Transit operates buses and ferries. **Buses** leave Fremont St. between Mission and Howard and travel via McAllister, Van Ness Ave. and Lombard, with stops on all streets, to various Marin County locations. For information on times and fares call 332–6600. Feeder service is also provided from Larkspur ferry terminal at no extra charge.

Ferries: *Larkspur* and *Sausalito* ferries leave from the terminal at the foot of Market St. The adult fare between Larkspur and San Francisco is $2.20 Monday through Friday and $3.00 Saturdays, Sundays, and holidays. Half-price fares for youths 6 to 12; children 5 or under, accompanied by an adult, travel free. The adult fare between Sausalito and San Francisco is $2.50 weekdays and $3.00 weekends and holidays.

Red and White Fleet (546–2810/2815) operates ferries to *Tiburon, Sausalito,* and *Angel Island.* The Tiburon service leaves from Pier 43½ and the Ferry Building. Roundtrip fare is $6.00; children under 5, free. Sausalito trips, leaving from Pier 41, Fisherman's Wharf, cost $6.00 roundtrip; $3.00 for children 5–11; under 5, free. Angel Island trips, departing from Pier 43½, are $6.00 roundtrip, for adults; $3.50 for children 5–11; under five, free.

TELEPHONES. The area code for Marin County—as well as for San Francisco, Oakland, and Berkeley—is 415. From outside the area, directory information can be obtained toll-free by dialing (415) 555–1212. Dial (800) 555–1212, directory information for toll-free 800 numbers, to see if there is an 800 number for the business you want to reach.

HOTELS AND MOTELS. For double occupancy, *expensive* is $80 up; *moderate,* from $60.00 to $80.00; *inexpensive,* less than $60.00.

Alta Mira Hotel. *Expensive to Moderate.* 125 Bulkley Ave., Sausalito; 332–1350. 35 rooms. Stiff climb to superb view. Dining room perched over treetops; great for yacht watching. Major credit cards.

Casa Madrona Hotel. *Expensive.* 801 Bridgeway, Sausalito; 332–0502. Thirteen rooms and three cottages, Victorian style; 16 individually designed new rooms in a separate building. Excellent restaurant, featuring French cuisine and California wines. Major credit cards.

Golden Hinde Boatel. *Moderate.* Inverness; 669–1389. Overhangs Tomales Bay. Yacht mooring. Restaurants nearby. Most credit cards.

Holiday Inn. *Moderate.* 1010 Northgate, San Rafael; 479–8800. In Terra Linda sector. 230 rooms. Lounge, restaurant. Meeting rooms. Overlooks U.S. 101. All major credit cards.

Madera Village Inn. *Moderate.* 45 Tamal Vista Blvd., Corte Madera (near Larkspur); 924–3608. 55 rooms, kitchenettes available. Pool. Major credit cards.

Tiburon Lodge. *Moderate.* 1651 Tiburon Blvd., Tiburon; 435–3133. 97 rooms. Lounge and restaurant. Pool. Near ferry commute to downtown San Francisco. Major credit cards.

Villa Rafael Motel. *Inexpensive.* 1600 Lincoln Ave., San Rafael; 456–4975. 52 units overlooking U.S. 101 near downtown sector. Pool, sauna. Dining room. Most credit cards.

 BED-AND-BREAKFAST. The bed-and-breakfast establishments beloved of English tourists have surfaced in California. Marin County has its share, mainly on the coastal route. Most are older homes that have been renovated and furnished with appropriate antiques. Prices range from moderate to fairly expensive. Don't count on using credit cards. Most of these are small, family-type operations. For double occupancy, *Expensive* is usually $40.00 to $60.00 but can be higher; *Moderate* is from $30.00 to $40.00.

INVERNESS

Inverness Valley Inn. *Moderate.* P.O. Box 629; 669–7250. On large grounds including swimming pool and tennis courts. Nine units, each with a fireplace and kitchenette. Continental breakfast.

Ten Inverness Way. *Moderate.* 10 Inverness Way; 669–1648. House built in 1904; five guest rooms. Breakfast may include blueberry pancakes or tomato quiche.

MUIR BEACH

The Pelican. *Expensive.* 10 Pacific Way (State Rte. 1 west of Mill Valley); 383–6000. Authentic English inn designed and built by owner Charles Felix; six rooms, antique-furnished; sherry, morning paper, English breakfast. The inn also serves "pub" lunches, afternoon teas and full dinners; monthly Shakespeare at the Inn programs; closed Mondays. Reservations essential.

OLEMA

Olema Inn. *Expensive.* Sir Francis Drake Blvd. and State Rte. 1; 663–8441. The former Olema Hotel, extensively remodeled; three rooms, three baths; Continental breakfast, restaurant serving excellent meals.

POINT REYES STATION

Holly Tree Inn. *Moderate.* 3 Silver Hills Rd.; 665–1554. A quiet home in wooded grounds; three bedrooms, central living room; Continental breakfast.

SAN RAFAEL

Ole Rafael Bed & Breakfast Inn. *Moderate.* 1629 5th Ave.; 453–0414. The only bed-and-breakfast place in central Marin, it is in a historical registered home; three rooms, two with shared bath. Continental breakfast. Midweek businessmen's special.

TOMALES

Bryon Randall's Guest House. *Moderate.* On State Rte. 1, Tomales (north past Point Reyes National Seashore); 878–9992. Rooms only; operated by a noted artist.

Victoria & Albert. *Moderate.* On State Rte. 1 also; 878–2703. In twin Victorians, with the local charm of West Marin. Five rooms, shared bath. Full breakfast.

YOUTH HOSTELS. Golden Gate Hostel. 941 Fort Barry, Sausalito; 331–2777. Located in the Marin Headlands; 60 beds in 5 dormitories; one family room; kitchen, dining area, common room. Overnight fee $3.50 to hostel members, $5.50 to general public.

Point Reyes Hostel. Near Limantour Beach, Point Reyes National Seashore; 669–9985. Accommodations for 40 in dormitories with bunk beds; kitchen, dining room, common rooms. Overnight only; $3.50 for members, $5.50 to general public.

TOURS AND SPECIAL-INTEREST SIGHTSEEING. Dinner cruise to Tiburon, Sausalito: *Holiday Tours,* 340 Mason St., San Francisco 94102; 981–5100. There are walking tours of Mount Tamalpais, lasting about 3 hours, starting at the Sausalito and Larkspur ferry terminals: *Araglen Tours,* 3 West Seaview Ave., San Rafael (Marin Co.); 626–0955.

Bus tours: *Gray Lines* tours (771–4000) leave the Transbay Terminal, 1st and Mission Sts., at 9:00 and 10:00 A.M. and 2:00 P.M. for a 3½-hour tour of Muir Woods and Sausalito. Price $9.75 for adults. *Lorrie's Travel and Tours* (885–6600); daily tours to Muir Woods and Sausalito leaving at 9:30 A.M. and 2:30

P.M. The price of $11.75 for adults includes pick-up at your hotel. Those taking the tour may leave it at Sausalito, the last stop, and take the ferry or bus back to town if they want to stay longer than 3½ hours.

By car: Get onto U.S. 101 at Van Ness Ave., follow to Lombard, turn left, and keep going until you cross Golden Gate Bridge (no toll going north). You are now in Marin and on your own!

SEASONAL EVENTS. January/February. Whale Watching, Point Reyes National Seashore.

March/May. Marin Symphony Concerts, San Rafael.

March. Civic Light Opera, Marin Center, San Rafael; Annual Primrose Tea, Inverness; Antique Show and Sale, San Rafael.

April. Marin Civic Ballet Performs, San Rafael; Marin Antiques Show & Sale, Sausalito.

May. Pacific Sun Marathon and 10K Race—Kentfield—Mill Valley RT; Flea Esta, San Rafael; Marin Grecian Festival, San Rafael (Marin Center); Nor-Cal Conference of Handweavers, San Rafael, Marin Center; San Anselmo Country Fair Days, San Anselmo; Orchestra Piccola and Marin Civic Ballet in Concert, San Rafael.

June. Mountain Plays, Mount Tamalpais, Mill Valley; Home Show, San Rafael; West Marin Livestock Show and Parade, Point Reyes Station; Trade Feast, Novato (Museum of American Indians, Miwok Park).

July. Marin County Fair, San Rafael, Marin Center; Kiwanis and Native Sons Parade and Picnic, San Rafael in the Meadows.

August. Fuchsia Society Show, Marin Art & Garden Center, Ross; Renaissance Pleasure Faire, Novato.

September. Annual Sausalito Art Festival.

October. Marin Ski Swap (benefit), San Rafael.

November. Civic Light Opera, San Rafael Marin Center; Parade of Lights, San Rafael; Antiques Show and Sale, San Rafael Marin Center; Festival of Trees, San Rafael.

November/May. Marin Symphony Concert Season, San Rafael, Marin Vet's Auditorium; Explorama Film Season, Marin Center.

December. Marin Antique Doll Show, Marin Civic Center, San Rafael; Living Christmas Tree, San Rafael; Crafts Fair, The Dance Palace, Point Reyes Stn.

PARKS: Information on hiking trails, campgrounds, and special programs in national and state parks may be obtained by calling the following:

Golden Gate National Recreation Area: Marin Headlands Ranger Station, 561-7612. Tennessee Valley Ranger Station, 383-7717. Muir Woods information, 388-2595. Mount Tamalpais area; state park information, 388-2070. Muir Beach and Stinson Beach Ranger Station, 868-0942.

Angel Island State Park information, 435–1915. Olema Valley information, 663–1092.

Pt. Reyes National Seashore: Campground information and reservations, 663–1092. Drakes Bay Information Center, 669–1250. Lighthouse Information Center, 669–1534.

CAMPING. Campsite reservations, advised in season, in state parks, national forests and parks are available through Ticketron computer outlets. Telephone the Ticketron number in your area for information on local outlets or mail reservations with fees and $1.75 for each reservation period to: Ticketron, P.O. Box 26430, San Francisco, CA 94125. Reservation forms available by calling (916) 445–6477.

Marin Headlands–GGNRA, Kirby Cove, Battery Alexander, Hill 88, N.W. of Golden Gate Bridge. (415) 561–7612. Primitive. No fee. Hiking, biking, horseback riding, nature trails.

Mount Tamalpais State Park, Panoramic Hwy., W. of Mill Valley. (415) 388–2070. Primitive. $3.00 Hiking, biking, horseback riding. Dogs, $1.00

Point Reyes National Seashore, National Park Service Headquarters. Near Olema, Hwy. 1. (415) 663–1092 (Tel. for camping reservations). Backpacking. No fee. Swimming, fishing, hiking, biking, horseback riding, nature trails, group camping. No dogs.

Samuel P. Taylor State Park, Sir Francis Drake Blvd., W. of Lagunitas. (415) 488–9897. $5. Hike and bike camp, 50¢. Swimming, fishing, hiking, biking, horseback riding.

Tomales Bay State Park, 4 miles north of Inverness on Sir Francis Drake Blvd. (415) 669–1140. Bike camp only 50¢. Swimming, fishing, hiking, biking, nature trails.

FISHING. Rock-cod fishing is year-round, while salmon fishing is seasonal. For rates and information contact the following: *Caruso's,* foot of Harbor Drive, Sausalito, CA; 332–1015. *Ma-ru Sport Fishing Boats,* foot of Harbor Drive, Sausalito, CA; 435–4548 or 348–2107. *New Merrimac Charter Boat,* Star Route 603, Sausalito, CA; 388–5351. *Pacific Queen* (Capt. Ron Nass), 45 Unionstone Drive, San Rafael, 479–1322. Sails out of Sausalito. *Sausalito Sport Fishing,* 924–1367 for information.

MUSEUMS. *Marin Museum of the American Indian,* 2200 Novato Blvd., Novato, 897–4064; located adjacent to an ancient Coast Miwok village site; houses archeological and ethnographic collections representative of the Bay Area, California, and the Western Americas; gallery open 10:00 A.M. –4:00 P.M., Tuesday through Saturday; noon to 4:00 P.M., Sunday.

SPECIAL EVENTS. *Renaissance Pleasure Faire,* Black Point Forest, Novato; Fridays and Saturdays from 9:00 A.M. to 6:00 P.M. from mid-August through mid-September. A once-in-a-lifetime experience of roisterous celebration in the days of Good Queen Bess. Arts and crafts, succulent foods, games, and lively entertainment, plus daily visits from Queen Elizabeth I and her court. Produced by the Living History Center. For information, call 434–4625 or 892–0162.

DINING OUT. The price categories are for dinner for one, *without* drinks, taxes, or tip. *Expensive,* $15.00 and up; *Moderate,* below $15.00; however, none of the restaurants listed here will let you out for less than $7.00 for a normal-sized meal.

CORTE MADERA (NEAR LARKSPUR)

Marin Joe's. *Moderate.* 1985 Redwood Hwy.; 924–2081. Great hamburgers. Italian dishes; continuous service from 11:30 A.M., Monday through Friday; 5:00 P.M.–2:00 A.M., Saturday; 4:00 P.M.–2:00 A.M., Sunday AE, MC, V.

INVERNESS

Manka's. *Moderate.* Inverness Lodge; 669–1034. Czech and Viennese cuisine; open June through October, Thursday through Monday, serving breakfast, lunch, dinner. Also 5 cabins and 4 rooms. MC, V.

Talli's. *Moderate.* Hwy. 1 at Inverness Junction; 663–9015. Trout, scallops, chicken, homemade tortes and mousses. Open 5:00 P.M. Wednesday through Sunday. MC, V.

Vladimir's Czechoslovakian Restaurant. *Moderate.* 12785 Sir Francis Drake Blvd.; 669–1021. Dinner house with European décor. Closed Monday and Thursday; lunches noon to 3:00 P.M., dinner 5:00–9:30 P.M. Cash only.

LARKSPUR

Four Sixty Four Magnolia. *Expensive.* 464 Magnolia Ave.; 924–6831. International dinner menu 6:00–10:00 P.M., Tuesday through Thursday; 6:00–11:00 P.M., Friday and Saturday; Sunday brunch, 10:00 A.M.–2:00 P.M. MC, V.

Lark Creek Inn. *Expensive.* 234 Magnolia Ave.; 924–7766. Restored Victorian. Varied menu. Lunch daily, 11:30 A.M.; dinner from 6:30 P.M.; Sunday brunch 11:30 A.M.–2:00 P.M. Major credit cards.

Scoma's. *Expensive.* Larkspur Landing; 461–6161. Bay view; seafood specialties. Lunch Monday through Friday, 11:30 A.M.–3:00 P.M. Dinner Monday through Thursday, 5:30–10:00 P.M.; Friday and Saturday, 5:30–11:00 P.M.; Sunday, 1:30–10:00 P.M. AE, DC, MC, V.

Blue Rock Inn. *Moderate.* 507 Magnolia Ave.; 924–9707. Old stagecoach inn. Lunch served Monday through Saturday; dinner, 5:00–10:00 P.M. daily; Sunday brunch, 10:00 A.M.–3:00 P.M. AE, MC, V.

Yet Wah. *Moderate.* Larkspur Landing; 461–3631. Chinese food served 11:30 A.M.–11:00 P.M., Monday through Saturday; 4:00–10:00 P.M., Sunday. AE, DC, MC, V.

MILL VALLEY

Le Camembert. *Expensive.* 200 Shoreline Hwy.; 383–8000. Cuisine of Normandy: open seven days; lunch, 11:00 A.M.–4:00 P.M.; dinner, 5:00–10:00 P.M. AE, MC, V.

Da Angelo's. *Moderate.* 20 Miller Ave.; 388–2000. First-rate Italian food in attractive setting. Open 11:00 A.M.–3:00 P.M. and 5:00–11:00 P.M., Monday through Friday; 5:00–11:00 P.M., Saturday and Sunday. AE, MC, V.

El Rebozo Restaurant. *Moderate.* 115 Shoreline Hwy.; 332–5122. Excellent Mexican food and *simpatico* service. Open seven days a week; 11:30 A.M.–10:45 P.M., Sunday–Thursday; 11:30 A.M.–11:45 P.M., Friday–Saturday. Major credit cards.

SAN RAFAEL

Andalou. *Expensive.* 3rd and E Sts.; 454–4900. California food served in Victorian home. Lunch, Tuesday through Friday, 11:30 A.M.–2:30 P.M.; dinner 6:00–9:30 P.M. through Thursday; until 10:00 P.M. Friday and Saturday; Sunday brunch, 10:30 A.M.–3:00 P.M. MC, V.

Maurice et Charles Bistro. *Expensive.* 901 Lincoln Ave.; 456–2010. Rated among the top restaurants in the Bay Area. Women get menus sans prices. Dinner only, 6:30 P.M.–10:30 P.M., closed Sundays. AE.

La Petite Auberge. *Expensive.* 704 Fourth St.; 456–5808. French cuisine in garden-patio décor. Dinner only, 5:30 P.M.–11:00 P.M., closed Mondays. Reservations. AE, MC, V.

Dominic's Harbor Restaurant. *Moderate.* 507 Francisco Blvd.; 456–1382. On San Rafael Canal, with boat docking facilities. Lunch and dinner daily from 11:00 A.M.; brunch, Saturday, Sunday, and holidays, 10:00 A.M.–3:00 P.M. AE, CB, DC, MC, V.

SAUSALITO

Casa Madrona. 801 Bridgeway; 331–5888. Country French in the 1885 landmark. Dinner Tues.–Sat., 6:00–10:00 P.M. Reservations recommended. All major credit cards.

Ondine. *Expensive.* 558 Bridgeway; 332–0791. A perennial *Holiday Magazine* award winner. Spectacular, over-the-water setting; Continental food. Open 5:30 –10:30 P.M. Monday through Saturday; 5–10 P.M. Sunday. Valet parking; reservations advised. AE, CB, DC, MC, V.

Alta Mira Hotel. *Expensive to Moderate.* 125 Bulkley Ave.; 332–1350. Most popular for lunch and Sunday brunch on deck overlooking Bay. Reservations needed. AE, DC, MC, V.

Horizons On The Bay. *Expensive to moderate.* 558 Bridgeway; 331–3232. Ondine's downstairs neighbor. Good bar. Seafood, steaks, veal and chicken. Open Monday–Friday from 11 A.M.; Saturday–Sunday from 10:00 A.M. Brunch daily until 5:00 P.M. Valet parking. MC, V.

Seven Seas. *Moderate.* 682 Bridgeway; 332–1304. Seafood; open noon to 11:30 P.M., Sunday through Thursday; to 1:00 A.M., Friday and Saturday. AE, MC, V.

The Spinnaker. *Moderate.* 100 Spinnaker Dr.; 332–1500. Seafood specialities in a spectacular setting; open daily 11:00 A.M.–10:00 P.M. Reservations advised. AE, MC, V.

Zack's By the Bay. *Moderate.* Bridgeway and Turney Sts.; 332–9779. Dock-side patio, famous for "Zackburgers." Nightly dancing, turtle races on Wednes-days. Open 11:00 A.M. Monday through Friday; 10:00 A.M. Saturday and Sunday. No credit cards.

STINSON BEACH

The Sand Dollar. *Moderate.* On Highway 1; 868–0434. Lunch, noon–2:00 P.M. daily; dinners, 6:00–10:00 P.M.; Sunday brunch, 11:00 A.M.–2:00 P.M. No credit cards.

TIBURON

The Dock. *Deluxe.* 25 Main St.; 435–4559. Seafood and steaks. Open Monday through Friday, 11:00 A.M.; Saturday and Sunday, 10:00 A.M. AE, MC, V.

Caprice. *Expensive.* 2000 Paradise Dr.; 435–3400. Overwater setting; interna-tional cuisine. Open noon–2:30 P.M., lunch; 5:00–10:30 P.M., dinner, daily. Reser-vations advised. AE, CB, DC, MC, V.

Sabella's of Marin. *Expensive.* 9 Main St.; 435–2636. Seafood specialties. Open 11:00 A.M.–11:00 P.M. daily, except Christmas. AE, CB, DC, MC, V.

Sam's Anchor Café. *Moderate.* 27 Main St.; 435–4527. Long-established favorite of yacht people. Open daily for breakfast, lunch, and dinner. All major credit cards.

Servino Ristorante Italiano. *Moderate.* 114 Main St.; 435–2676. Veal, fresh fish, eggplant, pasta. California and Italian wines. Relaxing, intimate ambiance, attentive service. 5:00–10:30 P.M., seven days a week. MC, V.

Tiburon Tommie's. *Moderate.* 41 Main St.; 435–1229. Polynesian décor and food. Open daily, 11:30 A.M.–9:45 P.M. Reservations advised. AE, MC, V.

 NIGHT LIFE AND BARS. Marin County does a lot of drinking, but isn't famous for its saloons or entertain-ment spots, although a few are certainly worth mention-ing. There are a number of booze-and-music clubs buried back in "old Marin," but they are hardly part of the San Francisco scene.

Sausalito and Tiburon are pretty touristy, but after dark Tiburon especially has a few all-purpose music, singles, and just plain drinking establishments that attract the younger residents.

Alta Mira Hotel. Bulkley Ave., Sausalito; 332–1350. A venerable old shingled inn best known for its glassed-in dining room and adjacent deck. Very popular at noon, but a superb place to drink and chat in late afternoon. The view of Sausalito's boat harbor, of Raccoon Straits, Angel Island, San Francisco, etc., is breathtaking. You might recall the opening scenes of *Behind the Green Door* —they were taken on the Alta Mira deck. There are nibblies and nicely served good drinks, too.

Marshall Tavern. The Tavern is one of Marshall's handful (or less) of commercial establishments, situated on the east shore of Tomales Bay about an hour's drive out of S.F. A rather rowdy saloon, with good food and lusty drinks, with music most weekend nights and quite often also during the week when drop-ins (often rather famous) come by for the hell of it.

The Mayflower Inn. 1533 Fourth St., San Rafael; 456–1011. Has gradually become one of the Bay Area's best English pubs, complete not only with darts but also with Ping-Pong (oops, sorry, *table tennis*) and pinball games and electronic gadgetry. One night, too, there may be community singing with a crusty old pianist, the next night dixieland jazz. But every night there's lots of drinking. It's been said that the food, mostly English dishes, is excellent, but most folks never get beyond the bar.

No Name Bar. 757 Bridgeway, Sausalito; 332–1392. Acquired something of a Beatnik reputation in the late fifties, and more recently has been surrounded by touristy commercial ventures—neither activity did the place well. It is still, however, the best haven from the shopping hordes out on Bridgeway, and the atmosphere is relaxing, the drinks strong. Many of the No Name's saloon-neighbors (there are a dozen along Broadway) are splendid watering holes once the mobs have departed. Jazz, rock, folk, and blues performers pop up in Sausalito's saloons on a haphazard basis; equally haphazard is the constant changing of ownership and names of most of Sausalito's drinking establishments.

The Pelican Inn. Muir Beach; 383–6000. On one of the routes out to Stinson Beach, Mount Tamalpais, and other Marin Country must-see tourist attractions. As it happens, the Pelican is pure delight from the time you enter until you leave—filled with drink, food, and good memories. It's British all the way, with beers and ales and food dishes seldom seen elsewhere in North America, or at least in the States. If you're in reasonably good shape you can drink-and-dart, order your meal, take a half hour's walk down to the beach and back, have your meal, and then begin drinking again. Overcrowded during the height of tourist season and also on weekends (especially Sunday daytime), but on a foggy, chilly afternoon the Pelican Inn is, well, a marvelous experience.

Sam's Anchor Café (also **The Dock**). Main St., Tiburon; 435–4527. Sam's is the older, more popular, and somewhat less pretentious of these two waterfront dining-and-drinking spots in increasingly fashionable Tiburon. In both, according to their setting, one wanders through a bar, an indoor restaurant, and out onto a deck. Sam's food used to be outstanding, but lately neither place has maintained a superior menu. However, both Sam's and The Dock are magnificent places to have a light lunch and drinks and watch the waterworld of Marin County pass by. (The Dock is much higher over the water and has a better view. Service at both places is at best sluggish.)

Sleeping Lady. 50 Bolinas Rd., Fairfax; 456–2044. A great place to hear music, usually folky, bluesy stuff, and drink. A young crowd, mostly beer drinkers, makes the Lady their hangout, but it's a comfortable place to hear some of the best Marin music and Fairfax is a nice spot, especially during the fall and spring months. Very crowded weekends and in the summer.

Smitty's. 214 Caledonia St., Sausalito; 332–2637. A couple of blocks off the beaten tourist track in Sausalito, Smitty's has a continuous floating pool game going, a shuffleboard game (full-size, authentic), and a "let's get away from it all" feeling—withall, it's essentially a drinking establishment.

Sweetwater. 153 Throckmorton, Mill Valley; 380–2820. This is Mill Valley's answer to Fairfax's Sleeping Lady (see above). Blues and country-rock, a hip young crowd (heavy on beer), and good fun, especially after a heavy day of convention speeches and Sausalito shopping.

Uncle Charlie's. 5625 Paradise, Corte Madera; 924–9927. A bit tricky to find (although locals know the location) this is a superb saloon/music club. The emphasis is on country-blues rock, with a few "names" dropping in quite often. Nice atmosphere, low prices, dancing and plenty of parking. About 40 minutes from downtown S.F.

INDEX

INDEX

(The letters H and R indicate Hotel and Restaurant listings.)